JULIA SEGAL

PHANTASY IN EVERYDAY LIFE

A Psychoanalytical Approach to Understanding Ourselves

Penguin Books

To Mary and Allen

PENGUIN BOOKS

Published by the Penguin Group
Penguin Books Ltd, 27 Wrights Lane, London w8 5tz, England
Viking Penguin, a division of Penguin Books USA Inc.
375 Hudson Street, New York, New York 10014, USA
Penguin Books Australia Ltd, Ringwood, Victoria, Australia
Penguin Books Canada Ltd, 2801 John Street, Markham, Ontario, Canada l3r 1b4
Penguin Books (NZ) Ltd, 182–190 Wairau Road, Auckland 10, New Zealand

Penguin Books Ltd, Registered Offices: Harmondsworth, Middlesex, England

First published in Pelican Books
Reprinted in Penguin Books 1991
1 3 5 7 9 10 8 6 4 2

Copyright © Julia Segal 1985

Printed in England by Clays Ltd, St Ives plc
Filmset in Monophoto Photina

Penguin Books

PHANTASY IN EVERYDAY LIFE

Julia Segal was born in 1950 and educated at a girls' grammar school in Coventry and at Newnham College, Cambridge. In the course of her life so far she has had two sons and worked in various capacities including housemother in a girls' hostel, nursing assistant in a mental hospital and course tutor for a postgraduate diploma for Third World women at the University of London, and for an English course at the Oberstufen Kolleg. University of Bielefeld, West Germany. She trained as a marriage guidance counsellor in Manchester for four years and has taught for the Extra-Mural Department of Manchester University and for the Richmond Fellowship. At present she teaches on a freelance basis for several organizations in London. Her interest in psychoanalysis began in 1969 and has since been fed by a personal analysis, partically paid for by the Institute of Psychoanalysis, courses and seminars at the Tavistock Institute of Human Relations and work supervisions from several senior psychoanalysts. She has published a paper entitled 'Mother, sex and envy in a children's story', which appeared in the *International Review of Psychoanalysis* in 1979.

CONTENTS

ACKNOWLEDGEMENTS

I would like to thank all those who helped make this book possible: my family and friends; the many analysts and fellow counsellors who have taught me over the years; the people who have come to me for counselling or for teaching and who have themselves taught me so much; those responsible for arranging the classes at the Extra-Mural Department of the University of Manchester, where I began to formulate this book; those responsible for allowing me to work and train as a marriage guidance counsellor; the people at Penguin Books who encouraged me and did the hard work; and all those who read and commented on the various drafts of the typescript. I am sorry I cannot thank them by name. I am grateful to Posy Simmonds and the *Guardian* for permission to use the cartoon on p. 26.

ONE

INTRODUCTION

Psychoanalysis has been around for a long time now. What began in nineteenth-century Vienna has spread over the world and in the process has developed and changed. Many psychoanalytical insights have crept into everyday awareness, often with their origin forgotten. 'Freudian slips' and Jung's and Adler's 'complexes' have become part of our language, as have 'identification' and perhaps even 'projection' and 'denial'. The importance of children's play, the need for mourning and the value of emotional as well as physical care in illness have all become recognized in our culture partly at least through the work of people using psycho-analytical insights.

As psychoanalysis has become better known, psychoanalysts have been accused of all kinds of evil influences and suspect practices, sometimes with justification. For a long time the women's movement and others on the political left were strongly opposed to psychoanalysis on the grounds, amongst others, that it was aimed at making people fit into a sick, patriarchal, capitalist society. Recently it has become more acceptable to seek out analytical insights which can be used in other ways, to avoid throwing out the baby with the bathwater. There probably have been, too, so-called analysts who believed or claimed to believe that 'all she needs is a good bit of sex' and were prepared to recommend or even to provide it, claiming they were following Freud's teaching. Freud was writing bitterly against such people in 1910 in a paper he called '"Wild" Psychoanalysis', where he pointed out the misunderstanding of his work inherent in such attitudes. As he says there, the concept of 'sex' as used by him has more in common with the concept of 'love', including all the depth and complexity that implies, than with a mere physical act. But there have always been people who jumped to conclusions about psychoanalytical teachings on the basis of a little hearsay and a lot of fantasy.

Psychoanalysis has been attacked on many grounds. It has been dismissed as 'contemplating your navel', with the full scorn of a Protestant ethic which values only action, and preferably profit-making action, and decries thought, contemplation and spending money. The problem has been mistaken for the cure, so that analysis is accused of making people spend a lot of time thinking about themselves rather than working or thinking about others – when this is often the very reason people come to analysis in the first place: because they *cannot* work or think about others as they would like to. It has been condemned as a Bad Thing because it is expensive, and the insights it throws up have been condemned by association. It has been accused of being relevant only for nineteenth-century Vienna, as if no work had been done anywhere else since. It is accused of working – if at all – only very slowly, and being very limited in its possibilities, as if it should be a magic cure for the evils of life and people. It has been accused of working only by 'suggestion', as if it were some huge con trick. It has been denounced as 'unproven', as if drugs or ECT for example were more 'proven' – an idea which many doctors find laughable. It has been charged with being too concerned with infancy or sex at the expense of present-day relations, or 'only' concerned with the relation with the analyst; the way in which these issues are intertwined and dealt with in the context of daily life is frequently misunderstood. Psycho-analysis has been blamed too for a decline in moral standards and for the existence of the 'permissive society'; for making people too soft with criminals, too weak with the insane or with children, too interested in sex or too ready to talk about things which would be better unsaid. Some of the accusations have some truth in them; others are wildly exaggerated or just false.

In spite of all the difficulties involved there is, I think, a resurgence of interest in psychoanalysis, and a real desire to know what it can and cannot offer, what it does and does not claim. This resurgence of interest can be seen in several forms.

In the first place, there is growing awareness on the part of the ordinary person who works 'with people' that there are useful ideas around which can make the task easier. Many social workers, marriage guidance counsellors and nurses, as well as some prison officers, teachers, doctors and clergy, to name but a few, have begun to find in some of the psychoanalytical sources work which has a very practical bearing on the work they do. Whereas academic psychology, as taught in Britain, seems to many such people useless and irrelevant, the ideas of Freud and Klein and other analysts – often interpreted through the Tavistock Clinic and Institute of Human Relations – have been able to throw light on the real day-to-day problems of dealing with clients and with the workers' feelings about clients or patients. Whereas earlier attitudes towards feelings were to dismiss them and feel guilty if they did not just go away, there is a growing recognition that feelings towards one's work and the people involved are unavoidable and can actually be used. This, however, is for many people a new and scaring idea. Those brought up in the older way may be afraid that emotions are so powerful that they can only be indulged immediately, in their entirety, or be completely pushed down and smothered. The idea that painful emotions are better kept conscious and simply suffered until they go away of their own accord is one which may not have entered their heads. Psychoanalytical insights into such emotions and the processes governing them are at variance with many commonly held views. These insights are beginning to percolate into the common consciousness, but they are much less widespread among the general public than they are among the social work professions.

In the universities psychoanalytical ideas are becoming once again serious objects of discussion, and students are gradually becoming less likely to be taught only that 'psychoanalysis is wrong'. Even behaviourally oriented psychologists are becoming more interested in what goes on in the mind and its influence upon action and emotional states. Philosophy and English departments have always had some interest in psycho-analysis; in the past few years a school of French analysis has gained some popularity and has indirectly led to an increase in interest in the home-grown 'English school', including people like Klein, who in fact influenced the French Lacan. Just as there are many ways of reading the Bible, so there are many ways of reading Freud; academics may have a tendency to pick up the more abstract and philosophical aspects of his work which are of less interest to those who like the more human 'case history' sides as I do. But an interest in one may also link up with and lead to an interest in the other.

A further source of growing interest in the ideas of psychoanalysis is simply the spread of psychotherapy. When a friend rings up and says 'I've started therapy', ripples of interest are aroused. In the classes I teach in the University of Manchester Extra-Mural Department there are often people who have come along to make sense of what is happening to their sister in London, for example, or to see if analysis could help their brother or father who is behaving in a most peculiar way. With increasing awareness there is increasing preparedness to sit and talk to – and about – the brother who is behaving in an odd manner, and to feel there is some sense in actually listening to his 'crazy' ideas – since it will no longer mean just going into a mental hospital for the rest of his life if he is found to be really 'mad'.

Two further sources should perhaps be mentioned. I think the women's movement may have been responsible for some people beginning to look at psychoanalytical ideas or therapy to see if they can give anything to discussions about how children are brought up to be sexist or non-sexist, about the effects of having or not having a father, and about how conflicts can arise and be dealt with within lesbian relationships, to name but a few areas of interest.

Finally, the church too has in places brought in some psychoanalytical ideas where previously there were none. In Coventry, where I was brought up, the Cathedral was responsible for bringing an analyst to lead discussions between social workers and voluntary workers, when little else was going on from the point of view of psychoanalysis in Coventry.

Having said why other people may be interested, perhaps I should say something of the attraction psychoanalysis has for me. For me, psychoanalysis seems to offer a means of understanding both myself and other people in a way which leaves me more humble and yet of more practical use to others than I was before. It combines the pleasures of doing a puzzle, fitting together different aspects of a person or relationship before me and seeing how the pieces interlock, with the pleasures of seeing the changes this process can bring about in terms of people becoming better able to recognize and survive the conflicts in their lives. For me the key is the word *understanding* in both its intellectual and its emotional sense. My ninety-three-year-old grandfather told me with tears in his eyes that the worst thing about his deteriorating physical condition was his inability to make people understand any more; the loneliness which lack of understanding can bring about is not physical but it is extremely painful.

What I am offering in this book is an attempt to describe the ideas I have found most useful in understanding both myself and the world around me. It is not a cool unbiased account; it is not simply a description of psycho-analytical insights applied to everyday life, though it is that to some extent. Many of the ideas I am trying to explain come from other people, some I seem to have worked out for myself, some do not quite fit in either category. I am not discussing opposing views, nor the many experimental results emerging from clinical and academic psychology which may seem to confirm some of these ideas. My intention is to explain *what* I have found useful, both for myself and for others; *why* it is useful and whether it fits or clashes with other views of the world – held by different schools of psychiatric, psychological or psychoanalytical thought – I leave for the reader and other authors to examine if they wish. I have in mind readers who have never come across analysis before, or who have come across it in other contexts or from different directions, and wish to know more about it. All psychoanalytical ideas are controversial: this book is bound to give rise to agreement and disagreement amongst those who have some knowledge already, as well as amongst those who know very little of analysis. Such controversy can help to clarify and modify ideas. Meanwhile it need not prevent some of them being useful in the process of finding something better or as a means of sorting out your own opinions.

Having taught people about these ideas for some time now, I know that they can be useful in various specific ways. Utterly conflicting emotions, confusion and lack of understanding can often give rise to panic: reducing the confusion and the lack of understanding often seems to enable people to feel freer to make sensible decisions, or simply to do nothing. By making sense of apparently irrational behaviour these ideas often seem to help people to begin to understand how they can behave in ways which go completely against their conscious wishes and common sense. As a result the feeling of being completely out of control of oneself, or of being utterly at the mercy of people around, may be reduced. This kind of book is not going to help directly with very deep-seated problems, but it might help with ordinary daily problems of how to deal with people at work, in the family or otherwise in daily life. Many of the people in my classes have found that their ability to observe what goes on and to make some sense of it has been considerably increased. Teachers have told me that they have found themselves treating the children in a more relaxed manner and have as a result had fewer behavioural problems; social workers have found the atmosphere at work and with clients has altered as their own insight has improved. In my work as a counsellor I have watched many people find in themselves the ability to change their lives very much for the better, as a result of learning to look at themselves and others differently. Understanding how a miserable situation can arise does seem to make it more bearable, though it does have to be a particular kind of understanding. I come back to this point later.

What I intend to do in this book is to explain to the general reader some of the ideas and discoveries which have arisen out of the work of analysts, particularly in England, over the last fifty years or so. Basing their work on Freud's, they have uncovered evidence which was not available to him and have as a result developed certain differences from and disagreements with his ideas. The ideas have been developed initially by piecing together clues in the consulting room, but they have often been confirmed and discovered over and over again in work of all kinds with 'ordinary' as well as 'mad' people. Analysis is a very practical matter, with theoretical ideas interacting with detailed observations. As a result many of the ideas I shall offer are of the very practical kind: simple rules of thumb to try out. The complicated ways in which these ideas make up a coherent whole – still of course in the process of developing and being changed – are touched on in places in this book, but, as in any introductory work, they cannot be fully developed here. There is no substitute for the books written by and for analysts; in some areas all I can do is to help the general reader with the ground-rules and the basic language which make these books and papers seem hopelessly obscure. But many readers will have neither the time nor the inclination to read further and I am writing for such people too.

Some of the ideas I shall present consist mainly of new ways of talking about observations, new ways of describing thoughts and feelings people have about themselves and the world around their them and already know about in some other way. But just as the Arabic numerals we use today offered much greater possibilities for mathematics than the Roman ones did, so new names for ways we feel and think and make assumptions about the world can offer much greater scope for understanding and talking about what goes on. As a result of the new language, new observations can be made and a whole set of new connections and relationships between these observations can be established.

Some of the ideas represent in some sense genuinely new concepts. Understanding these may not be easy and takes time. The idea of unconscious phantasy, of projection in all its manifestations, of introjection, idealization and splitting all have new aspects to them, and new applications which at first seem strange. Understanding some of the ideas behind these concepts means that we are provided with powerful new tools for thought and action.

An extremely important aspect of what I shall be presenting is the importance and significance of words, both for communication between people and for communication within the self. Psychiatry and psychology in the universities have, I think, largely neglected the use of words; the animal studies which are so popular do away with them explicitly. But words can be used to deal with anxiety, for example, and to offer particular kinds of control over the world which are not simply hindrances to deep feeling or 'getting in the way' of our 'instincts'. Neither a purely 'rationalist' view of the world nor a purely emotional one does justice to the power of words to link and to separate, to hold together, to affect the sense of time and boundaries of pain for example, and to enable us to hold what we would otherwise lose or have to deal with in other ways. Looking at ways we deal with ourselves, both with words and in states where words are kept out or unavailable, we can make quite startling discoveries.

Analysis is unusual amongst intellectual pursuits in its insistence on the importance of both intellect and emotion, and the interrelationship between the two. The idea that we can use our emotions to detect the emotional states of others in a way which is not to be dismissed as 'merely subjective' and dangerous to 'scientific objectivity' is for many a startling one. There are indeed real problems with using emotions in this way, but so there are with using, say, an electron microscope. At least some training is required, and then the results suffer still from a particular kind of distortion. But the advantages and the increase in insight we can gain by using such imperfect and distorting instruments certainly at times seem to compensate for the lack of certainty in the result. Knowing the result is uncertain, we can then test it in other ways.

The ideas I present in this book are not hard and fast rules or theories; they do not give infallible answers. Often people in my classes complain that I have not told them how they 'should' behave. Non-judgemental observation of one's own and others' behaviour is a skill, it seems, which has to be learnt. I offer suggestions for new ways of looking, ideas as to the precise ways in which our perceptions may be at fault and new ideas as to the reliability of our complex feelings and perceptions. But I cannot look for you. I can show you a microscope and tell you what I see; you have to do your own focusing and choose what you will put under it. Your own emotions are something you can detect or not; how far you learn to detect them or to use them in ways I suggest depends on you. Once you have seen something you had not seen before, it is up to you what you do about it. My hope might be that it may develop your understanding, your love, your mercy and forgiveness, and your ability to stand up for yourself in a way which makes life better for you and for those around you; but this result I cannot guarantee.

As this book is intended to be an introduction to psychoanalytical ideas for the general reader, I have to discuss the methods of psychoanalysis. I try to use my description of being in analysis in a way which shows the interaction between theoretical and practical aspects of analysis. This section may also be helpful for those who have friends or relatives in analysis, and want to know what goes on. It can be very hard, if a person you love is turning for help to someone else; you may feel rejected, guilty, useless and extremely jealous, as well as relieved and hopeful. Or you may feel none of these – but simply behave as if you were.

Psychoanalytical insights illuminate and are illuminated by literature, social observation in settings other than analysis, and also the observation of babies and children. I touch on these, too, drawing many of my examples from ordinary day-to-day behaviour.

There are difficulties in all this. It is very important to recognize that the claims of analysts are not statistical ones. Analysts, in reporting cases, cannot be understood to be saying 'it is always like this'. In my view they have to be understood as saying 'I saw this, here, then, and this is how I understood it; is this of any use to you?' This is a different approach from that of other disciplines. Some psychology students I once spoke to criticized the methods of psychoanalysis and the truth of its insights (without actually knowing much about what they were, of course) on the grounds that 'n is not big enough' – that is, not enough people have been analysed to prove anything. The point is that analysts are generally working to understand individuals rather than to make large generalizations about populations which might or might not apply to individuals in them. Knowing that, say, 'ninety per cent of the population behaves like this, under these circumstances' does not tell us whether the person in front of us is one of the ninety per cent or one of the ten per cent. It may be more useful to have many detailed examples of how people *can* behave and feel which enable us to look more closely, with fewer prejudices, at how this person is behaving and feeling now. Analysts do indeed see patterns in behaviour, and try to point them out to each other, but the patterns are not rules: they have to be tested out in each individual case. My psychology students, I think, had a somewhat crude understanding of the process of proof of theories anyway; with the development of our theories of methodology my impression is that no academic would ever claim to have proved anything, except in mathematics. All that is claimed nowadays is something like plausibility, or reasonable certainty – a much more subjective and less certain claim. But it takes time for the more sophisticated academic ideas to percolate; many people still believe that what the doctor offers is in some way more 'proved' than what a psychoanalyst offers, though in many cases the analyst's methods may have been around for far longer than the doctor's, and, as far as doing harm is concerned, it is far more likely that the doctor than the analyst would do harm. Psychoanalytical ideas may be found to be more or less useful; the problem of testing psychoanalysis as a method of treating certain states of mind is quite another matter, and an extremely difficult one, since the criteria used by the analyst may not even be recognized by people trained in different disciplines.

There are other difficulties in putting across psychoanalytical ideas too. They are, for example, often rejected because they are not very pleasant at first sight. People disliked the idea that children might be sexual; they now dislike the idea that children might be born with some aggression rather than just having it thrust upon them. The ideas are simplified and so become much more frightening. Melanie Klein's view of infantile aggression was very firmly grounded in a belief in infantile love which struggles with it – but that bit gets left out. Her suggestions that some problems may have innate aspects to them is frequently misunderstood to mean that she was hopeless about changing such things, though her whole life was devoted to helping people to change their psyches. After all, a harelip is inborn, but that does not mean we cannot change it with surgery. Inborn aggression and love are always modified by the environment, and where that environment includes psychoanalysis, the changes can be quite startling. There is perhaps no reason why other life events should not have a similarly dramatic effect at times; Freud certainly likened the process of falling in love to that of being analysed in terms of the deep changes which could be undergone as a result.

Some analytical ideas get a bad name because people have adopted them uncritically and then misused them. The idea, for example, that parents have a strong influence upon their children's emotional development may be welcomed with open arms by those who wish to use it as a stick to beat their own mothers with; their own part in dealing with the problems which she set them may be totally ignored in the wonderful feeling of liberation which accompanies blaming mother for all their present-day problems. The fact that the problems continue may then be simply used to demonstrate how useless psychoanalytical insight is: 'I know it's all my mother's fault, but that doesn't stop it.' Similarly, other people get stuck in the 'knowledge' that 'it's all my fault' – because analysts have pointed out how much we contribute to our own miseries. Others may even misuse the idea that 'talking about things' can often make them better; talking about things is not in fact the only way to make them better, and other methods – including keeping silence – should not be neglected. At times too much talking becomes persecutory; even the truth is a two-edged sword. 'Being open' is not always the wisest thing to be, if, for example, it includes subjecting children to watching their mother having sex with someone else. (Children can often get frightened of the excitement, jealousy and envy this arouses in them.)

It is not only the unpleasantness or the attractiveness of some analytical ideas which makes for difficulties, but also their strangeness. Analysts make connections which people find very strange indeed. We have begun to accept, perhaps, that there is a link between how we feel about our sexual relationships and how we feel about other aspects of daily life, but it may come as a shock, say, that the death of a parent may trigger sexual problems for several years after the event. What has that got to do with it, you may ask – unless it has happened to you, in which case you may be heaving a sigh of relief. The idea that small boys want to have babies in their tummies, and that this may be contributing to a grown man's inability to behave decently towards women is one which may seem incredible. I am very aware that the first contact with analytical ideas is often a disbelieving 'Nonsense!' I had this reaction myself at first too. It takes time for the ideas to become less strange and for them to start making sense, if they ever do. A remarkable number, however, do eventually turn out to be extremely sensible and useful. But in order to get to this stage an initial period of suspension of disbelief may be useful; a period when you are prepared to read and try out some of the ideas without committing yourself to believing them. With many of the ideas, my own experience has been that I have read and only half-grasped them, but that they have suddenly made sense, years later, when something happened to make them fall into place and fill a real need I had.

Before I move on to a summary of the contents of this book, let me return briefly to the question of how understanding can be helpful. People often question me about this, and it is not easy to explain to someone who has never experienced it themselves. Often people have experienced an immediate sense of relief from a piece of understanding which has been mainly in terms of 'it's not my fault'. When a friend is bad tempered and you ask why and discover that it is something quite out of your control, there may be a sense of relief connected with the fear that it was you who made them bad tempered. Sometimes such relief is long-lasting, but sometimes it is only temporary: you begin not to believe it after a while and the anxiety comes back. Sometimes the relief never comes because the understanding is of the wrong sort – only 'intellectual' for example, and not in terms of feelings – or is actually mistaken. A woman who came to me because of depression was angry with herself for crying bitterly a lot of the time. She described her very difficult childhood circumstances, and I pointed out gently that she had a lot to cry for. She said afterwards that that statement had suddenly made her understand what it meant to say that her problems were to do with her difficult childhood. Previously she had known this, but only in an intellectual, rather dismissive and hopeless way, as if it could not actually affect her. That her present crying might be a kind of mourning for past griefs had never struck her. But reading about such incidents is not the same as experiencing them and may mean little to you. The feeling of really understanding, or being understood by another person or yourself, can be a giddy, whole-body experience. As with falling in love, it may be based on an illusion or it may be the beginning of something lasting; either way it can have far-reaching consequences in terms of physical and mental states. Where it remains in a part of your mind which is not in contact with other parts, or is disconnected from your body, in some sense, understanding does not have these qualities. The 'intellectual' and more 'cold' kind of understanding can, however, precede the other kind.

Finally, I want to list the people who have most influenced me in the ideas I put forward here. They are all people who have worked in England in the last fifty years or so, and they all base their work on that of Freud and Abraham, one of Freud's followers who worked in Berlin. Other people in other places have also made contributions to psychoanalytical thought and have also produced useful insights and ideas, some similar to these and some very different. Rather than use a lot of people's work in a half-digested form I have concentrated in the last fourteen years on more fully digesting and understanding the work of a relatively small number – those I liked best. As a result my own ideas are influenced largely by the Kleinian group of the British Psychoanalytical Society. These include in particular Melanie Klein herself, and then Wilfred Bion, Hanna Segal, Susan Isaacs, Joan Riviere and Herbert Rosenfeld. I do not agree with every word they ever wrote or spoke, and they do not agree totally with each other or with their own earlier ideas, but substantially there is an agreement amongst them on the ways of working and the larger part of the ideas arising from this. The experience of being in analysis which I describe is also based upon Kleinian techniques.

There are many disagreements within the psychoanalytical world, though a surprising amount of agreement can be found too amongst all those who claim any kind of influence from Freud. It is fascinating to me to see how many different schools of thought – not only within psycho-analysis but also Primal Therapy, Gestalt, Transactional Analysis, and followers of Jung and Wilhelm Reich – have come up against similar problems and have found their own solutions which often bring them round towards old opponents. There are, too, real differences which arouse powerful emotions: after all, the ideas of analysts touch very deeply on our feelings about our own parents and our own selves, our own guilt and innocence, our own effectiveness as workers and parents and children, and as therapists and teachers. Here I do not attempt to criticize other people's work nor to look very much at criticisms of the Kleinian approach. Space would only allow a very superficial attempt and I prefer to devote my space to describing what there is to criticize. I sometimes feel that university courses neglect a full understanding of the content in their hurry to criticize and pull it to pieces. Too critical an approach can prevent understanding, though so can a too uncritical attitude. There are disagreements and criticisms which may be important; in the bibliography I give some sources where these can be found. There is no Bible for psychoanalysis: there is no one 'psychoanalytical viewpoint'. Each analyst has to some extent their own personal view which the reader then interprets through their own personal view. Some people are put off by this sense of disagreement, as if they wanted something they could really trust and believe in wholeheartedly, knowing that it was definitely true and right, and abdicating their own responsibility for checking each individual statement and seeking out the truth and the falsehood in their understanding of it. I must ask the reader to be responsible for assessing the validity and usefulness of this way of looking at the world: such judgements cannot really be left to others.

Let me now summarize some of the main ideas I include in the rest of this book.

The most important and basic idea is that of phantasy. Phantasies are unconscious fantasies, in a sense, which control our assumptions, our thoughts, our emotions and our behaviour. I devote the whole of Chapter 2 to getting this idea over and making it comprehensible. In some ways the word 'phantasy' seems to me to give a similar freedom to the freedom a child gains when it learns the concept of 'pretend'. What is 'pretend' can be subjected to different laws from what is 'real'; as a result the child is free to play and to experiment in a way that it could not do if it did not make the distinction. With the concept of phantasy we have a word which takes away many of the problems of talking about what is reality; phantasies can be more or less realistic and we treat them as if they were real and true.

An example of a phantasy is the idea that was popular in the sixties that some people 'had a policeman in their head'. Clearly there was no real policeman in their head, but they were supposed to behave and think as if there were.

The rest of the book will be concerned with following through some common phantasies which seem to me to be useful ones to know about. The first half of the book is concerned mainly with daily life; the second section more with theoretical issues.

In Chapter 3 I describe some of the phantasies which can lie behind particular feelings such as anger and falling in love: ways we can 'interpret' these feelings and thereby make problems for ourselves or others.

In Chapters 4 and 5 I look at some of the ways we use other people to help us to change our phantasies about the world and about ourselves. First I concentrate on phantasies whereby we put parts of ourselves into others, either just 'seeing' them there or actually indulging in behaviour which will provoke another person to express some feeling or ability of our own. In Chapter 5 I concentrate on the phantasies whereby we take over from other people their characteristics, and use them for our own purposes. Both these chapters are closely connected with processes of learning and changing which go on in everyday life. Many marital interactions and parent–child interactions can be understood in terms of combinations of such phantasies.

In Chapter 6 I take up the issue of blame and responsibility: this is a problem which often seems to cause considerable misunderstanding. Different kinds of intention are discussed, and the questions about the sharing of responsibility for the way we are as adults.

Chapter 7 looks at some of the phantasies which arise, particularly around the stressful times of birth and death, in the family. I show some of the unrealistic assumptions we have at such times and suggest that there may be a link with strongly frightening phantasies about what it means to be dependent as a baby is.

Chapter 8 takes a similar look at phantasies to do with work and earning money. The way the phantasies of an individual interact with those of the wider world around is touched on.

Chapter 9 takes us out of everyday life into the consulting room; I look at some of the ways in which phantasies have been uncovered in analysis, and discuss some of the issues which worry people about the process.

The question of evidence for the apparently strange ideas of analysts is taken up again in Chapter 10, where I look briefly at the ways we can observe babies and make quite surprising discoveries about them. I also discuss some of the difficulties of a theoretical and emotional nature which disturb such observations.

I end with a short classified bibliography, which is intended partly to fill gaps I have left in explaining the ideas of analysts, especially Kleinian ones, and partly to provide some critical or opposing views.

TWO

PHANTASY AS PERCEPTION

In this chapter I want to introduce the concept of phantasy which is basic to the rest of the book.

Our heads are full of phantasies. Not just *fantasies* – by which I mean stories we make up to amuse ourselves – but 'stories' we are deeply involved in and convinced by and which go on independently of our conscious awareness or intention. *Phantasies* make up the background to everything we do, think or feel: they determine our perceptions and in a sense *are* our perceptions.

I do not at the moment intend to go into the evidence for this statement nor to try to define phantasy in a rigorous way. I want to show how I *use* the concept, and I ask you, the reader, to bear with me for a while by taking it on trust until you are in a position to look for your own evidence, make your own definition if you so wish, and – more importantly – learn to use it yourself. As I said in the introduction, this process may take a little time and you may need patience. Wilfred Bion describes the effect of an analyst giving a 'deep' interpretation to a patient in a way which may describe what happens to those coming across some psychoanalytical ideas for the first time. 'The immediate reaction, from my experience,' he says, 'is that it is so much nonsense, a foible of the analyst. I cannot see what other preliminary reaction there can be. But after a time you begin to think there may be something in it and to be suspicious that you do behave in this peculiar manner and that therefore there is much to be said for that theoretical formulation. But to speak of a theory as if it were "absolute truth" is ridiculous.' The ideas I am offering – including the idea of unconscious phantasy – I am offering for you to play with, to try out and to speculate about. Whether you find them convincing or not depends not only on my efforts to make them convincing, but also on whether you are prepared to do this with them.

All perceptions, so neurologists tell us, are in a sense 'interpretations'.

We receive very limited data in terms of signals picked up by our eyes, ears and other sensory organs: it is the brain which puts two and two together with experience and makes not only five but fifty. The brain relies to an enormous extent upon previous experience, expectations and the ability to spot a slight but sufficient likeness between widely varying situations. There are many experiments which show how easy it is to fool the brain into making a wrong interpretation. But without this ability to make immediate, automatic judgements about the world and to treat them as if they were the truth, we would be unable to go about our everyday lives with the confidence and competence we do. Normally we do not need to be concerned about the inaccuracies of our rather rough-and-ready estimations. It does not usually matter that straight lines may seem to bend or bent lines appear straight, or even – usually – that a conversation on the telephone relies to a very large extent upon guesswork by the listener. But what can matter very much is that we perceive ourselves and other people also in this rough-and-ready manner.

Using very slight data we jump to quite unjustified conclusions about people. Quite unconsciously, without turning our attention to it, we search around for an existing pattern or phantasy which has sufficient points of similarity for it to be used as a 'completion' for the new data. And this is very important indeed. I can get along quite well enough with my common-sense perception of tables and chairs. but I far more often find that my perception of other people – or myself – has led me wildly astray. Not only do we take one generous or one foolish act as evidence, for a few seconds at least and often for much longer, that we *are* very generous or very foolish in spite of our knowledge of our meanness or our good sense, but we also take very slight similarities between people as evidence, quite without questioning or even thinking about it, that these people are in other ways identical. And we then treat them accordingly.

Just as, presented with 'yeserday', we unthinkingly insert the 't' and may as rapidly find a completion for 'recnt' without perhaps noticing that there is a choice, so, presented with an old lady, a small child or a young man, we 'complete' according to what is already available in our heads and so endow them with a lot of extra characteristics which may or may not turn out to be justified.

Described in terms of how our brains work, this sounds plausible enough perhaps, but – you may be wondering – is it true? It may not feel like that; perhaps you are thinking how you see everybody as different and never mistake one person for another. On a conscious level this may be so. The fact that two people have red hair says nothing about what they are like as people and nobody would claim that it did *really*. And yet there may be ways in which you do in fact, in part of your mind which is not so 'sensible', make some kind of identification between two people like this.

Let me show you this process detected in real life.

I worked for a while as a nursing auxiliary in a mental hospital on a ward for those physically ill. There was an old lady there I was drawn to and, after a while, I realized that she reminded me of a great-aunt of mine. I had stayed with this great-aunt as a child and she had accused me – unjustly, I thought – of being ungrateful and inconsiderate. The old lady in the mental hospital was a heaven-sent opportunity to prove that I was not ungrateful and inconsiderate. I loved that old lady. I fed her and protected her from the other nurses' impatience. All the time she never spoke and I built up for her a character. To me she practically *was* my great-aunt, though I did not realize this at the time. She seemed a dignified, rather prim old lady: her mouth, which she would scarcely open, even to eat, was pursed up in a prissy way. I fondly imagined that, unlike my great-aunt, she was feeling gratitude and affection for me too. Then one day she did open her mouth – to emit a stream of obscenities in a foghorn-like bellow. The bubble burst and I learnt in a very practical way just how convincing 'transference' relationships can be. On the basis of a look on her face and a need in me to show that I was a good girl, I had 'transferred' to the old lady a whole character which had nothing to do with what she was really like. I had 'completed' my perception of her with my own phantasies. I never felt the same about her after that.

Throughout this book I shall be using examples from my own experience with myself and with other people (I have of course disguised identities at times). But clearly my experience is insufficient evidence for the processes I describe. I hope that you will 'complete' your reading of the book by being stimulated to think of your own experiences which have similarities to mine. It is these products of your own mind which will really make sense to you and change your perceptions. You may, for example, remember being on some occasion amongst a group of people you did not know and yet wanted to get to know. Did you find yourself drawn to some, wary of others, uninterested in others? You may remember some initial expectations you had about some of the people which turned out to be disappointed or to be confirmed later. If you think about it you may be able to discover where your expectations came from.

When I moved to a new area with a new baby I had to find other people to talk to during the day. Daily visits to the park finally provided me with a collection of people to look amongst. I liked the look of one woman with a child like mine and gradually got to know her. Over a period of time I made a series of discoveries about her which gave me quite a shock and which forced me to reassess both her and myself. In spite of my initially knowing nothing about her beyond her appearance and the way she treated her child and me, I had assumed that she would in certain ways be like the friends I had recently left behind. The reality of her age, her politics, her job and her education all made me do a 'double take' and gave me an immediate reaction of anxiety: had I done or said anything I would not have done if I had known? This was not simply a matter of what *anyone* would have assumed, since the thing about her which might have been expected to surprise – the fact that she was not living with a man – did not surprise me in the slightest; it simply made her more like my friends and acquaintances. As far as that was concerned I had no expectations either way.

In the two examples I have given here we can see that I fitted new acquaintances into patterns which were already there. I did not at first consciously think 'she is like so-and-so'; I simply treated the new people as if they were people of my phantasy; hence the shock when I discovered that I was mistaken. There are in fact many different kinds of interpretation or completion we make where we may be quite ready to see our own contribution. But they can still subject us to this kind of shock, or by their inaccuracies or insufficiencies amount to quite serious errors of judgement.

We can quite consciously 'complete' by interpreting an ordinary conversation.

'I'm sorry, I can't come round tonight, I've got to wash the bathroom walls.' (Believe it or not, this was reported to me as a real incident.) This statement was understood to mean: 'I don't actually want to come round tonight'; and further: 'because I don't like you and I can't even be bothered to think up a more convincing excuse'. The interpretation may or may not have been justifiable; the person whose invitation was thus refused did not stay long enough to find out. She was so convinced by it that she did not pursue the matter further in case she was given the hint even more plainly. If she had been more confident in herself or the relationship, of course, she might have found that the statement was made with quite another intention.

Posy shows this process of interpreting conversations better than I can (see next page).

Not only conversations but also behaviour is interpreted quite consciously as a matter of course. A husband who suddenly began coming

Posy Simmonds, *Guardian*, 12 May 1980.

home at three o'clock in the morning might be suspected of having an affair unless he had very convincing explanations to the contrary. A grandmother who talked incessantly of one grandchild to the exclusion of the others might be suspected of having a favourite, however much she denied it. A girl who stepped on the foot of a good-looking but unknown young man might be suspected of acting with intent, however profusely she apologized.

All these events are 'understood' to mean more than they ostensibly 'say', by being fitted into patterns of behaviour which make sense to us. We may have conflicting patterns so that the girl's behaviour may simultaneously fit into a pattern of 'clumsy' behaviour as well as a pattern of 'seductive' behaviour. In some situations we might perceive only one interpretation where other people might perceive the other or both. We can imagine a jealous father who might see his daughter simply being clumsy and *therefore* (or so he might say) be angry with her: an observer might suspect that his anger is more appropriate to the denied interpretation which suggests that the girl is seeking a lover who might replace her father in her affections. The observer is putting an interpretation on the behaviour of both of them, and the father would probably not like it.

The patterns we recognize and use every day vary considerably from person to person. Some people are very quick to see signs of pregnancy, or of distress or hostility in others with uncanny accuracy. Some people always interpret behaviour in the worst possible way; others are always giving the benefit of the doubt. Some see romances everywhere; others do not see the most obvious flirtation going on under their noses. Some people seem to have an enviable ability to see things realistically, without jumping to conclusions or missing significant clues. What you see depends not only on what you want to see – and 'there's none so blind as them as won't see' – but also on what you have learnt to interpret in a particular way. My son was prone to vomiting and I rapidly learnt to interpret the preliminary signs – other people were much more likely to have to clean the carpet. Psychoanalysts teach each other to extend their interpretative powers by showing each other what they have seen, just as a mother or teacher or friend might pass on their own interpretations of the world around. The peculiarities and the unacceptability of psychoanalytical interpretations arise more from what analysts see than from the way they look, which is itself no more than a refinement of everyday behaviour. Even in everyday life there is sometimes a feeling that it is not *fair* to take people literally or to assume that even a part of them intended to make a tactless remark or an embarrassing slip. (As my mother says, with people like me around you have to take out your words and look at them: you're not safe any more. In fact you never were safe: the everyday need to 'take out your words and look at them' gave rise to the expression in the first place. I was frequently accused as a child of misinterpreting some remark which was not supposed to be taken seriously. As she also used to say: 'You should *know* that when I say fridge I mean oven!' One of the side-effects of understanding your own phantasies a bit better is that you are less likely to say fridge when you do mean oven, or, more seriously, yes when you mean no. However, I am straying from the point.)

One of the ways analysts teach each other to observe involves what is known as 'counter-transference'. The feelings a patient arouses in the analyst can be used as a sensitive response to something in the patient. Learning to distinguish between more appropriate or realistic feelings in the situation and less realistic ones, the analyst learns to use his or her own emotional responses not as immediate signals to act upon, but as a kind of diagnostic tool.

An important part of learning from experience through building up internal phantasies is that we can also learn what 'ain't so'. Having been twice usurped in love relationships by blonde girls, a friend of mine learnt to view *all* blonde girls with the deepest suspicion, though there was no reason to suppose that her husband should prefer them to dark-haired girls. We generalize from the particular; we say 'I can't stand people like that', or 'everybody says ...' when the basis for the statement is no more than bad experiences with one or two people. We tend to judge a school by a few noisy pupils on the bus. We may judge communists by Stalin and Americans by their presidents or by their behaviour during a war. All this is obvious and not quite true. We do equate people who cannot realistically be equated; we do lump together 'policemen' or 'teachers' or 'the unemployed' or 'the rich' and view them with certain prejudices. But the prejudices do not simply arise from learning by experience of real people, nor from what we read in the papers, though both of these sources may have their influence. We see people through phantasies which are the end-result not only of learning but also of a lot of working out in our heads and a lot of distortion of and addition to perceptions of internal and external reality.

Phantasies sometimes approximate quite closely to reality, using the word reality in a common-sense way. We can distinguish on one level at least between father and husband, brother and son. At another level, however, things are not so clear. We may refer to husband, employer and father all by the same phrase, 'my old man', or we may call our children accidentally by somebody else's name – often a younger brother's, for example. When we do anything like this we are clearly making links between people at a level which influences our behaviour – what we call people – and this suggests that we are using phantasies which are somehow common to the linked people and which may be distortions of one or other of them. These distortions can arise in many ways.

One obvious way in which our phantasies of people may become less than realistic involves the way we carry on relating to them when they are not there. Many people away from their mother, especially in their twenties, find that their picture of her changes. They may have arguments or discussions with her in their heads, and experience some kind of shock on discovering that she has in fact had no part in the conversation. Many people have told me how they do this: parting from their mother perhaps in some bad feeling, they work on the relationship entirely in their own heads so that the next time they meet or speak on the phone there is the same hope and expectation that *this* time she will understand – only for the pattern of disappointment to be repeated all over again. Misunderstandings between husband and wife can happen in a similar way, where one is quite convinced that they have told the other something, only to find it was a conversation which was never spoken aloud.

Distortions can happen in other ways too. Since we always understand something new in terms of what we already know, my present-day adult phantasies must be related, however distantly, to phantasies I developed not only in childhood but also in earliest infancy when perception began. Sometimes there may seem to be a relatively obvious connection: my experience of seven-year-old boys was virtually limited to the experience of my brothers until my son reached that age, and this may contribute to my calling him by my brother's name. In fact this is not enough as an explanation, but it has some part to play. But there are other ways in which childhood phantasies can set the ground rules which seriously affect and distort all subsequent perceptions in a particular area.

If I learnt at my mother's knee that Men Are Not To Be Trusted, I might never trust one sufficiently to find out if it is true. If I learnt that I would never have anything unless I fought for it, I might never dare sit back long enough to find out that some things come of their own accord. If I learnt that everything I struggled for would be taken from me, I might give up struggling very early on. Equally, memories of being once loved might bear me through terrible experiences later on. The kind of trust in the environment built up in the very early days affects how much the child can lay itself open to experiences and so to receive and give love. Too much early suspicion can prevent any reassuring experiences from 'getting through'; if the only expectation from the environment is harsh treatment, all attempts to break into the child's reverie will be experienced as frightening and threatening and to be determinedly resisted. Sometimes these expectations seem to come from inside the child's own mind: a child who is treated with only the utmost love and care may still have extremely terrifying phantasies about the world.

Children's phantasies are in fact often extremely unrealistic, looked at from the standpoint of an adult. Some have obvious roots: at the age of three, my sons both expressed the belief that they would have babies 'in their wombs' and were slow to give the idea up. Others are less obvious; one child told his mother, with a charming smile, that he wished she were dead so he could cut off her breast and have it all to himself. I came in from the garden once with my hand dripping blood from a cut, and Paul, then two, who had been sitting in the kitchen all the time, half asked and half stated: 'I didn't do it, did I mummy?' Such unrealistic views of the world betrayed in children's words may leave their traces in unconscious phantasies influencing our whole lives, if they have for some reason resisted being judged and tested by the common sense of the child or adult as they grow older.

I once saw a woman relieved of the phantasy that she had killed her brother forty years earlier. She 'knew' that he had died of diphtheria but she also 'knew' that she had killed him by giving him a 'poison' of Yorkshire pudding mixed with orange juice the week before. In a discussion she suddenly realized that she had carried this around as a secret burden of guilt all these years. Such ideas, which are so convincing and frightening to the child, may be kept out of conscious thought and so avoid being tested against later knowledge. Many people seem to suffer from a terrible nameless fear or guilt, just on the edge of consciousness, resulting from some such misinterpretation of events which they dare not reconsider, in case thinking about it simply opens up an old wound.

Sometimes traces of infantile phantasies seem to be maintained in physical symptoms. People with asthma often complain in analysis of feeling 'suffocated' by their mothers. In their breathing difficulties they may be both experiencing and expressing the feeling of being unable to breathe because their mother is all around them – that they have no free space to breathe in, that she might be breathed in and would then control them from the inside as well as by her intrusive and prying behaviour outside. Such a phantasy, expressed in the asthma, remains outside the realm of thought and thus maintains its conviction in the face of knowledge that it cannot be so. Often with asthma, removal of some of the anxieties arising from such phantasies can be sufficient to prevent attacks recurring, however they arose in the first place. It is important to note here that I am not saying that asthma is caused by over-solicitous mothers: the phantasy of the intrusive mother may just as well arise from the child's own desire to get into or take over its mother's body, which the child uses to 'interpret' perfectly normal concern on the mother's part. Nor am I saying that the asthma has no physical origins: there are often physical triggers which affect the body and the subsequent phantasies. All I wish to point out is that physical behaviour and bodily symptoms are endowed with meaning by phantasies and that phantasies can be 'felt' as bodily symptoms. Mind and body are not independent of each other: changes in one may arise from and cause changes in the other.

Other phantasies which may be felt as physical symptoms are those expressed in such phrases as 'a burden of guilt', 'a stab in the back' or 'a slap in the face'. 'Stinging' words may cause the recipient to wince: some people seem to go around looking as if they are weighed down by a physical burden, or they walk furtively, looking over their shoulder both metaphorically and perhaps physically. Someone who goes to a counsellor feeling – on some level – that they are 'unloading a lot of shit' may leave feeling temporarily 'relieved'. Body language as well as metaphors can be seen as an expression of phantasies at work within.

In the next few chapters I shall be looking at some quite unrealistic phantasies people seem to have about themselves and about the world. One group of such phantasies are those which involve the idea that a part of you, or you yourself, can get inside someone else. A small boy I knew once said to his mother 'I shall get right inside your breast and snuggle up.' The idea of 'giving your heart' is an expression of such a phantasy: John Donne's poetry is full of it. The desire to put the most treasured and life-giving part of yourself into the person you love, and to receive theirs in return, is a desire which may in phantasy be enacted and satisfied: the wish and the action may not be distinguished. It is also, of course, a phantasy enacted in a practical way in bed.

The internal logic of such lovers' phantasies is in fact often detectable as it works itself out in real life. After the initial excitement of the 'putting in' has worn off, feelings connected with being trapped inside, or controlled by somebody who is inside you, or 'always on your back' may emerge. Married couples often say they feel their spouse is watching and criticizing everything they do as if they were inside their head; some people feel like this about their parents or about other people who are important to them. Teenage children fight to 'escape' from the parents they previously were only too keen to keep near them. Mothers find that their delight in being a mother gives way at times to terrible feelings of suffocation and being caught in a trap where they must play the parts assigned to them by other people – of mother, daughter, wife – but are unable to hold on to any sense of their own identity apart from this.

There are many responses to this kind of feeling, just as there are many ways in which parts of yourself can be in phantasy put into someone. The putting in and the separating out can be done gently or violently, guiltily or kindly, harshly and destructively or carefully and with the eventual creation of something stronger and better. I shall be looking at these in more detail later on. Uncovering such phantasies in everyday life can sometimes be very enlightening, both in the sense of making a burden lighter and of throwing light on a gloomy situation. Phantasies are experienced as if they were reality; the feelings they arouse are real even if the events they portray are not. Finding and naming the phantasies can enable them to be changed and made more realistic so that they no longer add to the problems of daily life.

Partly because of these phantasies of putting parts of yourself into other people – as a gift, for help, for love, to keep hope alive or in order to spoil and mess something up, for example – there are many phantasies in which ownership of feelings or characteristics is confused. I may only recognize my own scorn, my own harsh critical eye, my own obstinacy, when I see it in someone else, and I may treat them the worse as a result of the phantasy that it *is* my scorn, or whatever, in them. This is of course projection, which occurs in many forms and which I deal with more in Chapter 4. Here I want to point out some of the powerful emotions which are involved in the process of creating and using phantasies.

Phantasies are selected, used and created under the influence of extremely powerful emotions. We do not 'give our hearts' unless we love passionately. When I sought out the old lady in the mental hospital part of me was still seething with rage against my great-aunt, and full of anxiety that she might be right about me. I would probably never make a fuss about someone else's obstinacy if I were not somehow preoccupied with, and probably terrified of my own. But the emotions do not simply govern which phantasy will be brought into operation – whether the father will see his daughter being clumsy or seductive, for example, or which part of reality we will be interested in and which part we refuse to recognize; they also govern the nature of the phantasies themselves.

Let us suppose for a minute that as a small child I phantasized that I had taken my mother away from my father and had taken her safely inside me, depriving him of her food and love and understanding. The internal logic of this phantasy might lead me to imagine that my father was out to get me for it. If the desire to maintain the phantasy of having my mother all mine inside me was strong enough, I might work very hard to make sure that I only saw my father in this way. All the things I saw him doing would be coloured by this phantasy, and I could 'perceive', perhaps in an utterly inoffensive man, a raging monster. If I then see all men as potential rivals for my mother, using this phantasy as all I know about men in general, I might run from them so fast that I can never find out that they are not all like this. But note, in terms of the phantasy I do not *want* to know that men are not revengeful monsters. If I discovered that they were less powerful, for example, I might feel a need to 'give back' my mother to them, out of pity or guilt or love perhaps. Or worse, I might find they were not against me because I had not in fact got my mother all to myself at all. And if I feel very strongly that I desperately need my mother inside me to keep at bay the terrible dangers of my own fury, my own stomach aches, my own badness and weakness and other unimaginable evils, both inside and outside, I may well feel I could not face being without her.

This particular kind of phantasy would survive intact only if for some important reasons it seemed more rewarding, more satisfying or safer to keep a relationship like this with an unrealistic internal mother than with real men. Normally, more realistic phantasies of men seem to win out.

Here we see a phantasy with a built-in mechanism for maintaining itself; there are many such. They provide protection against undesirable and contradictory information from the point of view of the phantasy, though from an outsider's point of view they may seem to be perversely limiting and crippling. They may also be perceived by the sufferer as problematic: people who are unreasonably terrified of men are sometimes themselves aware that they have a problem. The ramifications of the roots of such phantasies and the power of the emotions which help to maintain them should not be underestimated: they make it understandable why people can be so reluctant to even look at their behaviour and feelings, let alone at the phantasies which govern them. One woman who came somewhat reluctantly for help was terrified of what the therapy would uncover in her. Very quickly it emerged that she felt she had such a murderous rage that she had been responsible for the suicide of her sister, the subsequent misery of her whole family, and had nearly provoked her husband into killing her too. Such feelings are not to be considered lightly.

It may seem far-fetched that people might have phantasies such as this one about their mother being inside them and protecting them while laying them open to furious jealousy and attack from the outside. But there is a very common, perfectly conscious shared belief in something which is not so dissimilar. Christians believe that there is an all-powerful, all-knowing being, whose location inside or outside the self may be argued about, and who provides enormous help against internal and – to a lesser extent – external dangers. In phantasy, the mother's breast, just like God, may be deeply felt to be a real source of life and goodness and hope, giving strength which far outweighs the strength of the individual. Such phantasies can lend the most powerful force to adult experience and behaviour. Great deeds have been done, great sacrifices made and great crimes committed in the name of God the Father. Just as a phantasy of having the mother inside can be linked with terror of men, so the belief in God can be linked with terror of large categories of people, or with a desire to punish and attack them. The Infidel, Jews, Catholics or Protestants may all, in the name of 'the true religion', be fervently feared and attacked as 'the devil himself'.

Before I leave this chapter I have to make explicit an extremely important point. In talking about phantasies in the way I do I am rather in the position of a physicist introducing the subject of the nature of matter. To begin with and, under certain circumstances, later too, the analogy of billiard balls is close enough to give some idea of how electrons behave. But there is a lot more to electrons than this, and there is a lot more subtlety to the origins and nature of phantasies than my words so far have allowed. There is a particular distortion in the use of words to describe the most primitive phantasies. Christians agree that words are not enough to do full justice to the nature of God; they can at best only evoke something of him. Music and flavours too cannot be adequately described in words. With some of the deeper phantasies naming actually changes them. Words are used to take away fears, to modify phantasies which arose before words could be used.

Susan Isaacs once described a little girl with poor speech development who at the age of one year and eight months was terrified of a shoe with a flapping sole her mother used to wear. She would shrink away and scream whenever she saw it, so her mother hid it away. Fifteen months later she suddenly said to her mother in a frightened voice: 'Where are mummy's broken shoes?' Her mother hastily said she had sent them away, and the child commented: 'They might have eaten me right up.'

This phantasy was clearly active well before the words were. But part of the phantasy – the screaming terror which accompanied it – no longer belongs to the verbal version. This is very important when it comes to trying to imagine how things might seem to a tiny baby. The earliest phantasies are of incredibly dangerous, unnamed, seemingly unnameable dangers and powers – of perpetual bliss, of fusion with the loving and wonderful world for ever, of being suspended in total horror for ever, of disintegration into a million painful fragments – as well as relatively less powerful emotional states, when the world can be looked at and examined for what it actually contains. But in using words I am forced to reduce the horror and the beauty, and to describe something which cannot even be evoked easily since we have forgotten these experiences ourselves – for good reasons. What early infantile phantasies were like may very occasionally be glimpsed or physically felt in flashes, perhaps in response to playing a piece of music, watching a play, reading poetry, falling in love or in a religious experience, but, like the size of a subatomic particle, normally, for most of us, it is easier to talk of them than to imagine them.

In some ways perhaps it is unimportant if these experiences remain no more than words on a page. Some kind of information can be gleaned. But when it comes to being convinced by them, or to finding your own or someone else's phantasies, to sorting out those primitive perceptions of the world which are not only unrealistic but are also causing trouble in one way or another, the evocation of the experience is essential. Words which name phantasies are a tool which can make the experiencing of them in a more conscious way possible and bearable: it is this experiencing in a new and safer context which effects change, and also makes sense of the words.

Perhaps this explains partly why large generalizations are often of little help for those who work 'with people'. Generalizations are even further, it seems, from experience than concrete and detailed descriptions. The jump needed to translate from a generalization to personal experience seems to be larger than the jump we have to make, given one concrete experience, to translate it into something similar of our own. Our minds work naturally to seek out similarities and we can use this process to our advantage. I am trying to trigger off in you memories, and abilities to observe, which will give you some idea of the kind of processes I am describing. But it is this which perhaps offends some whose understanding of scientific observation is different. The testing, the proof or the criticism has to be undertaken by you, the reader, and unfortunately your task is by no means easy. Phantasies are by definition *unconscious* fantasies: you cannot simply look into your conscious memory and say 'Yes, I remember wanting to marry my mother and kill my father'; this does not constitute proof, nor its absence disproof, of psychoanalytical ideas. That you cannot see something does not, unfortunately, mean that it is not there.

Summary

I have tried in this chapter to give some idea of how we perceive by means of phantasies which we treat as if they were true representations of reality, just as a religious person may perceive the world through the beliefs of his or her particular sect. I have tried to show how some phantasies come quite close to reality (as the picture we have of long-standing friends may be a reasonably good approximation to how they are) and how others are wildly inaccurate as statements of fact, such as the phantasy expressed in 'I'll eat you up!' And yet these larger-than-life phantasies can have just as strong an effect upon our thoughts, feelings and actions as those which are more realistic. As we grow up we do not and cannot get rid of phantasies: all we can ever hope to do is to make them more realistic than they were before.

I have tried to show how phantasies derive not simply from 'pure' memories but from people and events 'taken in' or created under the influence of strong emotions, and that these emotions continue to influence perceptions in ways we simply do not notice. It is the relation between emotions and phantasies which I want to look at in the next chapter.

THREE

PHANTASIES AND FEELINGS

In this chapter I want to look more closely at the links between phantasies and feelings. I want to show how phantasies are triggered by events and sensations arising from the internal world and from the external world, and how they then mediate between the raw data and the feelings which are aroused. I want to show why some people seem to respond to situations with apparently inappropriate emotions or exaggerated ones: too much or too little feeling; despair or euphoria which goes beyond the reasonable; guilt where we might expect anger; or anger where we might expect an apology. I want to show how some feelings can seem intolerable and to look at some of the possible effects of attempts people make to avoid them.

As we go about our daily lives things happen to us, or we do things, which we interpret in our own ways. Having an accident in the car may feel like the end of the world, at least for a brief moment. Losing a job may 'mean' we are totally incompetent and will never get another one and do not deserve to live. Getting a job may 'mean' that we are the most wonderful person in the world, able to do the job far better than it has ever been done before. All of these 'meanings' quite naturally lead to particular emotions. Very often we are aware that we are responding to something rather different from the actual, simple event. Often we may be able to say to ourselves, 'Don't be silly, it's not the end of the world', for example, and so restore a sense of proportion. The pleasure and humour in discovering such 'silly' phantasies may make us laugh with relief, when once we have named them closely enough. 'When I started this job, I really thought I was going to be the saviour of all my clients' is a comment I have often heard from social workers; it is often said with a laugh of amazement.

Sometimes the interpretations we give to events are nastier than this, and do not lead so easily to being made more realistic. A very 'naughty' child, seeing another working hard and being praised by the teacher, may 'understand' that this child is 'just' being good to make the naughty one feel worse. There is no hope of being able to emulate such industry and getting such approval, only the terrible conviction that such bliss is for them unattainable. The perfectly 'natural' response may then be to disrupt the working of the 'good' child and so remove the agony of the contrast between them, and punish the good one for making the 'naughty' one feel so bad. Vandalism and all kinds of disruptive behaviour can arise from the interpretation of situations in such a way that goodness is unbearable.

Once a particular event has triggered a phantasy, this phantasy leads perhaps to action, perhaps to a particular feeling: to revengefulness for example, or despair; to hope or delight. This feeling itself may then trigger other phantasies which act to wind up or wind down the feelings.

Let us suppose that I have lost my favourite coat or handbag. This will have given rise to a sense of loss, of wanting something badly and not being able to have it. There will also be feelings of extreme anger and irritation with myself for my stupidity, and so on. A lot of feelings will be aroused, some of them tending to crowd out others. Just taking the sense of loss as an example, this feeling quite clearly will have arisen in me before. Since similarities of virtually any kind can act as triggers, previous experiences of loss are likely to come flooding into my mind. Memories of having lost handbags before, memories of losing favourite toys when I was small, memories of losing anything I cared about may come to mind. These memories are not usually static; they are like a film unrolling. The memory of losing my purse may be followed by the anger I felt when my mother refused to reimburse all the money I lost in it, and the sense of grief and guilt about losing a present given to me by somebody I never saw again, for example. The sense of loss in each particular memory or phantasy will change as a result of the unrolling of the film. This is important, since it gives me a rapid idea of the kind of changes I can expect as a result of this particular loss. If previous experiences of loss ended up as not too disastrous, then I may have some hope that I will survive this one. If previous experiences of loss led to a feeling which was too unbearable, I may expect such a feeling again.

One of the previous experiences of loss which I must have suffered, and which analysts find is in fact triggered by any deeply significant loss, is the experience of being deprived of my mother's breast, or her comforting presence, when I was very small. When I was that small, the world around me consisted of huge, enormously powerful people and things: I was not entirely clear about which were alive and which were dead – such distinctions probably did not have much relevance to me. I was utterly dependent upon these enormous beings for everything relating to my own comfort: food, warmth, being held or being given attention. Clearly, the phantasies I would use then to interpret the loss of my mother's breast would be formed in a world which was very different from that of an adult. Quite realistically, it might mean to me the loss of my mother's interest or affection, if, for example, she did not very much like older babies. Or it might mean an improvement in my relationship with older siblings, if they had found it very hard to cope with my special relationship with my mother. It might mean relief from hunger if breast-feeding was not going well. Or it might mean that I determined from that moment on to feed myself and never to be mothered again, in order to protect myself from the horror and fury of being so cruelly deprived of something I wanted. Or it might mean that I convinced myself that I should rely only on men for love, and never again on a woman. The possibilities are endless and will of course depend very much on the environment, as well as on such matters of chance as my own physical responses, my digestion, my tolerance of frustration, and my age and circumstances at the time.

Where previous experiences of loss have not been too horrifying, I might not mind too much feeling it. I will be able to suffer for a while, knowing that the experience is bearable and that every cloud has a silver lining. If previous experiences of loss were too terrible, I may not allow myself to feel this one: I may cut the agony off short. If I did this as a child, the feelings of loss may trigger extremely raw phantasies: ones which were not allowed to develop into anything less painful, but remained out of touch. Where this has happened, the phantasies which have been cut off have, for example, a sense of timelessness about them. A sense of time is the product of conscious working with phantasies, of being able to hold on to past and present together, without using one to destroy the other. The sense of loss which is timeless will of course be much more horrifying than one which is firmly embedded in a sense of time, and which we know will gradually develop and change into something more bearable.

Phantasies which we consider unbearable have a nightmare quality about them. Not only are they timeless, but they are utterly horrifying. It seems that we have in us phantasies about totally disintegrating, about falling apart and being frozen in a permanent state of being exploded in agony; these phantasies are not reasonable. We get a glimpse of such phantasies when people say things like: 'She couldn't cope with that!' or 'You'll kill your mother if you tell her that'; or 'He'd collapse', or 'He'd go to pieces', or 'I was afraid I'd fall apart.' In phantasy these metaphors have a horrible sense of reality to them: we really believe them – or worse: the phantasy may be not only that we are falling to pieces, but that each piece is screaming in agony; not only are we being torn apart by pain, but someone is actually cutting us up or sticking knives into us deliberately to punish us for some utterly unnameable crime. These phantasies may never be allowed into conscious feeling: we may keep them wrapped up and hidden, and feel only a sense of fear or guilt or horror, connected with hiding something extremely dangerous, both to ourselves and to everyone we love.

Part of the problem with these unspeakable phantasies is that they remain in their raw state, ready to be triggered by any new situation. Part of the horror of being faced with a new pain that we have not felt before, be it the pain of a toothache or the pain of a divorce, involves the fact that we have just such agonizing and timeless phantasies ready to be triggered, to be applied in our quick mental search for something which will make sense of the new situation. As long as we are actually in a state of 'not knowing', in our phantasy world we are likely to be in a state of 'knowing' something really terrifying and terrible. This is why even being told 'You have cancer of the jaw' can give a sense of relief and make the pain more bearable. The agony of the cancer is indeed caught up with the misery and sorrow of dying perhaps, and leaving loved people without you, but some of the more horrifying phantasies of being punished, of bringing it on yourself, of suffering from an invasion by cruel beings, like Frankenstein's monster, created by you, are stilled. Where the pain is identified as plain toothache, it becomes, as my husband says, 'only physical' – but we may need to remind ourselves of this.

When we are very small we sort out our experience with the phantasies available to us. A baby suffering from a pain in the stomach may try the breast, since it has found that the breast can take away pains. If the pain is wind, not hunger, the tiny baby will scream as if all the devils in hell are attacking it: and this, it seems, is something like the baby's feeling. The breast has become a source of agony, and a shocking disappointment. All hope of gratification has been destroyed. The mother, too, if she is new to motherhood, may feel 'something is wrong with the breast'; she too has little experience to help her to sort out what is going on. With any luck, someone else will come along and show her how to bring the baby's wind up: with that burp, mother and baby have dramatically increased their stock of phantasies, much to everyone's relief.

In this case, the original phantasy, that a breast would be a solution to the problem, proved false, and a new solution was found. Frequently, older, less accurate phantasies may be sufficiently good to continue being used long after they could be accepted consciously. My mother used to give us something to nibble while we waited to eat properly, saying 'This'll keep the worms quiet.' The phantasy that my stomach was full of worms which bit me when they were hungry and lay still when they were full was one which I discovered was still affecting my behaviour when I was twenty. It was not me that was hungry: it was the worms. This phantasy was for years perfectly adequate to make my behaviour consistent with keeping me alive. Until such phantasies for some reason give trouble, and are then actually discovered, they will not change.

One of the phantasies we use to get rid of very painful feelings attached to an unbearable, unnameable phantasy is the phantasy that we can make it not exist. There are many versions of this. We can imagine we are sicking it out, like we sicked out food we did not want as a baby. We can imagine we are building a big wall around it and sealing it in. We can 'place' it in part of our body, and then 'numb' that part so we have a permanent reminder not to feel whatever it is. If we feel our sexuality has brought us nothing but trouble, we may numb our genitals, perhaps, and so avoid feeling sexual ever again. We can close our eyes to something in ourselves, so we 'see' only a blackness, full of menace, but have no idea of what lies in or behind it. We may try to drown it: a feeling of guilt may be 'understood' to be 'my father telling me not to do it', and I may drink or drug myself silly in order to drown his voice, or him, inside me.

In the next chapter I shall be looking at ways we use our relations with other people partly to help along such denials: 'seeing' our own feelings in other people, as I saw my hunger in the worms, is a common way of attempting to get rid of painful feelings. Here I want to emphasize the fact that such phantasies are no more than phantasies, and the feeling which is thus denied does not in fact go away – it may be simply reinterpreted. My 'hunger' felt like 'being bitten'; the pain was still there. This is an extremely important point which many people fail to recognize.

Nicholas, aged three, came into the kitchen looking guilty. His mother asked him what was wrong and he said, shaking his head, 'I haven't broken John's spaceship.' This 'protesting too much' behaviour makes it clear that denial does not actually work. The need to state what is being denied gives us the clue. All the phantasies of denial include some acknowledgement of the reality of whatever is being denied.

A feeling of enormous rage, so enormous that I must deny it, may exist in the form of a phantasy of me actually taking a hatchet to the person I love best. If I cannot bear to allow this phantasy to live, to move on to the point where I in phantasy kill them, triumph over them, and then miss them and want them back – whereupon the reality that they are still alive can come as a pleasant relief – I am left with a conviction that I am somewhere actually killing them. However much I then deny this phantasy, it is *this* phantasy which is being denied. Keeping this phantasy out of conscious awareness, I am simply preventing it from becoming more realistic; I am not actually destroying it. I am still vulnerable to it in a way I could never be vulnerable to a more bearable phantasy. Nicholas could only relieve his feelings of guilt and fear in the long term by actually looking at the broken pieces of spaceship and asking for help in mending them or in telling John what he had done. My knowledge of internal reality tells me that I am actually killing the person I love, and I cannot escape this in any way while it exists in this form.

It is this kind of process which is at work when, for example, somebody seems totally unable to be angry with anyone. Michael was like this. He discovered that one of his colleagues was pilfering from the food stores in the hospital he worked in. Instead of feeling angry, he simply felt tremendously guilty himself. With some help, he traced this to a feeling that his righteous anger consisted of blowing up the person concerned, making them crumble to dust before his all-powerful fury. What he was then feeling was the guilt attached to actually destroying his colleague: his anger was denied because it was too powerful and dangerous. Denying his anger, he was left feeling guilty in a way which did not make sense in the situation.

Frances was unable to ask anyone to do anything for her because she was terrified they would be angry with her. When I asked her what anger meant to her she talked about people throwing cups and plates around the room, and about her father beating her mother when she was a child. For her, it seemed, there were no phantasies of a more constructive kind of anger: only a choice of 'no provocation' or total terror. Whenever she felt she needed help she was unable to hold on to the feeling: what she felt instead was a sense of fear towards the people around her, based on her understanding of their potential reactions to her need. She too never felt angry herself: such anger is hard to bear in the self, and she only felt it in others.

A similar process can happen with excessive guilt. A little bit of guilt *now* can trigger past situations in which guilt was felt, if only very briefly. Suppose, for example, that as a child I had said to my brother 'I wish you were dead' and he had been run over the next day. If I were small I could well believe that I was responsible for killing him or injuring him. I might then have terrible nightmares of him – or some frightening monster – coming to me and demanding my life for his, perhaps; or some enormous sacrifice which would make amends, as in fairy stories for example. My guilt could give rise to a terrible fear of attack; in my terror I might strike out at the accusing monsters and try to kill them before they kill me. If I am stuck with this phantasy waiting to be triggered every time I do anything I am afraid is wrong, I might then respond to any sign of my own guilt with an immediate attempt to ward it off, and in particular to fight off the person who accuses me. Instead of feeling guilt and sorrow in more reasonable proportions, I might be the kind of person who straight away strikes back with a counter-accusation of great bitterness.

The consequence of such a situation may well be that frightening phantasies appear to be confirmed. The person who has been attacked so bitterly for pointing out what seems to them a small, unimportant mistake may then in fact become an accuser in a more serious way. The frightening phantasy of being accused of a terrible crime then comes closer to realization.

Part of the belief in the most primitive and frightening phantasies depends on the way the real world has responded to your phantasies. If something has happened which seems to fit – if your mother has gone off for ever, or been run over, or become ill or had a miscarriage for example – at a time when you were still testing out the reality of your ability to make such things happen, your 'reality testing' may well seem to have produced the answer that your powers are indeed enormous. To this extent chance has a lot to answer for.

Looking at the roots of phantasies in infancy can make sense of the unrealistic enormity they often have. For a week-old child, being angry with the mother or her breast (for not being totally under the child's control, for not preventing all pain, for actually inflicting the pain of hunger or the discomfort of a wet nappy, perhaps) *is* being angry with the whole world. At this age the destructive aspect of anger phantasies is evident in the tone of the scream, which sounds as if the baby really feels attacked. Adults respond to such a cry very quickly; it is actually experienced by the listener as painful too. After a short while the tone of the baby's cry changes, as if the experience of anger and misery has begun to change too. But just as the breast at times fills the baby's world and field of vision at first, so phantasies of attacking this breast can seem to involve attacking the whole of existence, and trying to stop the baby-self being attacked out of existence itself. Normally we do not feel our adult anger like this, but sometimes schizophrenics do, attributing an earthquake in Guatemala, say, to their personal influence. Even if we have modified our phantasies somewhat, it makes sense that some people might still feel that they have the ability to shatter the world if only they let themselves go, and so never dare to feel their own anger or to arouse somebody else's.

I would like now to look at some phantasies connected with being in love or with loving. These phantasies too can range from the wonderful to the utterly unbearable: from ones which have an extremely happy outcome to ones which lead inexorably to horror and fear, so that love cannot be borne and may be attacked and thrust out of consciousness as soon as it threatens to arise. With love, the fact that a denied emotion is not necessarily lost for ever may seem more cheering. People often fear that they have lost their love for their spouses for ever when they have actually only lost touch with it for a while. Events later may bring back some of the love which was buried under disappointments and furious anger. Once the covering feelings have been worked through in some way, the buried love may re-emerge, albeit in a different, perhaps more realistic form.

Just as phantasies of anger and destructiveness have roots in babyhood, so too of course do phantasies of love. People often talk in terms of 'being one', of being united, merged, wrapped up in each other when they fall in love – or of a longing that this might happen, and a disappointment that it does not last. This sense of unity seems to be a common element which probably stems from the earliest love relationship with the mother's body, before she was felt to be a totally separate person. Or it may be a defensive attempt made by the baby initially, and later repeated as an adult, to create an illusion of oneness to fend off frightening phantasies connected with being separate beings. Just as a child I knew once said to his mother 'I shall get right inside your breast and snuggle up', so in a love relationship there may be a sense of being held and contained; of boundaries going round more than just the lonely self; of anger and fear at enforced separations; of timelessness and total absorption in each other. Listening to music or having a religious experience or belonging to a 'body' of people – as in a work or voluntary organization with 'members' – may be able to recreate for us something of the earliest phantasies of blissful unity with the source of all pleasure and life. Just like the baby, the adult has at times to face the limited nature of these phantasies, but may struggle to avoid it. With people we love, the emotional separation between them and us may be strongly fought off.

A mother may be utterly convinced that she knows what her teenage daughter wants or believes, just as she may have been convinced that she knew what her husband believed and felt when she fell in love with him, and may still. It is almost as if such people really felt they could get inside the head of someone else, and this 'knowledge' may fly in the face of all the evidence. 'I know she wants an abortion really, though she says she doesn't.' 'I know he doesn't like me working, though he found me this last job.' 'I know she wants me to give up seeing my mother, though she says she doesn't.' There may of course be elements of truth in these 'I know best' statements.

However, not only are there feelings of being united with the loved person, desires to merge with them, perhaps to control them totally or to hand over all responsibility for the self to them, but there are also at the same time some limits. There seem to be strong phantasies which at times conflict with these desires and which allow the other person to remain outside the self, different from and able to be of help to the self. If the mother and the breast become in phantasy too merged with the baby, a consequence may be that she is found to be no more use in times of difficulty than the baby-self is. It may be very nice at times to feel that you are the sole support of somebody, that they depend utterly upon you, so they can never go away from you and leave you, but there are other times, like at the first burping, when your need for somebody else is far more powerful than your need to do it yourself. If the other person is felt to be taken over and controlled entirely there can be a fear of losing the extra bit of them which is different and which is at times longed for and can give real cause for gratitude.

Recognizing the independence and separateness of the people you love involves recognizing the pain of knowing that they are not under your control, but it is essential for more realistic behaviour and phantasy. It also allows the pain and the pleasure of recognizing your own dependence and vulnerability, and making the phantasies triggered by these feelings more realistic and less frightening. For some people the sense of being dependent and vulnerable is extremely frightening. Where any sign of separateness between the self and loved people is interpreted as, perhaps, total desertion, as being left to disintegrate, as the destruction of the self and the whole world, this separateness may be intolerable. Dependence may be understood as being vulnerable to sadistic and angry attacks, the only defence being to unite with the attacker. But where dependence and vulnerability can be experienced in a situation where they do not lead to disaster, some of the earlier and more violent phantasies may be weakened. A husband or wife who promises to be faithful, in a way your mother never could be faithful to you, may enable you to experience dependence as an adult in a way you could not allow yourself to experience it as a child.

For some people loving does not seem to be separable from greed. The fear may be that no one, given free will, can or could possibly love you and give you all you need; partially perhaps because of a sense that you spoil and mess up what they do give you because you never acknowledge that it is enough. As a result of this fear the loved person is controlled and *made* to love you – but this of course messes up and spoils the relationship, so contributing to a vicious circle. The despair, and the sense of not being good enough, may be used to devalue or 'put down' both the self and the loved person. The lover is seen perhaps as no more than a pretty decoration for the self, or a supplier of goods or respectability, or a means of arousing envy or jealousy in someone else, but totally under the control of their lover, you. In these relationships, the 'real person' aspects of the other person, the part of them which is different from you, has been swallowed up and spoiled in the phantasy of taking them over. The phantasy that people can be devoured and destroyed in this way then adds to the despair and the hopelessness and the sense that no one, given free will, ever *should* enter into a loving relationship with you.

Love and loving may be attacked too by envy, either of the ability to love or of the loving person. Envy often betrays itself in the form of putting people down in various ways. Anything which someone else has and which appears – perhaps because it is not looked at properly but is slotted into an unrealistic phantasy of something wonderful – as much better than something you have is put down and mocked. In this way the feelings of longing for it, which seem unbearable, are translated into feelings of triumph and superiority. Other people may then be seen as longing for what you have: your own feelings of need or deprivation seem to disappear. People often do this with attributes of the opposite sex, which they can quite clearly never own. This kind of envy may then get in the way of a heterosexual love relationship, transforming the love into mutual attacking. Everything that is imagined to go with being a man may be subtly or less subtly derided, or everything which is imagined to go with being a woman. Some people are more specific in their undermining of something once valued: just the penis or just breasts or just wombs may be seen as not worth having, as causing no more than trouble for everyone, and far better if they did not exist.

Two teenage boys I once knew were past masters at turning everything which seemed happy or loving into something not worth having. Love was for them never more than self-interest; being cheerful was never more than a manic defence or 'superficiality'; good actions were never more than showing off; attempts to understand always failed dismally; and any kind of loving behaviour was turned by their bitter cynicism into a failure of some kind. Their power of observation of other people's faults and failings was extremely acute, but their total failure to observe or recognize any goodness anywhere amounted to a real block and gave them a permanent sense of utter gloom and despondency. Part of the problem, I think, was that they continually compared real life with some mythical kind of perfect love, perfect understanding, perfect bliss, and they turned their considerable powers of invective to destroying anything that failed to match up. Both suffered a kind of 'mental breakdown' in their early twenties, collapsing in tears and withdrawing from the world in bitter anger and misery, and in a furious sense of having their love rejected.

However, in spite of these difficulties, not all loving is spoiled in some way. The fear that the self is not big enough or good enough may be dealt with, not by taking over the other person and diminishing them too, but by valuing their separateness and independence and real or apparent 'betterness'. Where the other person is not being idealized too much, mutual, realistic dependence can also be recognized and the burden of responsibility on either is manageable because it is not made too great. The longing for a lover, or for a child who will carry on where you leave off, both physically and in time, can involve a longing for someone who will be more than you and can give you something like that first gift of milk and burping, which you could not give to yourself.

The desire to say 'I can manage on my own: I can look after myself and need nothing from anyone' is a strong one, since it would remove the difficulties of being dependent and vulnerable. But the loss it involves is a serious one, since it means losing the other person's ability to give to you. The desire to look after everyone else rather than be looked after yourself may also stem from an inability to allow others to be responsible for their own and your happiness. But the loss it involves is a real one. This can be a real struggle at the basis not only of falling in love, but also of remaining in love and being creative – having children or ideas or making things – too. The desire to take some part of the world and fashion it to your own image, to your own specifications, to make it 'be' a part of you and no more, must be tempered with respect for reality; for the way lovers, children, words, materials, musical instruments and pupils, for example, have a life and characteristics of their own. The ability to allow others to contribute to your world is essential for creativity.

Phantasies of loving where the fear is that the 'not-me' part of the other person will be destroyed can lead to fears of being trapped, of having to give up your own personality for your spouse or your children, or to demand that they do this for you. The passionately loving relationship can turn into one which feels like mutual destruction. Equally, absolutely no demand may be made upon each other, for fear of destroying this independent part of the other. Each may be totally unable to ask the other to make any changes in themselves, for fear of being left with only a passive and totally controlled lover who would be despised and then left.

Where there is more faith in the ability of each to maintain their independent integrity while accommodating the other, there may be extremely powerful loving phantasies of being able to contain and be contained by the lover. Each may be able to hold problematical parts of the other: the 'not-me' and the 'me' parts interact in a mutually supportive way. The fear that you can destroy the whole world in general, and your marriage in particular, can be calmed by the knowledge that you are not alone, that your attempts in your bad moments to destroy your marriage will have to contend with a real and solid force exerted by the other partner against this. Fears that you are totally useless and unlovable can be contained in the sharing process with a lover who knows these feelings too, and can show how unrealistic they are. I shall be looking more at these processes whereby people help each other with disturbing phantasies later on.

Loving phantasies involve phantasies of giving and taking, feeding and being fed, fertilizing and being fertilized, containing and being contained by someone else who has power to affect your whole internal world as well as your external world. They include anxieties about the safety and good intentions of these processes; about the ability to lose the self in the other, or the other in the self. Where they are working to mutual benefit they provide a context in which extremely creative processes can occur; where they are working to mutual destruction these processes can lose their loving aspects and this loss is felt to be a most terrible disaster.

Summary

My main point in this chapter is simply this. Emotions give life to and are understood, perceived and organized by quite concrete phantasies of things happening in and around the self and people you love or have loved. These phantasies are subtly and not-so-subtly different for different people, and they all add something to the experience of the present situation and the present emotions. Hidden phantasies left over from infancy, when the world was enormous and emotions shook your whole body, may be triggered by present-day events and feelings, so changing the situation and in the process being themselves changed. In particular these phantasies from past emotional situations can play tricks with the sense of limits: to people, to time, to responsibility, to power, to guilt, to anger and to love. The distinction between the world outside and the world of perception, of phantasy, is by no means obvious and is often misunderstood.

We can see that the concrete phantasies representing different states of mind are sometimes going to be experienced as intolerable. We can see that one phantasy is then going to be worked upon by another, perhaps to get rid of it, perhaps to change it into something different, so that the experience of an event gives rise, not to an appropriate feeling, but to another one entirely. If anger is felt to mean inevitable destruction of the person I love most, I might well put away the phantasy and the anger just as it is, and experience only the sense of guilt and anxiety connected with hiding something dangerous. If love is felt to lead to inevitable disappointment or to greedily devouring the person I love, I might well reject them before they can reject me or be destroyed by me. If guilt is felt as somebody beating me mercilessly over the head for something I have done and can never undo, I might well prefer to deny my own responsibility and beat them over the head instead.

Thus our conflicting emotions emerge in contradictory ways, and we may find ourselves rejecting the person we love the most, hating the person we would like to lay down our lives for, saying not a word to someone who has given us real cause for anger or irritation. Much of daily life seems to be made up of such 'irrational' tangles.

FOUR

PHANTASIES IN RELATIONSHIPS

(1)

In this chapter I want to look at some of the ways people use their relationships with other people and with the outside world.

Just as the inner world of phantasy is likely to confuse what has happened in phantasy with what has happened in reality, so it is likely to confuse what happens in the self and what happens in other people. Ownership of characteristics, emotions, abilities and parts of the self can be attributed or actually given in phantasy to other people, to inanimate objects or to animals. In our attempts to get rid of parts of ourselves – 'good' or 'bad' parts – we may help along the denial of our ownership by emphasizing their presence in other people. To gain reassurance and help from outside against the terrors and fears of destruction within, we may use the external world, just as we may at other times escape from the external world into fantasies. We may endow other people and objects with meaning derived from our inner world and watch what then happens, as part of our struggle to deal with terrifying anxieties.

In the process of using the world in this rather self-centred way, we may discover that the real characteristics of the external world have a potential we never dreamt of but can perhaps use. Sometimes we cannot use what we perceive at the time but store it up for the future. Trying to make a giraffe out of soft Plasticine we may discover that it falls naturally into a dinosaur which looks even better than the giraffe we had planned. Trying to make my husband into the loving father-mother-brother-sister I always wanted, I may discover that he has his own characteristics which are even better. The initial contact with him and with the Plasticine was motivated partly by my desire to find some approximation in the real world to phantasies in my inner world, but, if I am lucky, I may be able to take back into my inner world modifications to the phantasies which give even more satisfaction.

There are many specific phantasies to do with relationships; in this chapter I want to concentrate on phantasies of putting parts of the self into others; in the next I shall be looking in more detail at phantasies of taking parts of others into ourselves.

One of the most straightforward ways in which we confuse the inner world and internal perceptions with the outside world and external perceptions shows up when we attribute our own desires and feelings to other people. We tend to make mountains out of molehills, interpreting a slight piece of evidence for someone else's feelings with our knowledge of such feelings which comes from our own experience. We know what feelings of rejection are like: we may see other people's feelings as being just the same. We know what it is like to be jealous: we may use this knowledge by assuming that other people feel just the same in similar situations. We can sometimes sympathize and empathize with other people because we know what we would feel in their situation. Most of the time this is necessary, useful and sufficient.

But often our own feelings are exaggerated in one of the ways I described in the last chapter, and sometimes we do not allow ourselves to feel certain emotions at all. This will interfere with the process of understanding others too. When we use these exaggerated phantasies about what feelings mean to interpret other people's feelings or behaviour we may be making quite false assumptions and getting into all kinds of misunderstandings. Often our own acknowledgement of such fears or feelings is prevented by the enormity of the phantasies behind them, but this does not prevent their being perceived in a 'safer' situation – where they can be attributed to others, for example.

Margaret was quite unable to refuse to be 'on tap' for a friend whenever the friend wanted her. Talking with me, she rediscovered that when she was six her own mother had gone out to work, and Margaret had been furious that her mother was no longer always available all the time. She quickly realized that she was expecting the friend to feel the same kind of powerful feelings Margaret had felt at the age of six if she was ever not there when the friend wanted her. After this discovery, Margaret was able to laugh at herself, and make more realistic choices about when she was available and when she was not.

Sometimes there can be a phantasy that we have actually 'handed over' a certain set of feelings. Watching someone else get passionately excited, I may find myself becoming cool and reasonable as I feel or think to myself 'I wouldn't get *that* excited!' The excitement I would otherwise feel might actually get lost as I see it expressed by somebody else. When my son's friend became bad tempered and cross one day, my son suddenly became a paragon of virtue. His own tired bad temper seemed in some way satisfied by seeing his friend express it, and only emerged when his friend went home.

People do this in the adult world all the time. Feelings not recognized in ourselves are attributed to others – with many consequences. Seeing my own selfishness in someone else may help me to feel I am not so selfish. Accusing them of being selfish, I may be able to reassure myself that the selfishness in me is 'not the real me' – 'I' do not approve of selfishness. The need to state what I am not, just as Nicholas needed to state that he had not broken the spaceship, may lead me to find a representative of whatever I want to deny, in order to enable me to deny it firmly. Unless I care very much about my own say, stupidity, I am not going to bother about other people's. Seeing it in them I reassure myself that it exists – elsewhere, not in me. Samuel Beckett's brilliant monologue *Not I* depends upon this mechanism.

Partly, this mechanism can be seen as an attempt to do away with an internal conflict. The conflict between being selfish and not being selfish is a real one which can cause us trouble. Sometimes we simply try to set this conflict up in the outside world rather than bear it ourselves. Paul, when he was three, said to an adult friend: 'My panda used to be afraid of you, but he's not any more.' He had never actually shown any fear of her, and I think he had been partly afraid, partly not afraid. The panda was to carry one side of the conflict, and he was to carry the other. This happens frequently in marriages.

One partner may express one set of feelings, and the other its opposite, as a means of getting into the outside world an internal conflict. The desire to attack people, to be sarcastic or mocking or indignant or critical may be expressed by one, and the desire to protect people, to keep them safe or impotent or placated by the other. One can say 'no' all the time, and the other 'yes' – to spending money, having sex, letting the children stay out late, lending things, or whatever. One can be soft and the other hard; one mad and the other sane; one wild and the other boring. Each may use the other to express a hidden part of the self; in phantasy they may actually feel they have handed it over and no longer need feel any responsibility for it. Sometimes, as with policemen using the 'hard and soft' technique, partners realize what they are doing and are grateful to the other for acting as a brake, or for 'giving permission' for something which would be hard for themselves. Sometimes one of the partners may get increasingly angry – for example because the mother gets all the disciplining and the father all the fun with the children. Frequently, both partners are actually maintaining such situations, even if they complain bitterly about them. The phantasy 'getting rid of' or 'lending out of' feelings is often helped along by provoking behaviour of some kind to make sure that the other behaves in a way which fits the phantasy. Where the sharing out of the feelings like this remains temporary and disowned feelings are not denied in the long-term, this can be a useful way of making phantasies lose some of their exaggeration.

If, in phantasy, I hand over my own 'wildness' which scares me too much to my sister or my husband, I may be able to gain considerable reassurance from their ability to be a bit wild without going over the top. As a result I might gain the confidence to try out my own. My husband showed me that it was 'all right' to 'waste time' – to read the newspaper, not to work every minute of the day. I showed him that it was 'all right' to spend more time working. Each of us could show the other that latent desires in ourselves could be expressed and fulfilled without taking over entirely; work need not entirely drown out play and vice versa. (For a time it seemed we had simply changed over, that he had learnt to work all the time, and I had lost the ability entirely. This kind of feeling is common in these situations: it is not so easy to lose the fear that something can take over completely. As in this case, the fear, on closer inspection, turns out more often than not to be unrealistic.)

For years we lived with a friend who was very much tidier than we were and who used to get upset when the kitchen was in a mess. I used to go to great lengths to keep the kitchen clean 'for her', being prepared even to battle with other members of the household on her behalf in a way that I would never have done for myself at the time. It was not until we left the house that I discovered that the need to have the kitchen clean and tidy was mine as much as hers. In the process of fighting for her I had learnt that it was possible to demand the right to a relatively tidy kitchen for myself, both from myself and from other people I have lived with since. Through the phantasy that a denied part of myself (which liked a tidy kitchen) was in her, I came to modify my attitude to that part of me, becoming far less ashamed of it and frightened it would take over my life.

What can happen is that in this kind of way we learn to accept parts of ourselves which previously scared us too much, or were felt to be unrealistically important. It is as if we have inside us at times desperate, unspoken, conflicting demands: 'I should keep the kitchen extremely clean all the time' and at the same time 'I should be doing really important work – that is, not housework – all the time.' The difficulty is to recognize these demands and to become able to speak them – at which point they become quite clearly incompatible and probably exaggerated. Once spoken, they can be modified into more realistic longings or wishes: 'I'd like to ...' Such realistic wishes can admit the possibility of being given up; failure to achieve them then becomes cause for regret rather than huge guilt and blame. We can be helped by other people to recognize these demands inside ourselves; other people by their existence and their way of life can show us how we feel about things and how we could in fact change these feelings.

Where both partners in a marriage can come to share their acceptance of the part of themselves they previously put into the other, each can modify their expectations and discover that it is not possible nor necessary to be as perfect as they previously feared they had to be. There is no longer a need to deny wanting the kitchen tidy; both can regret that it is not tidy, and perhaps actually tidy it up. There is no longer a need to deny the need to keep back some money for bills; both partners can regret the necessity and enjoy spending what they can spend, where previously one took responsibility for spending and one for saving, and each attacked the other and the 'dangerous' part of themselves in the other. It seems that we often fight off the need to see discrepancies between logically incompatible desires, and may go to some lengths to maintain that both are possible. By fighting the battle between one person who 'wants' one and another person who 'wants' another, a modification of both positions may eventually be worked out.

Often these incompatible desires, especially those fought out between husband and wife, represent ones which in phantasy stem from fears for existence.

The need to hang on to money may be a way of keeping at bay deep anxieties about starvation which would be triggered by not having enough: being unable to keep any money may be a way of denying this fear, and continually 'proving' that other people will in fact bail you out. The need to be mad and the need to be sane, both in slightly excessive ways, may arise from deep anxieties about insanity in each, and from anxieties about not deserving to be loved, having to 'earn' love or having to prove that it will be given in spite of being very strongly tested. The need to keep a house excessively clean, and to struggle with a partner who makes a mess all the time, may be related to infantile phantasies about being capable of messing up the whole world and being left utterly uncared for. Where one partner is expressing dependence and the other independence in ways which lead to continual conflict, there may be powerful fears of being unable to survive on your own and being unable to love and value the separate existence of people who have the ability to hurt you, where this hurt feels so dangerous it could kill.

For some people these anxieties are so enormous that it is very difficult to 'disprove' them in everyday life. But where they are not too powerful, a husband or wife or a friend may be able to show that the fears are unrealistic, that food and love and understanding will be given in spite of terrors to the contrary. Other people can also force the recognition of one's own destructiveness in reality, and so bring about a modification of some of the underlying phantasies. Edna had for years allowed her husband to treat her like a doormat until one day she left him for another man. Her husband was suddenly faced with his own love for her, which previously he had totally failed to recognize in his scornful ill-treatment of her. Suddenly it seemed that he was the one who was being 'trampled all over'. For years, it seems, neither of them had admitted that his behaviour was extremely destructive, partly because it fitted in with their expectations of men. Consciously he had never been aware of loving feelings – except when drunk – and also that his behaviour was bound to destroy any love anyone could have for him. (I suspect that one of his fears was that his love could swallow his wife up completely and that she would die, just as his mother had died when he was fifteen. It was not until he actually lost her that he could feel safe enough to love her wholeheartedly – by which time it was too late to mend the marriage.)

The conditions under which people can help each other are interesting and of course complex. For this kind of phantasy to work there needs to be some kind of agreement about what aspects of the self another person can or will 'hold' and how they do this will affect the process.

If a woman starts complaining about her husband to a woman friend, the friend who defends him may find he is attacked even more; the friend has refused to 'hold' the attacking part of the wife even temporarily, but has taken over the 'defender' role for both of them. If the friend responds to the complaints by adding her own – 'Yes, I know he's dreadful, do you know what he said to me?' – the wife will probably begin to defend him, and may take the husband's side against the friend. If the friend manages to 'accept' or 'hold' the attack, without either adding to it, endorsing it or denying it, she may enable the wife to look at it as part of what she feels, and so to discover other parts of herself which feel quite differently about him.

This is part of understanding. Understanding does not add to or subtract from feelings or behaviour, but states them as they are, complete with real guilt, real anxieties and real fears. Understanding in this way helps to reduce the power and the volume of what has to be hidden. Reassurance does not change the truly frightening feelings if it simply covers them up; it does not offer the same 'holding on to' capacity which allows them to come into contact with other feelings and so to be changed of their own accord. Reassurance of too quick a kind may in fact be understood to be confirming the risks of considering the bad feelings too carefully.

When a friend accused me in a letter of treating him aggressively in a seminar, other members of the seminar tried to make me feel better. Some said 'You weren't aggressive to him', and this was comforting as a statement of solidarity and intention to reassure. But as a statement of fact I knew it was false, and it left me with my fears and my guilt unchanged. Other people said 'Yes, you were aggressive, but ...' The discussion of just how and why I had been aggressive, how misunderstandings might have arisen and how other people had actually enjoyed the challenge of similar treatment was much more helpful. I could sort out where I was in the wrong and where I had nothing to be ashamed of. This kind of understanding was helpful in two ways. It left me feeling I had really shared my burden of guilt and that it had been recognized for what it was, no more and no less. And it also enabled me to get beyond my immediate preoccupation with my own guilt and bad behaviour and to begin to think about the friend himself. Seeing it from his point of view, and also actually criticizing him, was only possible after I had had help with bearing my own guilt.

Similar interactions take place between children and parents and between husbands and wives. The parent who helps a child to recognize the extent and limits of the pain, the guilt, the misery it is suffering and has inflicted on others will engage the child's anxieties about it all and be able to help the child bear it more. As a result the child will be able to feel real concern for others and will learn to be more realistic about pain in itself and in others. 'Don't be silly, it's not really hurting' is likely to be less effective in general than a serious, matter of fact enquiry about how much it is hurting, or exactly how long it is going to go on hurting: until bedtime, or until tomorrow, or until next week. A parent who lays the guilt on thick – 'You're a monster, you've really hurt Johnny!' – when Johnny is not seriously hurt at all, is likely to confirm the child's enormous guilt and fears about having damaged Johnny for ever, and having tremendous power to inflict serious injury. As a result the child is likely to respond by denying the pain and the guilt: 'I don't care!' is a natural response, when caring seems too painful and hopeless. Not only is Johnny likely to become an enemy, but also adults lose their ability to help and become persecutors who make things worse. The child may simply learn to lose touch with its loving feelings, so that it can really inflict injury without caring. One of the people who treated my mother for a back injury earned her undying respect by telling her just how long and how much she would suffer from pain after he had treated her. His precision and accuracy enabled her to bear with fortitude several days of pain, knowing that it would be over.

This can even apply to death. It does hurt when someone dies: being able to talk about the pain somehow does create a feeling of having shared it, and in phantasy this may have happened. This can also be a reason people give for not talking about their pains. Sometimes there is a fear that another person would suffer too much, and there is a desire to protect such people from the agony. The very concrete nature of this feeling comes out in the assumption that the listener would actually suffer as much as the mourner, even though a more 'reasonable' view would be that no one can ever suffer as much if they are not personally involved. Once such fears are spoken they may lose their power, just as the other fears and secret agonies associated with death can lose their power to some extent when brought into the realm of common sense and allowed to be felt and then to pass.

It seems that a necessary condition for someone to help by 'holding' fears or anxieties or other feelings for us is that they understand them, that they can recognize them fully. It is far more comforting talking to someone else who has suffered as we have – be it with a serious illness, with the death of family members in a war, with the troubles of having a handicapped child in the family – than it is talking to someone who does not 'really' understand in this way. In order to enable a lover or a friend to help me to get in touch with and use parts of myself I previously could not bear, or to engage with my deepest fears and anxieties so that I can feel them for a while as unlimited, I have to find someone who understands them from the inside, someone whose own fears and anxieties are sufficiently close to mine. It is no help if they really do not see the problem in any way. But the risk is that I will simply find someone who will join me in playing out my worst anxieties and will in fact add to them.

The process begun as a normal method of trying to make phantasies more realistic may instead 'confirm' their exaggerations. Not only is there a risk of losing part of yourself when you hand it over to someone else, but the way they treat those parts of you may be no better. And you may also find yourself in a situation where you have to worry excessively about what you are doing to the other person.

Let us look at some examples of this.

Valerie seemed for a while to 'carry' the calmness that her husband could not accept in himself. But her behaviour just 'confirmed' to him that this calmness meant almost total withdrawal, apathy and being utterly boring. As a result, her husband's own calm was denied even more. His frantic behaviour then 'confirmed' his wife's phantasies that doing anything at all was too much. Similarly, Ursula was expected by her husband to carry excessive responsibility for being sexually experienced. The internal and external pressure to do this was felt to be so great that it could not be given up; she had to seek more experience outside the relationship to avoid having to admit that some experience goes along with some ignorance. And her husband, who 'had' to deny his own sexual knowledge, received confirmation of the feeling that such knowledge is dangerous indeed – it drives you to seek out new partners. And so his own approach to sex became even more inhibited and 'innocent', so encouraging Ursula to feel even more alone with her sexuality.

In each case the partner in the outside world had been used as a testing ground, but not consciously. In each case, the problem involves the fact that parts of the self are not acceptable and accepted. Other people's behaviour is being interpreted in a phantasy world which is full of excessive phantasies and which includes a refusal to see a part of the self which is being attacked or seems dangerous. And the message received from the outside world is a confirmation of the frightening phantasies.

The difficulties involved in handing over parts of the self to others do not end here.

In the process of handing over unwanted or feared parts of yourself (your sexual desire, your meanness, your insanity, your cold reason, your rejection of others), you may also hand over parts which are valuable and necessary (your aliveness, your control over your generosity, your spontaneity, your knowledge of realities, your ability to be a separate person, say). Not only do you have to work hard to deny your ownership of those characteristics, but you also need to keep a close eye on the part of yourself which you have disowned but cannot live without. In the process you may get involved with keeping a very tight rein on the person to whom you have 'given' that part of yourself: you may need to watch their movements closely, or try hard to influence them in one direction or another, for your own purposes, which may not be in the interest of their welfare.

You may feel a great need to worry about or actually control the person who is 'holding' or 'looking after' the part of yourself you are rejecting or even trying to attack. You may, for example, worry excessively about the sex life of your neighbour or your husband or your daughter or the French, depending where it is that you 'see' your own denied sexuality. (Attempts to control, watch or attack homosexuals are often interpreted in this way, as forms of excessive zeal on the part of members of the establishment or teenage boys whose own sexuality gives reason for anxiety. There may be good reasons for some laws about homosexuality, but some of the enforcing of such laws does smack of protesting too much.) You may be unrealistically concerned that other people's sexuality would lead to terrible trouble, like your own would, you fear, if you did not control it so tightly. You may watch or control your husband's or wife's behaviour with money jealously, to see that they do not overstep certain limits which are more to do with unrealistic anxieties than with real ones. You may be excessively concerned with your child's deceitfulness or obstinacy, while your own is apparently quite acceptable or totally denied. You may complain incessantly about your husband's or wife's lack of desire for excitement, maintaining that it is only your consideration for them which causes you to lead such a boring existence. In all of these cases there may be a realistic worry or complaint as well as the less realistic one.

The desire to deny your own jealousy or your own tactlessness may well latch on to some real example of someone else's jealousy or tactlessness; there may be real reason to worry about your child's behaviour at school or your husband's or wife's or sister's sexual behaviour. But the phantasy that you have landed the other person with a part of yourself that you cannot bear may considerably add to the real worry. Sometimes this extra burden simply increases your sense of anxiety; sometimes it can make things seem so bad that you actually deny the feelings and fail to take the real worry seriously enough in an attempt to avoid recognizing your own share in it.

Sometimes people seem to believe that such processes of handing over have gone on to the extent of causing damage, when the damage is better explained by some totally different cause. Children who have a sibling with some kind of disability may easily believe that they have handed over their own (phantasied) disabilities and actually caused the sibling's problems. Girls may believe they have handed over their own penis or 'masculinity' to their brothers, and brothers believe they have handed over their 'femininity' – whatever that means for them – to their sisters. So, for example, a girl may feel responsible if her brother is hurt fighting another boy, even if she has nothing to do with it: in her phantasy it may have been her physical aggression which 'made' her brother fight. Or the boy may feel guilty when he sees his sister crying, as if it is his own sensitivity which is causing her trouble. Here we can see more precisely something I mentioned in Chapter 2.

The excessive need to watch over or control others which arises from these phantasies may itself be denied in the self and 'seen' in others. This may give rise to a strong sense of being watched – by your brother or sister or spouse or parent – or feelings of having them 'on your back' all the time. The sense of being trapped comes from these phantasies. You may 'know' what someone else demands that you should do, without them ever telling you – so there is no real discussion, no real opportunity to challenge the assumption. 'The kitchen must be precisely *this* clean for him/her – much cleaner than I would bother to have it.' 'I cannot buy that pair of socks without asking my mother or my husband first; I *know* they would consider it extravagant.' 'If I look at myself in the mirror I can "feel" my sister saying "You are too fat."' 'I cannot go out because I *know* my children need me at home.' The trapped person may feel they cannot do what they want for fear of what the other person would say. Sometimes the other person would not say it at all: the conviction is often so strong it never gets tested out. Sometimes the external world has been so arranged that somebody is found who will say what is expected and so prove that the self is in fact 'controlled' by somebody else. In extreme cases, there is always prison. In these ways, the controlling part of the self may also have been successfully 'put' into someone else.

One of the most frightening parts of this kind of phantasy is the fear of being utterly depleted. If bits of the self are continually being left around in other people, like possessions left by a guest, the self may well begin to feel rather empty and weak. This feeling of weakness may well have been at the root of the process already, the stronger parts of the self being felt to be too dangerous because the acceptable parts were so weak. Some mothers feel they 'give' their lives and their strength to their children: in return the children may 'give' their weakness and helplessness to her. Emotionally and physically she may feel drained and exhausted, perhaps at the mercy of her children and the world in general. Unless she keeps hold of enough of her strength, she may die early; or her children may never dare show their own weakness for fear it 'means' this incapacitating weakness. Some mothers may be felt by their children to be utterly rapacious, draining them of all their strength and resources: the truth in this phantasy may be matched by the simultaneous truth that the child wants to do precisely this to her. The fear of being depleted is matched by a fear of greedily depleting those you love. Where the demands made by the world are felt to be too much, there may be a sense that one or the other has to happen. It is only by finding out that the world can be satisfied with something less than this that the fears can be calmed and both the self and the loved person can be felt to be safe.

Where parts of the self are being seen or evoked in others as a means of denying them in the self, not only is there a sense of injustice at the hypocrisy involved, but there is also a real danger of empathy being destroyed. Instead of saying 'I know how you feel, and I don't like feeling it either', and so sharing the guilt and shame and painfulness or whatever, both partners may be saying 'I don't understand you at all'. Sympathy and understanding are not allowed in, for fear of having to acknowledge one's own share of the real burden. In one sense it is true that neither understands the other; in another sense it is a lie, and felt as such. Consciously there may really be a lack of understanding, but on a deeper level, in those thoughts which flash through our minds and are then gone, perhaps there is a great deal of unrealistic understanding. And the price of denying this kind of understanding may be a gradually increasing sense of loneliness.

The kind of man, to take an example, who claims he does not understand how his wife can be so emotional and unreasonable may himself be highly emotional and unreasonable in other relationships: he does understand only too well how difficult it makes life. By being reasonable with his wife, he may be not only 'showing her how to behave' but also reassuring both of them that someone in the family can remain cool. Both of them may believe that it would be only too easy for both of them to explode together, and so destroy everything. But by behaving in such a cool way when his wife is getting upset, he is also (on one level unintentionally) provoking her to become more emotional and making her feel guilty for expressing the emotionality which he is disowning and fighting off. He may also be making her into an enemy when she could be an ally, sharing the burden of guilt and emotionality, and making it seem less threatening.

Often this kind of interaction can be traced by looking at how people feel they used to be. A man who worked in a remand home for boys told me how he used to be a naughty and 'dirty' boy but had changed drastically at the age of twelve. His life was now devoted to helping the boys in his care to change too, he said; but it appeared to me and some of his colleagues that his life was in fact more directed at punishing the boys in his care for being like he was. His frustration was the greater, I think, because he had not fully separated himself out from the boys; in his phantasy they were not real people but were seen as *no more than* a dirty and dangerous part of himself. He dared not view that part of himself with anything more than disgust and fear in case it regained its powerful hold over him. The attraction of being 'like that' was denied, not defused.

Another man I knew had to be away on business quite a lot of the time. His wife used to get so upset about being left on her own that he made great efforts to come home early, travelling long distances late at night or early in the morning to be at home with her. He claimed that he knew she got anxious when he was away but it was not something he could really understand: he liked being away from home. He was finding her anxiety a terrible tie and was seriously considering leaving her. But when we were once talking about our school days he remembered crying hysterically at primary school whenever he knew that his mother intended being out for the day. As a result the school would send him home and his mother was unable to go out. It seemed that he did indeed 'know' what his wife's feelings might be. By in phantasy putting into his wife that crying child part of himself he seemed to have bolstered a picture of himself as a very independent man struggling with a dependent wife. His picture of what it meant to be independent was in fact somewhat lacking: it could not incorporate dependence, but had to fight it off. He so disowned the dependent part of himself that he was able to consider leaving it and his wife entirely. My feeling that his attempts to leave would not succeed was confirmed when I met him again several years later and he was still living with his wife. It is interesting that a man who showed such anxiety as a child should take a job which took him away from home so often, and a wife who found it so difficult. It is possible that he was trying to use the real world to help him with some very deep anxieties about being left.

One of the sad things about this kind of interaction is that the harder people work to change the behaviour of their spouse, the worse things may seem to get. The more my friend tried to show his wife that she was 'all right' on her own, by going away and leaving her overnight, the more upset she got. The more the 'cool' husband tries to show his wife how to be cool, the more emotional and unreasonable she may seem to get. The more the 'mean' partner tries to control the spending of money, the more the 'generous' or 'spendthrift' partner may feel it is safe and necessary to show that spending money is all right. I sat in the back of the car once with my son behind me. He was shouting in my ear and I was being deafened, so I spoke more softly to make him lower his voice. But, as I was facing forward and the car was noisy, he could not hear so he shouted louder in my ear to make me speak up. This went on for a few exchanges before I realized what was happening and was able to *say* to him that I wanted him to speak more softly – whereupon he was able to say that he wanted me to speak up. We both found our extreme irritation changed to laughter. This can happen in marriages too, when fighting couples realize that they have been doing something like this to each other for years.

It seems that the 'showing' kind of behaviour is more primitive and more automatic than the 'telling' kind. When the phantasies involved are very excessive there may be a lot of hidden fear which makes it hard to stop and think about them and to let them go. Sometimes there is a feeling that 'as long as I don't talk about it it isn't true'. Sometimes the difficulty arises from the fact that such primitive mechanisms often have a secret, denied punitive element in them, stemming from early beliefs that someone must be to blame for everything. The other partner may recognize only this blame element and fail to see a real desire for change all round.

The paradox is that it is only by sharing the responsibility for unwanted characteristics that the excessiveness can be reduced. Only when the 'cool' husband or wife shows some emotion may the 'emotional' partner cool down a bit. Only when the partner who saves all the time begins to spend can the partner who spends begin to save. Only when the partner who 'wants sex all the time' learns to say no when they do not want it can the partner who normally says no make the first move. Only when the partner who claims to want to keep the marriage together admits to the advantages of separation can the partner who wants to leave admit to the parts of himself or herself which would suffer from the separation.

But here it is clear what a risk is involved. If both partners start saying that they want to separate, what will keep the marriage together? If both get emotional, when will it end? If both say no to sex there will never be any; if both say yes, they will never get any sleep. It takes knowledge, courage, belief and trust to accept that desires are not just 'on' or 'off'; that holding one does not mean having to give the other up entirely; that expressing *both* desires, and the conflict between them, will most likely lead the other to express both too. And the risk of losing what you have, however unsatisfactory it is, may seem too enormous.

The phantasy of putting parts of the self into others can work to increase the excessiveness of the phantasy part, not only because of the way the other person deals with it but also because of the lack of practice and experience of the denied part. Where a husband 'puts' all his understanding into his wife and never uses his own, he may well increase and confirm his own weakness of understanding. Where a wife 'puts' all her ambition into her husband and never tries out her own, she may well maintain a picture of success which does not quite fit with reality. In the course of having a job or a career, or using one's understanding, the realities of life force a gradual modification of aims to fit the possibilities. Where the wife or husband (or parent or anyone else) does not experience the constraints, she or he may be less able to accept that they are real. Similarly with housework and childcare: some husbands seem to expect a quite unrealistic level of cleanliness and tidiness, particularly when they have never tried to do the job themselves over a long period of time. Lack of such experience may mean that they have not had to modify their picture of how to live, nor discovered the costs of maintaining the standards of their mothers – or, more likely, their phantasy mothers. It may particularly be men who spent large parts of their childhood in institutions who have an unrealistic idea of keeping house. I must confess that I came across this problem more in Germany: men have been doing housework, and treating women better for it, for longer in England, I suspect – Engels reports it in Victorian Manchester, for example, though with true Germanic horror.

These excessive demands – for cleanliness or power or money – may give rise to excessive guilt when they are never confronted and modified and given up in their pure form. The guilt then feels like an attack and is fended off and denied, as I described before. To the guilt of never living up to an impossible ideal is added the guilt and resentment of loading the other person with unbearable parts of the self, and the fear that they will be damaged as a result. The guilt becomes far too heavy and unrealistic to be borne. As a natural next step, the partners may deny their own guilt and try to make their partners feel sorry. But the more they try to do this the more each is likely to feel utterly hopeless and helpless about ever making sufficient amends. Each fluctuates between depression and 'I don't care!', between accusing the other and accusing the self. Neither can help the other reduce the burden of their own guilt, for fear that any admission that one is not totally guilty will lead to an assumption that they are not guilty at all. In which case, the other 'must' be guilty. It seems that the concept of 'a little bit guilty', or 'a little bit sorry', or 'a little bit sad' is one which some people do not recognize. For them 'a little bit' always means 'this is just the tip of the iceberg'; there is no alternative to 'on' or 'off' when it comes to guilt, sorrow, sadness or anger.

What can often happen goes something like this.

The husband, for example, seems not to care very much for the family and the wife takes over more and more responsibility for everything to do with it. Because she takes over more and more of the responsibility her burden becomes bigger and bigger as time goes on, and her husband never learns to care for the household as she has learnt. He loses all the skills he ever had for caring for people, perhaps, and all his self-respect too. As a result he seems to care less and less for the family, though somewhere inside him he does care very much and he feels hopeless and guilty about his failures. The discrepancy between his behaviour and hers widens and it may seem an impossible task ever to make up for his wrong behaviour because she has been by comparison so enormously good and long-suffering. His hidden guilt may become increasingly intolerable and his wife's attempts to make him feel guilty and show him how to behave simply exacerbate the problem. Confessing his guilt to her would lay him open to quite unrealistic demands for recompense: if not quite the death penalty, at least total slavery for life – as his wife seems to have accepted – in his phantasy. He may fluctuate between trying to live up to the high standards set by the two of them in her, and giving up entirely. Every time he tries to be a 'good' husband his attempt is doomed to failure because their standards are so unrealistic, and his wife is likely to use it as an occasion for pointing out his normally bad behaviour. She is also likely to criticize his efforts partly because her own sense of worth for her depends upon the comparison with his lack of worth. Every time he 'fails' he receives confirmation of his fears that he is guilty for all the problems in their lives, including all his wife's: her own fears and resentments may well make her deny *any* share, and she will use the on/off principle to support her: 'I am not as guilty as him so I am not guilty at all.' Since she knows, however, that she *is* partly responsible (and in phantasy this may be more than partially; perhaps she believes that she drives him to drunken irresponsibility single-handed, just as she felt she drove her father that way when she was small), she cannot discuss the whole thing with him reasonably. Both see the other as blaming them unrealistically, and expect the huge blame they feel is their due and at times put on the other. Very often this blame and the guilt are quite out of proportion to the events and arise from some earlier situation being daily replayed.

I have seen this kind of scenario being played out in many relationships; it is by no means always the husband who is 'irresponsible'. Where it is the wife she may turn to drugs rather than drink to drown her sense of her own inadequacy and unworthiness which her husband daily pushes down her throat. Sometimes it is possible to help such people to regain some hope in their ability to make some recompense, partly by helping them to grasp the more realistic nature of the grievances, teasing out the unrealistic aspects and enabling both to confess to their enormous sense of guilt. They may be surprised to find that the other feels guilty at all. However, where the denials are too strong these relationships can be very hard to change; as soon as one confesses to guilt of any kind the other takes it as confirmation that they themselves are 'really' innocent. The possibility of sharing any painful or conflicting feelings – blame, guilt, anger, love, hopelessness or responsibility – may seem a totally alien concept. Good and bad may be kept so far apart that they do not affect each other, for fear that a little bit of badness would totally destroy all goodness. Such couples seem to believe that the only hope for keeping any goodness is to keep it well away from the badness, locked up in one partner at a time. For such couples, there may be a lack of sense of time and memory; they find it hard to remember their own sense of guilt when confronted with their spouse's, or their own sense of being all right, or being good, when confronted with their own badness.

In this kind of relationship, there may appear to be a problem of 'breakdown of communication'. Husband and wife cannot talk to each other at all because each is terrified of discovering their own (unrealistically exaggerated) guilt, and each is terrified of damaging their picture of perfect goodness, either in the self or in the other, and so being left with nothing. But it is only verbal communication which is stopped; on a non-verbal level there is only too much communication. The phantasy of putting parts of the self into others is a form of very primitive communication.

Non-verbal communication has great potential. Making love with someone can convey all kinds of messages; giving them a black eye or a wink or a hug can convey something which words would express differently. Listening to music and dreaming are both forms of non-verbal experience which have deep effects at times. But the potential for misunderstanding non-verbal messages is also enormous. Messages about the past or the future cannot be directly communicated by actions which take place always 'now'. Memory and a sense of time cannot easily be included and may be actively denied by non-verbal behaviour. Interpreting other people's messages through our own phantasies we may well pick up one or more parts of their behaviour which were not intended to be communicated, and we may not see or understand whole areas of meaning which the other person wants us to see. It is hard to convey reasons for behaviour by the simple activity or even by obvious moods, and the reasons which are supposed to be conveyed may be so conflicting that it is not surprising that they can be easily misunderstood.

Seeing that someone is clearly upset, it is very easy to 'understand' that you are responsible: your mind may immediately rush to something you have done which might have upset them. Seeing someone being withdrawn it is very easy to understand that they do not love you any more; perhaps they are thinking about a secret lover. In fact, of course, they may be withdrawn because in their phantasy you do not love them any more, or they may be miserable about something completely different. Asking someone what the matter is may produce a surprising answer, or it may produce the answer 'nothing' – which leaves the speculations intact. Many people have great difficulty in believing what people say about their reasons for the way they feel – this is partly realistic in that people often do not know or do not want to say what is going on in them if they do know. Often it feels too 'silly' to say. (A practical means for daily living with a person who has moods like this is to ask them a precise question about the cause which is of greatest concern to you: 'Did I upset you by ...?' for example. The answer in the look of incredulity on the miserable person's face may be far more convincing than words could be. Formulating the anxiety they are provoking in you can in itself be constructive: often the answer is clear without the need to put the question.) Once words have been put to such anxieties, there may be new possibilities for thinking about alternatives, or for sharing the anxieties. While such feelings remain unverbalized they simply get in the way of clear thinking, and especially thinking about things from another person's point of view.

Handing feelings over to other people by actually evoking them is a kind of non-verbal communication which has great potential and is used frequently without people being aware of what they are doing. It is perhaps the first method of communicating with someone we love; a tiny baby can only make people understand that it needs something by somehow evoking in them feelings which are close enough to what the baby is feeling for them to know what to do. A baby's first scream hurts the ears, physically, and evokes a very powerful desire to do something to stop it.

In counselling I have experienced many different feelings about myself as a counsellor which turned out on second thoughts to apply more to my client. These have included feelings of being utterly useless, of being watched in every move I made, of everything being too much for me to handle, of being extremely competent and capable. Superficially, the feelings experienced by the clients seemed in each case quite different from these, but thinking about what they had said it became clear to me that there was a strong possibility that somewhere they did have hidden feelings, unrecognized in themselves, which corresponded to mine. Asking the client if this was the case produced confirming evidence, and changed my perception of my own – and their – feelings. It was as if the client had been able to 'take back' their share of these denied feelings in a context in which I could help with them. The person who made me feel so competent and capable was someone who seemed to feel quite useless himself: when I suggested that my feelings perhaps 'belonged' to him, he smiled and admitted to all kinds of sensible actions which he had previously seemed incapable of performing. He had been doing this to people around him at home too, making them feel wonderful and very capable, but also worried about him and afraid that they had to support him in an excessive way. Quite often this kind of observation of feelings communicated non-verbally can be used outside counselling situations too.

In my seminars people often discuss work relationships with me, sometimes wanting help with a boss, a child, a colleague or a friend, or also with members of their family. In such situations I have often suggested that the person bringing the problem thinks 'What do they make me feel? And is there any way in which this feeling could in fact "belong" to them too?' (It is very important to recognize that there is likely to be a realistic aspect to one's own share of the feeling as well as an aspect which arises from the other person.) The answer is often quite striking. It obviously makes sense to wonder if a man who seems quite confident but who makes others feel totally lacking in confidence too lacks confidence himself but cannot show it. (As my mother taught me, a True Gentleman makes you feel wonderful: he doesn't *need* to make you feel uncomfortable.) A woman who seems prepared to bite your head off – is she afraid you will bite off hers? A child who makes you feel angry – might there be something making them feel particularly angry just now? Often this throws a whole new light on the problem; remarkably often some evidence is found immediately which suggests that this feeling – quite the opposite of their apparent feeling – might indeed 'come from' them.

Part of the mechanism at work can be understood as an attempt to get rid of a burden of feelings they cannot bear. Making other people feel them does two things: it may offer an opportunity to get help with the feeling – if the other person acknowledges it and deals with it in a different way; or it may simply help along the phantasy that the feeling is located elsewhere, not in them.

What is done with the new insight depends on the situation. Realizing that they too are (possibly) in some way suffering from this feeling may be enough to reduce your own feelings of being unjustly persecuted. Trying simply to accuse them of loading off their own bad feelings on to you may be appropriate for a quarrel, but not for improving relations. However you do try to 'feed' this back into the relationship the other person may be feeling vulnerable and may interpret what you say as blame or persecution. Quite often, though, the situation does ease up, as the enormity of your own feelings fades, not only with the idea that they might be shared, but also with your own 'naming' of them to yourself. This in itself is likely to enable you to look at the reality: 'Am I really as totally useless as he makes me feel? Would he really have offered me the job if I were? Am I *just* totally bourgeois and boring? And is that *just* an insult anyway? If I am feeling attacked am I attacking in self-defence?' Sorting out the truth from the excessiveness may enable an element of goodness and strength to be rescued from previously overwhelming feelings of badness or weakness or impotence.

Before I leave this discussion of handing over feelings to others I should like to mention jealousy in particular. One way of getting rid of feelings of jealousy is obviously to try to get someone else to feel them 'for' you. This does not in fact get rid of the feelings, but it may for a while create the illusion that it has. The sense of triumph against the jealousy-provoking person may temporarily cover up the feelings of loss and misery and helpless dependence evoked by them. Loving and caring and vulnerable parts of the self are actually attacked or buried in the excite-ment of making someone jealous. Unfortunately, in the long run this can lead to powerful feelings of being unworthy, unlovable and bad inside, as well as very often creating the actual loss of the jealousy-provoking person.

Sometimes people get their own back on each other's infidelities by indulging in some action which might reasonably be expected to produce jealousy in their lover, but both their own jealousy and their lover's are denied. This went on a lot amongst people I knew in my early twenties. There was a common belief that jealousy was the root of all evil; all we needed to do was to get rid of jealousy, and we could all have as many love relationships as we liked. Many people suffered considerably from this philosophy; where they could not deny their own jealousy they still felt very strongly that they *ought* to. Nobody was supposed to feel jealousy, and many people would not admit to feeling it; certainly they would not admit that their behaviour might quite reasonably produce jealousy. Where so much is denied, it can be hard to demonstrate that this is what is happening. Sometimes what happened is that the denial broke down eventually, and people began to admit to feelings they previously did not know they had. (I suspect this happens to quite a considerable extent as people enter their thirties and forties; denials which could be maintained during their twenties no longer retain their credibility. Men who in their twenties cared not a jot for their children suddenly discover what they have missed; women who despised childbearing and motherhood – or earning money and working outside the home – may suddenly wake up to a whole side of life which they previously found totally worthless. There are many similar examples.) Sometimes people suddenly found themselves enormously attracted by a partner who promised to be faithful. Sometimes relationships which were based on each partner sleeping around broke down for apparently trivial reasons, and it looked from the outside at least as if these trivial reasons in fact tapped the built-up frustrations and unexpressed, unadmitted confusion of emotions passing between the two. In counselling I find people are frequently very surprised at the strength of emotions which can be aroused in them on the subject of sex and sexual jealousy in particular. Quarrels in daily life about, say, who does the washing up, or how the children or the dogs should be disciplined, or how often relatives should be visited, remarkably often seem to gain their virulent passion from unexpressed and probably unrecognized feelings about sex.

Sexual feelings tap some of the deepest phantasies there are in us. They link up with infantile beliefs about putting parts of ourselves into our mothers and fathers in order to make babies or good things, or in order to destroy and punish them. They connect with our whole way of dealing with the world: how we take in and how we give; how much goodness and how much badness there is in us and in those around us. We seem to be very vulnerable to 'proofs' or 'disproofs' which we glean from our sexual relationships about how good we are, how bad we are, how loving and how destructive. This is why a good sexual relationship casts a happy glow, not only over the physical skin, but also over the whole outlook on the world. And this is why any sexual (or gynaecological or childbirth) problem can shake our faith in our own goodness to such an extent that we become sour or sadistic or seriously depressed.

Before I conclude this chapter I would like to give one detailed example of an incident where a child used his present-day relationships to help him with some painful feelings left over from a much earlier time. In the process he created a situation in which another child was 'made' to experience something like a situation he had experienced and the child then used this to gain help from adults which earlier he had been unable to use.

We left London for Germany when Peter, a friend of my son Joel, was just five years old. Three years later he came to visit us, now in Manchester, having visited us in Germany in between. One day he came running into the house and sat down at the table with his mother and me, looking as if he were seeking protection. Eventually we asked him where Joel was, to be told he was on his way. Some time later, Joel arrived in great distress, because Peter had left him behind in a strange part of the neighbourhood, and had run on home without him. We asked Peter in some indignation why he had done that and Peter replied 'Joel did it to me in London.' His mother and I looked at each other in amazement; here was an eight-year-old talking of something that could only have happened more than three years ago.

Neither of us believed him: there was no way that Joel could have done this to the older and more self-assured Peter. I then had an idea and asked 'You mean when we went to Germany and left you behind?' The striking thing was the effect this had upon Peter. He looked at me with an interest he scarcely ever showed and began firing questions at me: why did we go to Germany? Did Joel want to go? Why couldn't he go too? We had a brief discussion of why we had gone and how we had felt at the time, how we had not wanted to leave London and our friends at all. It was very clear to his mother and me that Peter had had very hurt feelings about it which were now, three years later, playing themselves out in his behaviour with Joel. Peter lost his fear of Joel and came out from behind the table, though Joel was still in fact quite violently angry.

It seems that seeing Joel again had roused in Peter phantasies which were left over from much earlier. He had re-experienced, but not, I think, remembered at first, the feelings his questions showed. He seemed to have no idea that we had gone because of my husband's work, though I am sure we would have told him. He might well have been convinced that we left 'really' because he and Joel were fighting: it had happened often enough in their day-to-day relationship. When these phantasies were aroused, he experienced the desire to 'get his own back' on Joel by running off and leaving him. It was a perfectly natural thing to do, and a natural way to find out what it felt like to be the person who left, for example. And it looked as if he believed – quite rightly – that what Joel would be left feeling was murderous. Not until we recognized and acknowledged what was going on – by seeking the element of truth in a child's lie, note – was he able to ask some of the questions that he had not asked, or heard the answers to, when he was five.

Joel was just one of several friends who played together, and Peter was left with closer ones. But I think the importance of our leaving may have been exaggerated for him because it triggered much more important desertions. Before he was two he had moved house twice and had lost his father and later a dog, both of whom he loved and missed. Reassurance he received from the incident with Joel might in its turn have cast doubts upon the other conviction he must have held, that he was responsible for his father leaving. If so, this would help to account for the quite startling change in his face, behaviour and body movements which took place after our discussion. He seemed to have been relieved of an enormous burden, of some inner rigidity, and I think he might have been. As far as the older losses were concerned, the relief may have been only partial and temporary, but it may have set in train other thoughts and feelings which could make it easier for him to ask the same kind of questions, if only of himself, about his father leaving. (This incident points too to some of the value to children of seeing parents who have left. It does give them a chance to try out some of their frightening and angry phantasies with the real person concerned. It can help quite serious distortions of reality to be modified.)

What happened with Peter shows up several aspects of phantasies. We can see the unrealistic nature of his worries. It shows in particular the self-centredness of the omnipotent phantasies of children which can cause great anxiety. He seemed to think that he could be responsible for a family of friends leaving the country; that we had done it to punish him. Piaget described these things too, from his experimental work. These phantasies are often noticeable in adults: many is the time I have been convinced that I was guilty of upsetting someone when they were actually upset for reasons which had nothing to do with me.

Peter's behaviour also shows a long-term effect on a child of an apparently minor event at the age of five. It shows how this event can be stored in phantasies which control behaviour and feelings, but may not directly enter conscious thought. It shows how a modified repetition of the phantasy situation can then be brought about, partly as a way of punishing people, and partly as a way of finding out what had happened. The value of this kind of re-enactment, or play, should not be underestimated. Peter was finding out, in the best way he could at the time, what the feelings were of the person who left. But this shows how misperceptions can arise: his enactment, based on a child's misinterpretations, instead of reducing the anxiety in fact heightened it. His desertion of Joel was voluntary and, I think, deliberately hurtful since this is what he believed had been done to him. As a result he became quite terrified of Joel. This was not normal behaviour for him and shows the strength of feeling aroused in him by the earlier losses, as well as the persecutory nature of them. His loss of fear after the discussion, when Joel's fury had not abated at all, shows too the unrealistic nature of his fear of Joel. What he feared was being on the receiving end of the murderous feelings *he* had experienced; when these murderous feelings in him were reduced, by making it clear to him that we had not left him behind out of malice, or to punish him, for example, he no longer feared Joel so much. But the real Joel was still just as angry as he had been: the discussion had not interested him in the slightest.

In this example we see Peter attempting to use the external world as a testing ground for his internal fears and anxieties. In the process he 'made' another person carry some of his pain, and in the event managed to get help with this pain and actually to change it: in this case, from feeling attacked into feeling regretful but understanding. Both his behaviour and his perception of his friend's feelings were strongly influenced by his perception of his own three years earlier.

We can see in the behaviour of Peter that there are actually serious dangers involved in the attempt to get rid of bad or dangerous feelings into other people. Peter was making Joel feel murderous towards him as a means of dealing with his own murderous feelings. Not only may there be a risk in such situations that the person on the receiving end may actually act out such feelings, but also, even if they do not, the person handing over the feeling is left scared. It is common knowledge that a fear of the opposite sex can be a result of hating them (and handing over that hatred to them – seeing/experiencing them as hating) as well as a cause of it.

I have been told of a man who drove his lorry into the back of a car which was stationary at red traffic lights. The lorry driver jumped down and ran round to the driver of the car shouting 'What the hell do you think you're doing?' Cases where people see their own faults in others are frequent and may be, as in this case, quite dangerous. A physical fight between the drivers could easily have ensued.

I have been concentrating on the more positive aspects of phantasies of putting parts of the self into others (which analysts call projection or projective identification, phenomena which have many forms) because they seem to me less well known and obvious than some of the more negative aspects. In Chapter 6 I discuss blame in some detail and take up some more of the dangers involved.

Summary

In this chapter I have tried to look at a specific class of phantasies which affect people's relationships with each other. Phantasies of putting parts of the self into others and taking over parts of them are very important indeed. They are intimately connected with learning processes as well as with loving and with hurting. Just how people see this kind of transaction taking place affects their abilities to give and to take, to love and to learn and to keep loving relationships going over a period of time. Such phantasies contribute to a lot of the difficulties in relationships. We have to be able to give and take back parts of ourselves; to borrow and let go parts of others. We have to learn to do it so that we and the others involved feel strengthened at the end rather than depleted and resentful and guilty. Too many of these phantasies can lead to feeling trapped and empty, controlled or impotent, in ways which are not simply determined by the practicalities of the situation.

I do not want to give the impression that I undervalue the effects of real life. Of course some people are really trapped in some way; some people are in some real sense under the control of others; some people have good reason to fear their spouse's reaction to their behaviour. All I am trying to say is that remarkably often what seems to be unchangeable becomes in fact changeable once the precise phantasies have been uncovered. I have seen quite startling changes take place in relationships when people realized what they were doing to each other in these terms, and recognized their own part in maintaining extremely painful situations. Once we can separate out the physical pain or the external situation from phantasies of what it means we frequently find that not only is the suffering more bearable, but we can discover means to change it or simply to allow it to change of its own accord. Naming the exact phantasy which is being used to interpret the world around is not an easy task. The phantasy is often dismissed too quickly as obviously implausible or foolish. Often it is impossible to find such phantasies without help. If it can be done it can be an extremely powerful method of dealing with the troubles of daily relationships.

In this chapter I have dealt largely with the less well known, more benevolent and positive aspects of such phantasies. Some of the more negative aspects appear in Chapter 6, where I discuss their involvement in blame.

FIVE

PHANTASIES
IN RELATIONSHIPS

(2)

In the previous chapter I described phantasies whereby what hurts, or causes trouble, or feels bad is put into the outside world in some form, perhaps to be modified and taken back in. But in order to grow, or even survive, we have to take in things which have not originated with ourselves too. Good things, both physical and mental, must be absorbed and digested.

(It seems that we understand the processes of getting rid of parts of ourselves, and taking parts of others in, in terms initially of bodily processes. Metaphor is a useful pointer to the phantasies which can be involved. Prototypes for phantasies of getting rid of something painful include defecating, as in the many metaphorical uses of the word 'shit'; urinating, as in 'piss off', to use one of the milder expressions; breathing out, as in 'a sigh of relief'; and also many kinds of muscular movement, such as hitting out. Bodily processes we use to understand 'taking in' phantasies include eating, digesting and also breathing in, as in 'taking a deep breath'. In phantasy we seem to believe on the whole that good things should come in and bad ones go out, except when things have gone wrong.)

Confidence in the self and in others

It seems that the very foundation of good feelings about ourselves and people around us is our ability and opportunity to take in good things, to appreciate them, to absorb and to enjoy them. We have to actually remember them or in some other way hold on to the fact that we have had them. A baby who has enjoyed good experiences with the breast or bottle is likely to be more able to enjoy solid foods offered later; a basis of trust in food and in people has been built up. A baby who could rely on people it loved to be sufficiently there and in touch – physically and emotionally – may be easier to leave later on as a child; the baby has learnt confidence in itself, in its own worth and value and in the people around. Ultimately such trusting phantasies give the baby a strong sense of internal and external security. Such a confident baby can allow others to offer comfort, food and love – though he or she may make it clear when they do not want to lose someone or something. The process of giving up the breast or the bottle or the presence of some loved person may not be without a struggle, since the baby or child actually values it and feels the loss. But other people and other foods will on the whole be expected to provide gratification, so loss of one good thing does not mean loss of everything worth having. New relationships and new foods may be greeted with some interest and hope even while the struggle over parting with old ones is going on.

Learning

It seems in particular that our ability to learn is related to phantasies of taking in good food and good people who love us as babies and small children. Difficulties in learning, just as difficulties with our digestion or eating habits or with friendships, may all be closely connected with the phantasies we developed as infants to do with the processes of taking in, and to do with what we felt we took in. Where we were sufficiently loved and fed as babies, even if we have consciously forgotten this, provided we obtained sufficient enjoyment we may have a firm basis to carry us through even quite severe difficulties later in life.

Inner security and projection

Not only do good experiences and the consequent inner security built up in infancy affect our learning and our self-confidence, but they in particular lessen the need to inflict our own phantasy problems on others. Many of the projection phantasies described in the last chapter function as some form of remedial work, so to speak. Where early and later experiences have been good enough the demands we make on others to work hard to contain our phantasies for us will lessen. Most of us of course are not in the situation of needing nobody to help us with at least some unbearable phantasies – and the emotional bonds forged in this process are in themselves often worth having. We are all bound at some time or other in our lives to push our own phantasies on to others, and in the process to create deep ties of gratitude and love, if we are lucky, as well as shame and anger or hatred in less happy situations. But it seems that more mature and secure people do this less than the immature and the insecure. This is perhaps one of the reasons why some people can be so pleasant to have around; there are people who almost seem to absorb tensions rather than add to them. I have met a few such people in my life; they were all over forty and realistically confident in their abilities. One was a midwife; she knew she was good at her job and had no need to prove it to anyone. She was able to work with mothers in such a way that their wishes and her skills were both respected.

The opposite extreme, of course, is the kind of person who feels so messed up inside that they seem to have to make everyone around them feel messed up too. In my chapter on work phantasies I have a section devoted to working with such people. Those who come up against some of society's sanctions may do so for reasons related to this kind of phantasy world. But, as I have said, I suspect that all of us do it at some time even in our adult life, especially when we are under any kind of pressure.

Difficulties

In order to be able to build up a secure, confident inner world we have to be able to acknowledge pleasure we have had, even if we no longer have it or even if it was not perfect. We must be able to hold on to good experiences without destroying the memory of them the minute they are past. We must also be able to tease out the goodness in a mixed experience without spoiling it either by too much emphasis on the bad or by 'blowing it up' and trying to pretend that the bad was not there too. This means that we have to be able to tolerate not having something we want, without denying that it or something else is worth having or wanting. This of course can be hard and painful. The process of taking in and appreciating, enjoying, absorbing and holding on to good experiences can be easily impeded. In the rest of this chapter I look in more detail at phantasies which involve some kind of taking over from another person in ways which do not lead to a sense of inner security and peace. In a deep sense these phantasies mean to us that something is wrong.

Using someone else's property, taking something from someone, can be done in a context of a gift, of borrowing or of theft. In a similar way we can use other people's attributes or other kinds of phantasy 'possessions' as if we were borrowing them or stealing them, and the consequences of the different kinds of phantasies may be quite different. It is important to note that I am talking largely about infantile and phantasy concepts of ownership which link up with adult ones but are not necessarily the same.

Ownership

For a child under three, its own teddy bear may actually seem to *be* a part of itself, or a loving and helpful parent-like figure. Later such things merely *represent*, say, security; in early childhood they may seem to *be* security. Taking away such a teddy bear or blanket, or losing a loved cat or dog, may mean to the child loss of part of itself as well as loss of real security. We cannot teach our children to be unselfish by depriving them too suddenly of such objects; if we try to, we are likely to increase their greed and their desire later to expropriate other children's teddies. Even if they learn to deny themselves the pleasure of taking other people's possessions, the more secure sense of having enough themselves (and thereby not needing to pass on strong feelings of deprivation) will be much harder for them to attain.

But because I would not make my sons give up their favourite tricycle to their friends, this is no reason for assuming that I believe in a capitalist view of property and ownership. Some people, reading drafts of this chapter, have tried to argue that ideas of ownership and possession, and guilt about theft too, are no more than socially determined concepts created by a capitalist culture. Some of them also, for example, see vandalism or burglary committed by teenage boys from particular subcultures as no more than a political act of revenge against those who have more. Or they see such behaviour as both meaningless and guiltless for the boys concerned, where their culture both encourages and condones it. It seems to me that when I actually met such boys the evidence was that acts of burglary, vandalism and rape, for example, arose from and gave rise to utterly despairing phantasies. The acts were seen and felt as destructive even if this was consciously – and certainly in public – denied. There was, for example, a strong sense of excitement – often of an overtly sexual kind – but together with this a weakly disguised deep depression. To dismiss this kind of observation as merely middle-class prejudices – as some people do at first – is not enough. It is important to distinguish between consciously felt emotions and emotions whose presence can be deduced, but which are being denied. It is important to distinguish political definitions of property or theft from quite basic feelings we have about fairness and greed, allowing people to keep enough of what they have, and making unfair demands on them or on ourselves. Too simple a view of the way we learn social or asocial behaviour can lead us to quite false conclusions about crime and punishment, as well as about how to bring up our own children with a strong sense of caring for those around them. One of the problems with our culture is that it frequently prevents us from strength-ening the loving and good aspects of ourselves and others, and encourages instead the more greedy, revengeful and destructive aspects.

Let us now look at an example of children's attempts to take over aspects of their parents.

A child may get enormous pleasure out of putting on its father's or mother's hat or shoes, partly because of a feeling that it is putting on its father's or mother's characteristics, such as the right to tell other people what to do, or to do adult work, or to buy everything it wants. These characteristics, exaggerated as they are by the child's-eye view, are clearly ones which do not belong to the child, and the child is normally aware of this. In such play the child may be able to find out something about what it is like to have such characteristics, and perhaps to modify its understand-ing in the process. Through ordering other children about, or ill-treating their dolls, children learn the limits of power, and the problems associated with exercising it. As a temporary measure such play is extremely valuable. But sometimes such phantasies do not remain in the realm of play in quite the same way.

Sometimes a child who is consistently ill-treated by a parent may in desperation try to 'become' that parent, and so lose touch with the hurt and damaged self which only seems to cause trouble. Or sometimes a little girl will decide to take over the 'mothering' of herself because she cannot bear to admit that her mother can do it better than she can. Such phantasies have left the realm of play and have serious consequences. Adults around are no longer allowed access to the vulnerable, dependent part of such a child, and the child gains a spurious kind of maturity which acts to cover up a very distressed, angry, hurt and destructive infantile self. The pleasures involved in playing at being grown up, or being someone else can lead to a loss of parts of the self as well as to phantasies of depleting and damaging the person who is in this way taken over or usurped.

Theft phantasies

Let us look at a perfectly conscious 'theft' phantasy expressed by a child of nearly three, who was being weaned. Melanie Klein found that such phantasies were common in the small children she worked with, and traces of them could be found in adults too.

Saul was sitting on the lavatory one day when he said to his mother: 'I wish you were dead then I could cut off your breast and have it all to myself.' While saying this he was smiling at his mother in a charming and apparently affectionate way: there was no sign of anger on his part, nor of a wish for her to go away.

In this fantasy, Saul has exchanged the painful situation of being dependent upon his mother's control and ownership of her breast for one in which he has it. As an apparently unimportant side-effect his mother appears in the fantasy as 'dead', whatever this means for him. The breast was obviously something very important and quite unrealistic for him: it meant much more than a piece of flesh. By his fantasy theft Saul has attempted to get round the realization that the actual breast does not belong to him – as he used earlier to claim – and he also manages to punish his mother for taking it away from him, though this desire to punish her is not clearly acknowledged. This attempt to create his own independence from his mother is clearly premature and unrealistic and is based not on realistic evaluation of his own abilities and possessions with regard to food, but on an attempt to enhance himself at the expense of someone else. In the process he has to deny at least temporarily his own care and concern for his mother: it is as if the longing for the wonderful breast has destroyed all his own realistic caring attributes, and left him just wanting to attack – in order to obtain a magical ability to care and love, represented by the breast. The price of recognizing his own caring feelings towards his mother is the realization that he cannot in fact have such a wonderful, magical breast, such an 'adult' kind of caring and ability to feed someone, and also the realization that this makes him angry and disappointed.

This kind of fantasy in one variation or another seems to be very common amongst children. A well known variation is the fantasy that the child can become independent by eating its own faeces, which are often represented as something like magical chocolate. The attacking aspect of such phantasies too may be kept separate, though children frequently use the word 'poo' as a magical attacking word, especially when they are being defiant. Roald Dahl's children's book *Charlie and the Chocolate Factory* captures this stage of childhood fantasy and turns it into an exciting story. Magical sweets and chocolate are made by machines which are extremely reminiscent of digestive processes, and their attacking and distracting effects are clear in the book: their purpose tends to be to cheat the appetite rather than to satisfy it; to take one's mind off unpleasant times in the classroom or to attack one's friends. The small hero of the story, Charlie, holds on weakly to his own concern for others, but he is swept along by the larger-than-life Mr Willie Wonka who tells him that such concern is unnecessary. The whole fantasy is set in a world of snow and ice, unemployment and cabbage water, with fifty-pence pieces but no Welfare State; the fantasy of eating faeces tends to work and be used most where the feeling is that the outside world really does not provide anything better. Mr Willie Wonka, a his name might suggest to you too, seems to bear some resemblance to phantasies of a penis belonging to an adult man and used for 'wanking' – that is, for satisfying the self when others have failed to do so. Just like Saul's cut off and stolen breast, a cut off and stolen 'willie' could give a child in phantasy enormous pleasure and power without him concerning himself for the real person providing it. (This relates to interesting ideas analysts have about masturbation, and the way it can be used to defend against misery and depression and a sense of loss and deprivation. I asked the boys in the remand home I worked in what they would do if they were put in solitary confinement and they answered somewhat predictably to that effect. The connection between such uses of masturbation and phantasies like Saul's, where an attempt to satisfy the self when others seem to have rejected and deprived you is intimately connected with an attack on them, may explain why it is that so many people have such unrealistically shameful feelings about masturbation, and are afraid they can actually damage themselves by doing it. It is not the masturbation itself which is the source of trouble, but the phantasies about what it means.)

Theft phantasies seem to arise, as one would expect, in connection with both real deprivation and with greed and envy, in the attempt to deny the lack of something which someone else is supposed to have. Feelings of not having something seem unbearable at the time; what the self does not have is perceived elsewhere, stolen or taken over without acknowledgement of its source in someone else, and the person who seemed to have the desired thing or attribute is then attacked, deprived and punished. This attack can serve to get even with them for taking or having the coveted thing, or to enable the theft to take place, or as a means of denying that they had it in the first place. Saul's picture of a 'dead mummy' perhaps serves to punish her for depriving him of the breast, and also to prevent her getting it back from him. Perhaps too it relieves him of the necessity of recognizing his care for her.

One of the problems with this way of dealing with situations of loss or lack in the self is that the satisfaction obtained is hollow. If the baby in phantasy steals the breast, this phantasy must then be modified by the next experience of hunger. Sometimes the phantasy develops in such a way that the child feels it has spoilt the breast by stealing it, and the hunger pains are simply a sign of the attacks the breast is now making on the inside of the body. When older children steal objects – often representing magical adult possessions such as unlimited food or penises or babies – the stolen object often takes on the meaning of a persecutor and has to be got rid of rapidly. Theft phantasies maintain the illusion that the wonderful thing is there to be had; they help to fend off the realization that such magical powers as children believe adults to possess do not in fact exist. As a result, they work against the child valuing what it has and being more realistic about what adults have. The child who is always demanding more presents does not seem to appreciate those it already has. Somewhere such a child has not yet understood that what it wants is something the present stands for – such as unlimited love and indulgence from the adults around, for example – and that this longing is for something which does not and cannot exist.

Caught up in such phantasies, the child or adult may be forever seeking to prevent feelings of hunger – for love or for food – rather than to feel them and then satisfy them. In the desperate attempt to prevent them there may be more and more attacks on people around who – according to the phantasy – have the means to prevent them, and are cruelly withholding. These attacks may then become a means of satisfaction; in Dahl's children's books the 'message' on one level seems to be that the main satisfaction in life consists in getting one's own back on one's enemies. This may be coupled with ownership of huge amounts of food, as the chocolate factory itself, or the vast numbers of pheasants which Danny and his father are to poach in *Danny, The Champion Of The World*, but the wonderful food which is so often promised is not in fact eaten. The triumphant attack leaves me feeling hollow and empty and hungry, when I read his books, though children seem to love it.

Taking over other people's abilities can often be done in a way which makes it clear that the main motive is to attack them for having them in the first place. Let me give some adult examples.

Steven used to do the housework 'for his wife' in such a way that he made it clear that she was totally inadequate and quite incapable of doing what both felt was 'her' job. Sometimes men can be afraid of loving their babies in case their wife should feel that they are taking over in this way, when their desire to attack their wives for being able to feed and have babies is kept under control, but is not fully mitigated by, their more loving and realistic attitudes to being a father. Sometimes women may take over what they see as 'really' men's work in order to show men they can do it better. In the process other pleasure in the work may be lost or spoiled. This kind of competitiveness between the sexes tends to be insecure, as well as destructive of more solid pleasures. It may be clear to other people watching but denied by the person who is doing it.

People who ask for help from counsellors or therapists can sometimes show evidence for phantasies of taking over and stealing what they are being offered, rather than allowing it to be given and having to acknowledge that someone has something they have not got. One client began her session by sitting in the chair the counsellor had been sitting in the previous week. She then described a dream in which she was showing the counsellor round a beautiful landscape – her internal world. Her desire to take over the abilities of the counsellor in order not to feel her own need for help included a hidden attack on the counsellor. It emerged eventually that in her phantasy what she was taking over was the ability to have so much insight into herself and other people that she could make everyone – in particular her nearest and dearest – feel very small, and herself feel enormously big and powerful in comparison. Sitting in the counsellor's chair, she was hunched up against the revengeful attack she expected from the counsellor.

Such people cannot immediately use what is offered by the therapist in a constructive way. The pleasure they get out of life is short-lived and insecure since it is dependent upon putting other people down and denying their own caring feelings for these other people. Whatever they are offered may be rejected or turned into a weapon to use against someone else. If they are offered love they are likely to feel that it is not enough, that it is only a pale shadow of the love offered to someone else, and they may reject it as such. Or they may use this love simply to crow over someone else supposedly more loved than them. If they are offered help, they may see it as implying that they need help, that they are not already enormously big, and they may reject this implication and with it the help. Whatever they feel they have inside them they may feel they have taken on their own account from someone else, and the 'victims', like Saul's dead mother, are waiting to get their own back.

Admitting to their own failings would mean for these people admitting to the terrible destruction they feel they have wrought upon all those around them, and the prospect may be too awful. In their attempts to distract themselves from these feelings, and avoid feeling them, they may get into situations where they are using other people more and more to bolster their feelings of wonderful superiority, and are caring less and less for these people. The trail of broken friendships and deserted jobs may become longer as they seek always to make others feel small and deprived and not good enough, and deny the terrible phantasies connected with their own sense of deprivation and lack of goodness.

Such people may be very greedy. Since nothing they are given is felt to satisfy them they are continually demanding more – and just as often making it in some way unusable or spoiling it. This greedy kind of behaviour may manifest itself in many ways.

Some people seem to be greedy about having lovers. They may move from one lover to another in a desperate attempt to deny their own feelings of dependence and unworthiness for love, and to pass them on to others. For such people the message passed in the sexual relationship is not one of love but of spoiling: 'You are just dirt', or 'I am just dirt.' There may be a sense of using the other person in some illegitimate way, such as to punish an ex-spouse or a parent who has suddenly 'shown' they do not love them. The initial longing for a new lover may include feelings of wanting to have and enjoy something they have: not only their body, but also perhaps, peace of mind and a sense of self-worth. But in the process of taking from them without real care for what goes with it, without recognizing them as real people with real emotions and real lives, this very sense of self-worth is likely to be damaged. The greedy lover's own sense of self-worth cannot be built up in this way; the increasing sense of worthlessness and 'dirtiness' may gradually refuse to be denied. For such people the value of the lover is lost once they are seduced: however much good loving they are offered they may be unable to make constructive use of it, because the greediness of the seduction process is suspected to have damaged the person seduced, who now becomes a potential enemy. In 'taking in' greedily, be it food or lovers, there is also an element of denial which prevents the object being looked at carefully and considered before being 'grabbed': closer inspection then may quite reasonably lead to the discovery that the person or the food was not actually good enough for the long term.

Sometimes, when people are greedy about food, this seems to be related to a feeling of having 'stolen' the ability to feed themselves, rather than having 'earned' it by growing up. Once again there may be feelings of being basically bad and unworthy. Sometimes people use food for 'stuffing' the self, partially in order to protect others from their emotional demands which are felt to be as greedy as their physical demands. The protection often fails since it is likely to be unrealistic: real needs are denied along with the greed; the protection may also be covering a strong desire to punish the very people who are to be protected. This punishment may emerge at intervals, just as the self-punishment of desperate dieting arises at intervals. Food is used to deny the need to depend on others and so keeps going the phantasy that such dependence would be dangerous for both parties. But the belief in the ability of the self to continue to feed and care for the self cannot be maintained for ever, as it feels, like Saul's would have been, an unrealistic independence. Being so scared of their own emotional hunger such people cannot bear physical hunger; the feelings are not experienced and satisfied, so reassuring the self that it is possible as an adult to feed and care for oneself, but are continually pushed under and denied. The real adult ability to feed the self is never allowed into contact with the desperate child's phantasies of being a bottomless pit. By continually depriving others of the chance to feed them emotionally and physically such people remain tragically caught in a phantasy that they must do it all themselves.

The unrealistic and 'theft' aspects of such phantasies may also be expressed in the way in which some people deal with their greed by eating too much and then being sick. If the food is felt to be stolen, it may indeed turn into a dangerous attacker inside, and may have to be ejected again. There are many other phantasies connected with greed for food, and at times these may be more important than the ones I have mentioned here; I am only giving examples of those connected with stealing the ability to feed.

There are many professions which provide opportunities to steal the work of others, or the result of their work. In daily life there are many opportunities to underpay or undervalue other people's contribution or your own. Some people use these opportunities and in the process build up an increasing sense of destructiveness inside themselves. Their illusion of being glorious and independent, the object of admiration, may (especially in mid-life) eventually crack, forcing them to admit to huge dependence upon others. The 'break-down' or 'crack-up' of apparently successful people may at times relate to such situations. Their real worth has never been valued by themselves for what it is; their real failings have never been confronted for what they are. The continual attempt to deny their failings and enhance their abilities has undermined their sense of self-worth, which at the time of the crack-up may have swung from exaggeratedly good to exaggeratedly bad. But sometimes people emerge from such crack-ups with a new sense of the value of others as well as of themselves. The triumphant glee in 'getting one over' other people may be replaced by a more realistic kind of ambition and caring. As a result the world may no longer seem such a dangerous place and the people in it may themselves seem more caring.

It seems that many people who resort to phantasies of stealing others' abilities or characteristics in one way or another suffer from a lack of belief in and confirmation of their real ability to care for people. Their behaviour then of course confirms their inability to care. Really loving relationships and satisfying work can enable a person to hold on to their sense of being able to care for others in a realistic and also a phantasy way. Not only the people in their outside world, but also 'the mother in their heads', for example, are known to be sufficiently well looked after for them to be able to go about daily life confidently. It seems to be loss of faith in this part of themselves which leads to and arises from the sense of the world being full of merciless and greedy people whose work and possessions can quite justifiably be stolen from them. Where the father in your head is a greedy and selfish tyrant, because you feel you have taken from him all his goodness and his power, not only is it relatively easy to steal from your boss, but you may also find yourself relating to your children as if they too were greedy and selfish tyrants – and so becoming one yourself.

Sometimes there is obvious reason why a person should have lost faith in this part of themselves. A divorce or the death of a loved person can lead to such despair: 'I wasn't good enough to keep them here.' The person who has 'left' in such a cruel way may become a maliciously punitive person in the phantasy world of the person who has been deserted. And without the help of loving adults in their inner world, all hope for strengthening and fostering the good parts of the self may be lost. Losing a job can also 'mean' that the self is not worthy of loving and being loved, not valuable to anyone else. One of the worst things about being poor financially often seems to be the frustration at being unable to give presents to people, especially children, and being unable to care for people who are loved. The ability to care for people such as your children or your parents in a realistic way seems to confirm the more positive phantasies about the self as a loving and worthy person, and to help to reduce anxieties arising from infantile phantasies of destroying the very people you love the best.

For teenagers who are put into remand homes it often seems to be that they have had no realistic way in which to discover that they could care for people. Their attempts to give have often been too mixed up with yet another attack, partly because they have little experience of realistic loving relationships, and partly because if they were to help or care for their mothers, say, the burden they would have to carry would truly be enormous. The external world and their internal world are such depressing and messed-up places, for reasons partially beyond their control, that they can have no hope of mending it themselves, and no hope of finding helpful adults to improve things either. As a result, by adolescence they may have learnt to reject any offer of help as if it were simply a pretence – which, of course, it may be. Even sincere offers of help may be unusable at first because breaking through the denial of dependence may unleash not a hope for a worthwhile dependent relationship, but despairing and envious destructiveness. The glimpse of hope offered by a loving and helpful person may seem too much for someone who feels they have never been offered lasting love or real help. The desire to smash it, to test it to absolute destruction, is understandable but may not be withstandable. Seeing even a hint of goodness may simply serve to arouse the fury and agony of feeling deprived of it over and over again.

But there is another kind of teenager who cannot easily accept help and who may grow into an adult who steals in one of the more subtle and disguised ways. Sometimes there are realistic economic and social reasons why people have a sense of being deprived; sometimes the reasons are more emotional. The feeling that the parents are, for example, cruel and harsh may be a reflection of reality, or it may be a very partial view which derives its strength more from the child's desperate need to get rid of its own cruelty and harshness into someone else. The feeling that the parents are ailing and damaged, in need of the child's care and protection, may arise from real illness on the part of the parents, or it may arise from the child's furious envy or greed, which convincingly 'stole' or spoiled the parent's ability to care for themselves and others. Sometimes it seems that real illnesses in the parents are attributed by the child to such thefts on the child's part. The child who took on the role of looking after other siblings or one or other parent may have done so because the adults around encouraged this. However, they may then have used this to deny their own dependence, or their need for (and jealousy of) the relationships between their parents, or between a parent and a sibling, perhaps.

Often, for example, a small girl may turn against her mother at the birth of a younger sibling: she may decide to take over all mothering of herself as well as of the baby, if she is allowed to. She may develop an apparently independent exterior appearance which hides a sense she has of being inside a small child, raging with envy of her mother's ability to have babies, and with jealousy of her mother's relationship with her father. This childish self may remain out of touch, in a cool and competent exterior which simply shows the world how much better she is than her mother on all counts. Her phantasy of having stolen the ability to create, to love, to care, may only cause obvious trouble later on, when she is faced with something which triggers her knowledge of her own 'badness' and her own disbelief in her real, owned abilities. She may for years function in the belief that the 'real me' part of her is no more than this raging child; all her apparent goodness may for her feel no more than a sham.

The attitudes of important adults who are around in childhood, and of close people later, can also contribute to the felt need to take over other people's possessions. Continual destructive criticism can undermine the belief in one's own goodness. Very moralistic partners or parents can in such ways encourage some kind of cheating behaviour, as belief in real goodness being sufficient cannot be maintained. Such partners or parents can also be a pale reflection of one's own 'moralistic' side, 'seen' in them in an unrealistic way, but they may add real weight to an otherwise manageable aspect of the self.

Idealization of the self is related to this. When parents continually exaggerate the goodness of their child, kindly overlooking its faults, the child may respond by feeling overwhelmed by its badness which is being denied, rather than recognized and made realistic. Ity may go in for sneaky behaviour, or for outright theft, partly in order to force its parents to recognize its 'bad' side, but partly in order to try to live up to an impossible ideal. One girl, for example, stole money to buy her mother a present: her own ability to give was not felt to be sufficient. The anger at this kind of idealization and the pressure it causes can also be expressed 'sneakily' by such actions which are guaranteed to make the discovering parent feel all the 'bad' emotions the child could wish, from disgust and fury to 'where did we go wrong?' and an enormous sense of loss.

Sometimes what is stolen is love: in some families there may be an agreement that one child is the good one and another child less loved and less good. It would seem obvious that the less loved child would suffer from this situation; what is less obvious is that the 'favourite' child suffers considerably too, from a sense of having more than their rightful share of a parent's love.

Alice suffered from this.

Alice was very concerned about her sister: her name kept cropping up as somebody who had stopped Alice from doing what she wanted to do or had upset her in some way or other. Among the complicated feelings between them was a strong belief that her sister was unloved and un-lovable; that Alice was the good daughter and her sister the bad one; that Alice cared for people and was loved for it and her sister was selfish and unloved. Alice spent a lot of her time caring for other people. She not only had a full-time responsible job, but she took on the sick-nursing of various relatives and neighbours, seemingly unable to say no to any request for help. I met her when she was suffering from nervous exhaustion and the doctor had ordered a complete rest.

It seemed that in Alice's phantasy – and perhaps in her sister's too – Alice was carrying all the good and dutiful parts of an ideal daughter, and the sister was carrying all the feelings of being rejected and rejecting for both of them. As a consequence, Alice was forced to do twice as much work in looking after sick relatives as she might have had to do if her sister had shared it. But Alice seemed unable to feel satisfied and comfortable with her own goodness; she felt enormously guilty that she had still not done enough, particularly for her parents, who had died recently.

I think that the feeling of guilt related at least in part to her feeling that she had 'stolen' the love of her parents from her sister, and her sister's (and parents') ability to care for others. Her good behaviour was devalued in her own eyes because on one level she felt it was being used simply to show everyone that she was better than her sister. Alice was desperately trying to live up to a picture of an ideal daughter who was totally unselfish. This was impossible, as her breakdown seemed to suggest, and in order to maintain it over the years so far she had denied her own selfishness out of desperation and had in phantasy 'put' it into her sister. Her sister was actively encouraged to be worse than she need be; whatever she did do was unappreciated since no normal daughterly behaviour could compare with Alice's utter selflessness. In this way too, the phantasies about what it meant to be a loved daughter, and what it meant to be selfish, were kept completely idealized and unrealistic. By her collapse, Alice actually forced her husband to give her some of the caring she had previously refused for herself, but in doing so reinforced her picture of herself as greedily taking more than her fair share of loving and being cared for. Phantasies of stealing the ability to provide all are usually accompanied by phantasies of getting rid of the needy and dependent parts of the self into others. When Alice had to reverse this process she found it extremely painful.

There are many apparently 'good' people whose 'goodness' does not quite stand up to examination – though of course not all good behaviour suffers from this. The kind of person I am thinking of may, for example, always do the washing up first in such a way as to make other people feel guilty or uncomfortable about not doing it; they may be always the first to say sorry, in such a way that other people can never make their own apology. The kind of person who is always the life and soul of the party may in fact be preventing other people from having their share of the glory. The kind of person who always 'supports' others may be preventing others from taking their share of the difficulties and the rewards of being supportive. The kind of person who always takes over a task which someone else is doing badly or slowly may in fact be preventing the other from learning how to do the task better, or undermining their self-confidence; the extra share of responsibility taken over in this way then may lead to mutual feelings of something being owed somewhere – but something which it is hard to pin down and actually 'pay'. Trapping people into working for you by creating debts they can never pay off is a ploy which is used not only on the international economic scene. There are many daily ways of taking over more than your share of socially approved tasks or roles, in such a way that other people are deprived of some satisfaction and gratification – in the name of being helpful. The greed such 'helpful' people seem to express is a greed for goodness, but because it does not include enough concern for other people as real people it remains unsatisfying. The 'good' member of the household may well, like Alice, and in spite of all appearances to the contrary, be convinced at heart of their own worthlessness.

Feelings of 'not having' something

It seems that some of the more frightening aspects of 'taking over' phantasies arise when feelings of not having something seem truly unbearable. The small child who cannot bear to be small, for whatever reason, is going to be much less able to develop its own real skills and so gradually to become really, securely 'big' in terms of what it can do, than a child who can accept how small it is, and can be patient enough to grow and learn at a more appropriate pace. Pleasure in being small, or awareness of what is to be lost by giving it up too quickly, can make the child more able to accept being at the age or stage it is. This is true of an adult in a learning situation later. There is no substitute for the acknowledgement that some people have something you want and cannot have, now or perhaps ever; the pain of bearing this situation is one which cannot ultimately be avoided without severe difficulties arising. Many of the struggles between mother and father and child around the ages of two, three and later, too, depend precisely on this problem. Not only are parents continually having to deprive their children of, say, the latest Space Invaders game, or toy, but on an emotional level the child is having to come to terms with the discovery that adults really can do things which children cannot do, and some things which the child will never be able to do. They are discovering that boys can never 'have babies in their tummies' or breast-feed; that girls can never have penises (though they may be able to have some, not all, of what the penis 'means' in their phantasy); that they can never marry their mother or their father; that they cannot yet feed themselves entirely;

and so on. A surprising number of adults seem to have avoided facing these facts, and somewhere continue to believe, for example, that their claim on their father or mother is still greater than that of the other parent, who is seen, in spite of evidence to the contrary, as a pale shadow of a person, hardly worthy to exist, let alone to live and love with their spouse.

To be able to tolerate and enjoy other people having something desirable that you have not got – adult abilities, a happy marriage, a child, the love of your father, a better job, say – you have to be able to admit to feelings about not having it yourself. If these feelings are too painful, so that in phantasy you would kill someone for it, for example, you may prefer to deny either that it is worth having or that you would like it. You cannot enjoy other people's pleasure in their children if your defence against the grief of not having them is to say 'Who wants children anyway? Nasty dirty things . . .' You cannot enjoy other people's better education or better fortune or marital happiness if you have to devalue it or them: 'What good does university do you?' or 'Married people are boring.' But where these things are devalued all hope of ever having them yourself may be lost, and with this, perhaps, all hope of having anything worth having, since you may well expect any kind of good fortune of your own to be subject to such attacks by others as well as by part of yourself which fears you do not deserve it. The devaluation also prevents a more realistic assessment of the value of the thing envied in this way. Admitting to the possibility of wanting it and not being able to have it, you may be able to look more closely at the implications and be able to give it up in fact more easily. University education may, for example, then be valued, but not over-valued; seen as something worth having, but not worth giving up three years of something else for. Regrets at having missed the chance earlier may actually be quite bearable when the other gains and losses of the alternative path you took are looked at in a realistic light. The ability to enjoy life and to have memories of enjoying it can be strong supports in facing many feelings of not having had something. Where this sense of enjoyment is missing it may be very hard to bear feelings of loss.

Devaluation is not the only defence against painful feelings of not having something someone else seems to have. The 'theft' phantasies deal with this pain by stealing. What is taken over in this way does not, however, feel as if it belongs to you; there is no sense of fully owning and deserving and having a right to it. As a defence against envy such greedy devouring of other people's possessions or qualities fails since what is taken over can be in fact devalued, spoiled and made useless once it has been taken. Alice's attempt to be superhuman failed. Her care for her sister was swallowed up, and actually destroyed effectively, in her attempts to be all-caring. The attempt to make her own caring abilities too big actually succeeded in destroying them and the satisfaction she got from them. The feeling of failure to achieve this superhuman caring was taken by her as confirmation that *all* her goodness was no more than a hollow sham; the realistic 'owned' part of her behaviour was never valued and seemed too insignificant to count at all. Envious destructiveness and devaluation seems to have won after all. 'Blowing up' and exaggerating or idealizing some characteristic or possession seems in fact to end up just as destructive as straightforward devaluation of it. It is this which probably makes it so painful to be 'put on a pedestal'; underlying the elevation is a strong sense of devaluation. Behind the image of the pure virgin is the threat of turning out to be the whore.

However, the greedy 'taking over' response is marginally more secure than the envious destructiveness, since it paves the way for a shift from the destruction of what was desired – the ability to love and care, to understand, to have children, for example – to an attack on the person who has it. This can at least seem to preserve the desired characteristic or object; Saul, by wishing his mother dead, was at least able to preserve the breast for a while as something desirable. An earlier and more feared scenario would involve punishing the actual breast itself, and being left utterly uncared for. Jealousy is in this way an advance on envy; the attack is deflected from the loved person on to the person who has taken their love from you. In this way the original love for the object of the jealousy is preserved, in spite of the shortcomings it has. Instead of attacking your mother for not being there when you want her, you may instead blame her absence on your father or your brother, and so retain her in your inner world as a good and loving figure who is merely temporarily absent.

In the long run there is no substitute for acknowledging the reality that the longed-for ability or part of the body does not exist in quite the form the phantasies gave it; that the ability of the breast to feed the child is dependent upon its attachment to a mother who not only can, but must, sometimes say no to the child; that the child can exist without the real breast; that the child's caring is enough and does not need to be enhanced since the world around can be relied upon to make up the shortfall or to help bear the loss of ideal phantasies.

The punitive aspects of greedy and envious phantasies arise in part, I think, from the age at which they develop; when the adult's ownership of riches is so convincing and the adult's refusal to give these riches to the child may almost reasonably be understood in terms of deliberate deprivation. The child's attempt to take over the adult's power can arise from the child's sense of being deliberately deprived; the feeling that the child is not being cared for enough may easily lead to the desire to take over the ability to care for the self – and for other loved people around. The loss of the child's own caring impulses then seems to be connected with loss of belief in the caring impulses of others. When the child in phantasy takes over any good parts of the adults around and leaves the adults carrying the feelings of deprivation, the picture of adults as merciless and revengeful and unloving is re-created. Such an adult is not one who can be asked for help, but can be attacked without mercy. A vicious circle may be set up in which all loving and caring parts of everyone concerned seem to get completely lost.

Often reality keeps this kind of phantasy down to a reasonable level. Real evidence of caring and being cared for, and being able to enjoy that, enables the child to hold on to its belief in its own and other people's goodness; the desire to punish becomes less pressing than the desire to give love and real gratitude to those around. The independence of other people, their resistance to being controlled, and their ability to give surprising pleasure, all contribute to trust and belief in some goodness in the real world both 'inside' and 'outside'.

So far in this chapter I have tried to look at some of the hidden aspects of phantasies of taking over and stealing from other people. I have tried to show how such phantasies involve an attack on the person who is supposed to be deliberately depriving, and how such phantasies can divert the attack from the desired thing or attribute on to the owning person. I have suggested that often what is taken over or stolen has the phantasy meaning of some kind of unrealistic and exaggerated ability to care for the self and others, but that in the process of stealing it, the real caring parts of the self may seem to be lost. I used the example of Saul's phantasy in which he said he wished his mother dead so that he could have her breast all to himself to illustrate the exaggerated and unrealistic kind of independence desired by those who steal in some way, and the denied attack behind it. However, since such phantasies do in some way allow the loved and loving parts of others to be valued, if only for a while, they are slightly less destructive than purely envious phantasies, and may be used either as a cover for such envy or as a means of growing out of it. By repeated phantasies of taking over and discovering that it does not work, the child or adult may be gradually pushed into a more realistic evaluation of the self and the attributes and possessions of others.

In terms of everyday life such phantasies are played out in many kinds of criminal and greedy behaviour, and in any kind of attempt to be more independent than is reasonable, or more helpful than is reasonable. The attempt to manage without other people may seem an ideal to some people, but it is likely to be accompanied by (apparently unintentional and probably totally unrecognized) the hurting of other people, if only by the rejection of whatever they would like to offer. The pervasive and general sense of self-dissatisfaction which is felt by many people, however apparently good and nice they are, may be related to a sense of not owning their own goodness, but believing that it has only been stolen by them from others to cover up their own 'real' badness.

'Containing' phantasies

Before I leave this chapter I would like to look briefly at an extremely important aspect of phantasies of putting parts of the self into others and taking parts of them into ourselves. This is to do with the way we endow the world with meaning and the way we get help with our deepest anxieties, including the way we actually structure our internal world.

What we seem to do is this. As I have said before, we search around in the outside world for some representative of important phantasies within. One example is the hungry baby seeking for things around it to put in its mouth. Sheet, fingers, knobs, pieces of plastic or furry toys may all be endowed with the meaning of 'nipple/breast' in some sense; in other words, they are treated as if they were the nipple or the breast. Having done this we then take back inside ourselves – physically for the baby in this case, but later only in phantasy – a new representative of the phantasy object. The baby finds and learns about 'nipples' made of plastic, or 'nipples' which will eventually be known as fingers or toes or (for a boy) a penis. Not only does the baby in this way develop new phantasies about the contents of the world but it also discovers – or confirms – something about the process of endowing the world with meaning, and giving out and taking in. Hope may become embodied in the phantasy, for example, that such processes are possible.

Let me repeat this in a different way. The baby can feel that it thrusts a lump of pain into the outside world, and receives back a loving set of arms and warm body and breast or bottle which 'takes the pain away' and puts warm contentment there instead. Not only has the lump of pain been turned into a new good feeling, but the baby has also been able to 'take in' a sense of the existence of a 'good container'; of something out there which can take lumps of pain and change them into something bearable and worth having, perhaps even enjoyable.

Obviously, anyone caring for a small baby can affect the baby's belief in such good containers. Where, for example, people around disappear, or deliberately or ignorantly 'mis-take' or ignore the baby's meaning – feeding it when the pain is misery, for example, or smacking when the pain is hunger – the baby may develop a strong sense that, say, its 'lumps of pain' are so powerful that they can destroy the good container – both 'out there' and the one which has been taken in with the milk. This is felt to be the most terrible disaster since it means that all hope of help for all bad pains (such as anxiety, grief, loss, fear, guilt) is lost, at least for a while.

Where, under more normal circumstances, the baby can feel it has lost or damaged but *regained* such a good container over and over again, belief in an extremely valuable object can be developed. The world can make sense of the raw data of pain, discomfort, passion, hunger and love. Under such circumstances, we learn as we grow older that the 'good container' inside us, and outside too, is tough, can bear attacks without crumbling or cracking up or exploding or being destroyed for ever; can be affected by what we do to it, but is not so weak and dependent upon us that it has no coherence or boundaries of its own; that we can mould it to some extent but we cannot simply control it and make it do what we want, careless of the way we treat it. We learn that such containers are neither completely vulnerable nor completely invulnerable; neither indestructible nor totally and forever destructible; not perfect, but usable. Belief in such objects in the world around and inside ourselves is extremely important for all our relationships. and especially for a sense of security, of sanity and sense, of hope and love and the worth or value of ourselves and others.

One of the important roles people around the mother can play for a baby is to become alternative 'containers' for some of the baby's unbearable fears and feelings. Fathers, friends and siblings, for example, can often be felt to protect and spare the loved mother/breast as a container in this sense, not only in reality, but also by helping to take some of the load of such painful and potentially damaging parts of the baby's inner world. These people then 'feed back' to the baby different messages about not only these parts of the baby, but also about the strength and weakness of the 'containers' around too. They may give the baby – and later the child or adult – hope that even if the mother or her phantasy breast inside the child is temporarily unable to help, there are other sources of love and help and understanding. A vital function they can perform is to help the baby to love and keep safe the first, most powerfully loved 'container' – the first representative of feeding and comforting understanding: the mother's breast. (The breast is of course endowed with an enormous amount of meaning by the baby, including, Melanie Klein suspected, phantasies connected with being held, warm and safe in the womb. Such phantasies can retain their strength even when the child is bottle fed. Bottle feeding does not necessarily 'mean' disaster for mother or child: it can be experienced as a huge relief for both.)

In our culture mothers – or 'mothering' – often come to stand for the good containing function; the ability to understand, to enclose and hold and love and nourish without destroying. Similarly, fathers and fathering may come to stand not only for our attacks on that good container, but also for our hope that we can preserve it, look after it, and protect it from our destructive impulses. Someone who loves and cares for our mother can give us the most enormous sense of relief from fears connected with these fundamental phantasies, as well as all the practical – and other phantasy – aspects of their help. The longing to have the mother well looked after is one which is very strong, and which can be powerfully affected in marriage break-ups. Teasing out the real mother from her structural place in the internal world may be an extremely hard task for a child and may contribute to difficulties and disturbances of all kinds which can emerge in children when the adults around them do not seem to be safe and loving.

When I had my first child, I experienced a sense of being overwhelmed by him and by the situation. My husband was able to come between us in a way which prevented me from 'falling into' the baby completely, and getting so entangled that we would never be able to extricate ourselves. This is how it felt for me, and, I suspect, for the baby too. Because my husband was able to take over responsibility for the baby sometimes, I could re-establish a sense of my own identity independent of my child. I suspect that he, largely simply by his existence, helped the child with the problem of separating himself out from me both directly and through his influence on my state of mind. He helped to establish boundaries between us and, later too, to hold those boundaries.

Words themselves function as containers of meaning; they too can stand for an aspect of the original 'good breast/nipple' phantasies. We 'fill' words with meaning: I remember at a stormy conference as a teenager suddenly understanding what the words 'the peace of God which passes all understanding' meant, as a furious quarrel ended in agreement and calm. Not until I had the experience together with the words could I truly feel I had fitted the two together, and the satisfaction involved was enormous. I felt I would never lose this experience, now that I had the words to encapsulate it. And this ability to hold on to experience is a large part of the value words can have for us; there is a sense in which they actually seem to prevent loss; at other times, as when a child learns to say 'bye bye' or 'mummy back soon', they enable us to contain and make bearable experiences of loss in a way which has deep reassurance about it. Some people feel words for them are always 'hollow'; they may feel actually cut off from their inner experience, or as if the only words that 'get through' are painful, angry ones. Children often struggle to *control* words and meaning, angry at the way they exist separately and apparently under the control of adults, independent of the child. This struggle can be related to their deepest anxieties about understanding. Our use of words, for internal as well as external communication, and for 'holding' meaning and understanding, affects our belief in our ability to use or destroy the boundaries between sense and nonsense, sanity and madness, love and hatred, protection and destruction. Feelings people have about structures, about limits and about links and relationships between people and things can all be related to deep feelings about the earliest containers they knew, which structured their inner world and their ability to enjoy the external world.

It is the way words can be taken inside us and used for reassurance, for help, for making sense of our inner world and our outer world which I wish to point out here. Words exist independently of us, yet they can be used and misused by us, to enormous passionate effect. The phantasies of putting parts of our inner world (parts representing both 'me' and 'not-me' phantasies) into the outside world and taking them back inside for comfort, for help, to change things or to keep them as they are, are daily expressed in our use of words. The words can be the means of conveying such phantasies, or they can be felt as things in themselves; the uses to which we put them are enormously complex and varied. Some of these I take up in Chapter 8. Some phantasies are never put into words: certain feelings may have to be 'put into people' or into things, because we have no words yet to express them. But these processes of giving meaning to our world, and taking in new understanding – on the model of a good feed – in a deep sense structure our world, and so affect our whole sense of balance, of security, depth, 'strength of character', and our ability to regain peace of mind after we have temporarily lost it.

SIX

BLAME, INTENTION AND RESPONSIBILITY

In this chapter I want to look at the concepts of blame, intention and responsibility, since psychoanalytical insights raise some interesting questions about them. All three concepts are concerned with ascribing guilt and with trying to make changes. Often very primitive phantasies are involved, and it is worth looking at some of these if we wish to use these processes constructively. In this chapter I shall restate some of the points touched on in earlier chapters in order to put them into a different context.

Blame

Psychoanalysis itself seems at times to provide evidence which is used in the process of blaming. Bowlby and other analysts have been accused of blaming bad mothering for all the troubles of the child. Reich and Freud sometimes blamed society for sexual repression and consequent neuroses. Other analysts seem to blame the individual for everything that happens to them, from being run over to marrying a man who turns violent, or from developing hysterical paralysis to having children who are ungrateful. But psychoanalysis has taught us quite a lot about the process of blaming as well as drawing attention at different times to different burdens of responsibility which may have been overlooked or exaggerated.

Let us look first at ways we may use blame.

From very early on, it seems, we discover that blaming someone seems to help for a while. The child – or adult – that can localize the source of misery, be it its mother or brother or the tree which 'came up and hit me', may find that some of the discomfort is reduced. Many people know the sense of relief, particularly common in adolescence, arising from the discovery that, say, all the problems of the world could be ascribed to Capitalism or the Nuclear Family, or, for other generations perhaps, Communism or the Devil, the Nazis or the Jews. Part of the mechanism involved is the containment of the badness and danger, which for a while makes the rest of the world or the self seem safer. If it is the fault of my bad education, or the British Class System, it is not my fault. If it is the fault of the government, I cannot be blamed and nor can my parents. A very small baby may have a phantasy that there is a Bad Breast which is responsible for pain, and that this is separate from the Good Breast which provides good and edible food. Localizing the source of badness may protect the phantasy of a good world or good breast and so allow real food and love to be taken in trustingly.

For a baby this may make sense for a while, and on a temporary basis it may help an adult too. Belief in a good source of love and help may be maintained in the face of anxiety that the good source is in fact polluted, and in danger from attack, by attributing the pollution to one part of the world which can then be attacked freely. Belief in a new lover may be maintained in the face of anxiety that he or she is not the answer to all life's problems by, for example, blaming problems on bad living conditions, on his/her mother, on the fact that you have no children or whatever. What begins as a rather unrealistic belief may be able over time to change into a more realistic one, and a certain blindness at times may not hinder this process too much.

Sometimes blaming can itself help to change things, particularly if, for example, I can bring myself to confess to doing it. Accusing someone of having done something to me, for example, can be a useful – if painful – way of discovering corrective views of myself and the world. If once I dare to blame my mother for what she did to me when I was five, say, I might find that she has a quite different view of what went on then, which changes my whole attitude and understanding. A less painful way which people often use is to 'blame' to a third party. I can tell a friend or relative what another person has done to me in such a way that they can help me find a different way of looking at it, or in some other way modify my feelings about the situation so that I can actually perhaps bring about a change in the real world.

But, in the long term, blaming which is kept hidden or in some other way protected from other views of reality does not help at all. Let us look at some of the problems involved.

One of the problems is that blame can be used as a means of denying responsibility. Using someone else's real (or imagined) guilt, we may try to claim that we have no guilt at all. This has several consequences which are problematic in the long term. Denying our own responsibility takes away from ourselves the power to change anything directly. Not only do we feel like innocent victims when we are not, but we also lose control over the extent of the injury being done. The 'sin' for which the other person is being blamed may take on enormous proportions, and this exaggeration can arise from two interconnected sources. Using 'their' guilt, we may jump at the chance to unload a large amount of 'our' guilt on to it. If my son is late for supper, I might unjustly blame him for its being ruined, when I know that it would have been ruined anyway and I am glad to be able to hide my own failure as a cook. But another source of the exaggeration lies in our perceptions of exactly what there is to be guilty about.

Sometimes people start blaming each other, handing over responsibility, precisely because they are so terrified of what has been done. Rather than look at what there is to be guilty for, they assume that they know this, and concentrate on who has done it. But this leaves the guilt quite unrealistic. It may supposedly be referring to, say, overspending this week; in phantasy the dangers of overspending may be understood to mean, say, the threat of total ruin, starvation, loss of respect from everyone and proof that your mother was right and you should never have married this person. It is these underlying anxieties – somewhat unrealistic ones – which give the force to the blame and give rise to the need to disown responsibility for it.

Sometimes the fear of what has been done, of what sin has been committed, is so great that it seems hopeless to try to save the self, and the 'guilty' person may turn their attention to saving the person they love. Here the powerful, unrealistic blame remains primitive and still attached to impossible scenarios, and in this case directed at the self. In order, perhaps, to maintain the phantasy that there exists some hope, some perfection somewhere, this terrifying guilt may be directed at the self and leave the other person innocent.

In both of these cases, the enormity of the guilt, its attachment to unrealistic situations such as total loss of everything you care about, has been responsible for and maintained by the process of concentrating on who it belongs to. By attributing guilt of this kind to someone who is not in fact *that* guilty, the fear and the guilt may even be raised, and so the 'need' to deny it increased. Blaming someone wrongly – another or myself – is felt to be a guilty activity. As a process of reducing anxiety, blame may in such cases fail in the long term.

In the long term, if anxiety about what has been done is to be reduced, responsibility has to be seen more realistically, both in terms of the nature of the guilty act and in terms of who is responsible for it. Sharing guilt can make a lot of difference. Blaming my mother for preferring an older sister to me, I may be making it very hard for her to show any love for me. Admitting my own share in the problems between us, I may be able to admit that she loves me enough: I may, for example, stop interpreting every gift she gives me as a guilty 'compensation' for the fact that she prefers my sister, and learn to be more appreciative of what she offers. If two people can share responsibility for living in a house they dislike, or sending their children to the wrong school, or having an unplanned baby, the sense of guilt and the fear of the consequences may suddenly become much lighter. If both are sympathizing with each other, the house may seem a less depressing place anyway, or it may be possible actually to leave it. If both agree to share the guilt about the children, it may be possible to look more closely at the actual damage being done to them at the school, say, and the child may even be able to cope better with an unsatisfactory situation at school if the parents are not fighting over it. On a more primitive but equally important level, parents (or others) who can share guilt successfully have an enormous bond between them in phantasy, and reason for real gratitude to each other. Blaming, either of the self or of the other person, can often be part of the mechanism which prevents this gratitude, and therefore love, being experienced.

Using blame to shift responsibilities while keeping them at an unrealistic level may have other consequences too. Protecting, say, my loved mother by blaming everything on my father may be useful in the short term if it allows me to live in relative harmony with my mother, and my father is out all the time anyway. But in the long term it must lead to an assumption that my mother is helpless or weak or stupid and my father a monster with an enormous amount of power. The responsibility then laid on me to care for such a mother may be enormous, and my task made far harder by my attitude to my father. My own ability to be a mother or father myself will also be seriously affected as the possibilities are so idealized. Whenever I want to do anything 'strong' I may feel I am being like my (bad) father; if I then remain 'weak' I may feel I will become as terrified and helpless as I feared my mother was. In order to survive reasonably intact, I may have to recognize not only the 'bad' side of my mother and the 'good' side of my father, but also my own guilt in overlooking those aspects before, and perhaps guilt about the way I treated them as a result of my idealizations. Perhaps I not only devalued my father's efforts but also attacked him for my mother's imperfections or my own.

By denying our own share of responsibility, we may also use blame as a means of punishment. This may at times include punishing in a quite unrealistic way. I may pick on someone's real fault and use it as an excuse to punish them for something completely different and far less realistic or acceptable. As a child of six, for example, I could perhaps determine to punish my mother for pushing me off her lap when I could not admit to wanting to punish her for having a baby. Small children often seem to 'ask' to be punished themselves, as do some adults who feel better after ECT because they have interpreted it as a deserved punishment. Such demands for punishment can be made in order to relieve feelings connected with terrible crimes committed in phantasy; by being punished in reality for something they have done wrong in fact, a child may feel their hidden guilt is assuaged. For a while this may seem to relieve the guilty party from the need to attempt to make better whatever it was they did wrong.

Blame is often unrealistic and primitive; it can work on the assumption that if I can make you suffer it will take away my own pain, or if I can make myself suffer, it will take away your pain. There may of course be an element of truth in this, but it is an uneasy truth: it may mean that the blamed person is waiting to get their own back, and is storing up vengeful hatred. This unrealistic punitive element can make it much harder to admit to a share of responsibility. The fear of being attacked by others as we attack them in our blaming phantasies may make it extremely hard to look at our own share. The fear of rising up against someone you have struggled for years to 'protect' may make it very hard to admit that they have some responsibility for the troubles in your life. Removing the death penalty may make it easier to convict the guilty: accepting faults as something people may be responsible for rather than as something which gives an excuse to attack, it may be easier to find the precise cause of the trouble. What can be repaired may then be repaired, and what must be lost may be grieved over.

In this way, a global guilt can give way to a more specific, less persecuting one. 'You never care about the safety of the baby!' can be honed down to 'You walked past an open safety-pin lying on the floor last night!' The blame becomes realistic and forgivable. 'I'm a terrible daughter!' becomes, perhaps, 'I did not realize that my mother was upset for her own reasons, not just because I was being nasty when I said that I did not want her to come for Christmas.'

Another problem with blame is that it may be a way of keeping alive an unrealistic hope which might be better made more realistic. I may blame myself for being a terrible daughter while keeping alive an unrealistic hope about what it means to be a good daughter. Something similar seems to happen in some people's view of the 'innocence of childhood'. By blaming the environment for children's greedy or destructive or jealous behaviour, they may keep alive an unrealistic hope about 'unspoiled' children, and about the human race in general. Utopia or Disaster may be seen as the only alternatives for the human race. Some of the objections to various psychoanalytical discoveries may be seen as responses to such fears about the future. Freud was attacked for 'discovering' childhood sexuality, and Melanie Klein for suggesting that children might respond to very 'good' environments with envy as well as with gratitude, or be born with inbuilt aggression as well as inbuilt love. In both cases, I think, some people felt that their hopes about the future of the world were being threatened. The liberal fallacy that, given enough freedom, a child will naturally turn out free of conflicts traded off present discomfort (from inconsiderate children) for future hope (somehow it will all turn out right, and sacrificing ourselves as parents is worth it for Them). In fact, it has been suggested that adults taking too little responsibility for keeping the boundaries, for controlling the child's aggression and greed, left the children with enormous problems and terrible guilt about their inability to control their more destructive impulses, rather than teaching them to handle them in a caring fashion. But the anger with people like Klein who suggested that we cannot get rid of these conflicts for ever was almost certainly connected with the fear of losing quite unrealistic hopes. Part of the fear lies in the lack of ability to think about more realistic alternatives: rather than turning attention to this, it was perhaps natural that attention should be focused on blaming the messenger for the bad news.

A very common way in which blame is related to idealizations like this one about innocent children involves setting up an ideal and punishing real people for not living up to it. A mother or husband or wife may be blamed for not being totally devoted to us. Many people feel that those you love should know what you want without being asked. They should always be there when they are wanted and go away when they are not wanted. 'She should have *known* I wanted comforting!' when the need was not very clearly expressed and may have been expressed in a distinctly confusing form. If someone retires into themselves or into their bedroom it is not easy to know if on this occasion they want to be followed or to be left alone. An ideal mother (or lover) is supposed to have magical powers of divining her children's needs – where a realistic mother can at best only help her children to learn to express them more clearly. An ideal mother should take away all pain, whereas a real mother can at best sometimes do no more than help her child acknowledge its existence; this discrepancy is enough to make any child angry.

It seems rather ironic that often in analysis it is found that such ideal mothers, when they are perceived by the child as totally self-sacrificing, may easily become the object of enormously envious attacks. Where a mother actually tries to be a servant for her child and take away all pain she may not be helping the child to cope with its own imperfections, with the discrepancy between the way the child would like to be and the way the child feels he or she is. When you are struggling to be good and failing all the time, a mother who is always good may seem to be a permanent reproach as well as an unattainable hope. The misery of being bad may be made worse if there is never a feeling that your mother herself knows what it is like to feel bad from the inside, as if her sympathy is always the understanding shown by superior mortals to those of lesser worth. The child is then in a deep sense left alone with its feeling of being bad, and may even use all the power at its command to punish all around for making it feel like that.

One of the problems with blame is that it stems from very primitive phantasies, where the anxieties being dealt with are extremely powerful. The earliest phantasies do seem to include the assumption that the baby self can destroy the world, like God with the Flood. Worse, there may be a fear more like the fear of destroying God too; of destroying all hope of goodness being repaired, of evil being overcome, of forgiveness and love. It is anxieties like this which emerge in a disguised form sometimes in blaming. The phantasy of total destruction may be got rid of into the outside world in various ways, becoming more or less modified in the process. It may be experienced in a fear of the Americans or the Russians being able actually to destroy the world, or a fear of a lover being able to destroy the relationship with them, and the self with it. These primitive phantasies may be involved too when a rape victim blames herself: she (and others) may feel she 'must have asked for it'; as if her power was so strong that she could make a perfectly normal man go suddenly wild. This belief may attach itself to feelings of, say, flirtatiousness she once felt, and her infantile confusion between reality and phantasy then takes over. In moments of excessive emotion, when we feel overwhelmed by events and feelings we seem particularly vulnerable to more primitive forms of phantasy; in particular to the sense that something can happen just because we willed it to. Our innermost guilty thoughts then become the focus for utterly unrealistic blame.

In such states, guilt and blame and punishment may become indistinguishable, and extremely painful. Later we may regain a more normal, realistic view of the world, but we may need help with bearing the primitive, overwhelming emotions before we can use our reason and common sense on the phantasies which lie behind them. In a very simple sense, the presence of another person offering silent or verbal support may function as a reminder that the world does go on, that there is still love and hope and help, even if we cannot at the time of crisis actually make use of it. The presence of another person can reassure us that we have not in fact done the equivalent of destroying God in our inner world.

Intention and responsibility

Let us turn now to the issue of intention and responsibility. Rape is a case where confusion is often expressed around these issues; as if a rape victim always 'asks for it', or battered wives deliberately choose a husband who will batter them. People in my classes sometimes ask if I think that accidents are always deliberate, or slips of the tongue always significant. There is often an assumption that such questions can be answered globally, once and for all, when of course they cannot. Each individual case must be considered in detail before anyone could realistically guess how much responsibility can be apportioned where, and what to do about it if anything. But people also get annoyed with me for implying that even 'unintentional' or 'accidental' behaviour may sometimes be in some way motivated.

Part of the annoyance arises from a fear of being held responsible for something you want to deny. A drunken man may well do and say things which he denies wanting to do when sober, and being accused of somehow wanting to do these things may seem very threatening. It feels much better to say it was 'the drink' not me. Many people do not like the implication that they might lose things or forget them or turn up late for some reason. And they do not like to think they might be 'giving themselves away', when someone who is supposed to have almost magical means of divining their inner motivations detects a discrepancy between what they say they want and what they then do, for example. The objections are well motivated: all such actions probably take place in the 'accidental' way they do partly because the person concerned does not like and does not want to take responsibility for the part of themselves which did, in some way, motivate them.

Freud had a patient who was extremely upset when Freud was driven to the unavoidable conclusion that her symptoms – pains in the legs –

were partly motivated by the fact that she had been in love with her brother-in-law for years. But as Freud pointed out, the symptoms had arisen because of the *horror* at the idea, not just because she had been in love.

It is important to bear in mind that saying that some 'unintended' action is probably in some way motivated by denied phantasies is not quite the same as saying you *really* wanted to do it. Where such events are motivated, the phantasies making them happen are part of a set which conflicts with another set of phantasies which very definitely does not want them. Both sides of the conflict, however, are part of 'you', even if you do not like the idea. What those phantasies are which did motivate some unwanted behaviour, an outsider cannot say and probably neither can you, though very often one answer will arise immediately.

I was discussing this point with a friend once and she told me how absent-minded her husband was, and that he made mistakes as a result of this which were caused, she thought, simply by his being absent-minded and preoccupied with his work. As an example, she told me how he had managed to misunderstand for more than a week when she told him that his favourite uncle had died suddenly. For the whole week he had been involved in long conversations about it, but had persistently understood that it was *her* uncle, someone who was old and ill and nowhere near so loved. It was quite striking how clear the evidence was for a perfectly good reason why her husband might have been in some way motivated to misunderstand, yet she would not agree. It seemed impossible to convince her, and I did not try for long.

Similarly, when another friend wrote in some annoyance to say he would not be coming to any more of my seminars because he did not have time 'but I do not expect you to believe that', he followed this up immediately with several good reasons why I should not believe it – reasons which took me completely by surprise. The feeling that someone psychoanalytically inclined might misunderstand 'pure' motives is often well grounded in the belief that such motives are being misrepresented.

Clearly people cannot always be held totally responsible for everything that happens to them. However, remarkably often we can discover a greater degree of responsibility than we liked to admit to, once we give up the idea that conflicting emotions and conflicting desires somehow cancel each other out. Once we realize that it is quite possible simultaneously to want something and not to want it – to want to have our cake and eat it, for example – understanding our 'unintentional' actions can become much easier. But it is still not easy. I may be suspicious that the ostensible motive – or apparent lack of it – is insufficient to explain some behaviour without in any way knowing what conflicts actually lie behind it. Given the uncertainty in real life I find it is usually best to take people at their word – if they say they did not want to turn up late, I believe them; I am sure this was one of the elements in their behaviour, and what other elements there are is probably none of my business.

When it comes to my own behaviour I might start wondering if I found myself seriously misbehaving in some way: always arriving late to collect my son from school, although I knew he would be upset, for example, or being rude to someone I thought I did not want to offend. I might try wondering what lay behind such behaviour; letting my mind wander over any pictures or ideas that came up in connection with my behaviour, for example. It takes an effort to do this, but in my experience it is the only effective cure for such problems. Even then I doubt that I would think of all the conflicts being expressed, though I might well learn quite a lot about myself, and enough to reduce the frequency of my 'bad' behaviour. The conflicts which cause us most trouble are not going to yield to self-questioning easily, though the evidence may be staring us in the face. This is why all the techniques for self-discovery which various schools of psychotherapy suggest can only go so far without another person with some training being there to help.

This point is important to bear in mind in quarrels. Couples sometimes go in for interpreting each other's behaviour in a way which simply adds to the injuries being done. The person who loves you best is not in fact likely to have a very clear view of you, though they may have considerable, *partial* insight. Their insulting interpretations – 'You just want me to be like your mother!' for example – may have some truth in them but they will never be the whole truth. The rest of the truth may well be extremely important and totally missed by both of you. (In particular, the direct opposite may often be equally true; in this case, that you also want them to be totally unlike your mother, for example.)

In counselling I think different rules apply. When someone asks for the help of a counsellor I think that help may well include some probing into alternative explanations for behaviour which should not stop at the most superficial, though I think they should probably also not stop at the 'first one down' either. Frequently the first explanation is felt to be hollow: 'I was being nice to my mother-in-law by asking her to stay.' The 'first one down', easily uncovered beneath this explanation, may be extremely nasty: 'I was only asking her to show up my sister-in-law and to punish my husband for being so rude about my mother', for example. If the counselling stops here there may be some relief but not as much as might be reached by further consideration, where real love, real sadness, real anguish can be found mingled in conflicting desires lying behind the action. One reason why I find that it is best to take people at their own estimation in normal life is that the superficial explanation may in fact be nearer to some kind of 'deep' truth than any quickly ascertained underlying one. Both distort. Quite often there seems a sense in which the feared, 'bad' reason which is felt to be 'the real me', making all my polite behaviour seem a mockery, only comes between a superficial reason and a deep grounding for *that* reason: after a lot of work, client and counsellor may discover a far deeper meaning to the apparently 'hollow' explanation. The 'being nice to my mother-in-law' may emerge, for example, grounded in a longing to be loved by her, and to love her as you always wanted your mother to love you. All the spite and revengefulness which was suspected and feared may emerge as an expression of despair at ever attaining this kind of love, for example. Discounting the superficial explanation too easily may give rise to a very depressing and no more 'real' view of the self than too easy a belief in it would support.

In marriage counselling in particular it may be important to discuss interpretations since the partners will all the time be interpreting each other's behaviour anyway, and some testing of these interpretations may be very useful – 'Is her backache just an excuse to avoid sex?' for example – and discovering that there are other possible hidden motives may be a relief; so too may confirmation of the fear in a more open way, so that perhaps something can be done about removing it or living with it.

I think in general it is valid to make distinctions between different kinds of intention. Drunken intention is different from sober intention, and the differences may be as important as the similarities. What we do without conscious 'permission' may be intended in a different way from what we do with conscious permission. We may or may not have conscious control over our behaviour – over bringing on backache, for example. Either way, it can really hurt. But I think we cannot disclaim all responsibility for any part of ourselves we do not wish to know or cannot bear to know. Some people really do talk as if it wasn't really them who, say, dropped something or even killed someone. 'I didn't mean it' is not always treated in adult contexts with as much scepticism as it deserves. The logic behind the assertion that people can make slips of the tongue, or knock things or people over without feeling in any way responsible, is not easy to understand. It seems to imply that one's body and mind can be taken over; it implies that we are the innocent victims of our bodies or of forces which have a life of their own inside us.

This of course does reflect a powerful phantasy, as all the stories of 'possession by the devil' bear witness. We do have phantasies of being inhabited by other people: by our parents, by our lovers, by Jesus or by people who left our real lives years ago. Part of this phantasy may well include a sense that one of these people can 'take over' for a time so that 'we' are not responsible for our actions: 'they' are. Many people who go for psychiatric help have this kind of feeling in some degree.

Someone with obsessions may be quite sure that someone else is telling them what they have to do; the inner voice which ensures that some ritual is done correctly may feel as if it has nothing to do with the self – the self is no more than an utterly helpless and innocent pawn. Here the strength of the self may have been in phantasy put into someone else – a father, it seems, very often – and then that father in phantasy taken back inside. Instead of the normal processes of psychic 'digestion', whereby father and self are confused and sorted out, mingled and change each other inside and outside, in such phantasy worlds it seems as if the phantasy of the powerful father has remained in some sense separate from the phantasies of the self. He remains as a 'foreign body' in the psyche, telling the 'self' – now very weak and drained of all strength – what to do. But such phantasies, which can feel extremely real, should not be confused with real perceptions. As with all denials of reality, psychic or external, hard work is put in to maintain such delusions; it is not an easy life being obsessional. And however much we would like to imagine that our right hand does not know what our left hand is doing, that actions which are extremely uncomfortable to others and ourselves bear no relationship to our own desires, we cannot I think allow such disclaimers of responsibility.

I think the point is that we must admit responsibility for whatever we do, drunk or sober, intentionally or accidentally. But we must also often be prepared to recognize that the way we are is the end-result of a long process which may be extremely difficult to change. I am not saying that we can have total control over our actions just by taking responsibility for them, nor by willing it. There is quite definitely a sense in which we have to learn to know ourselves: to find out what is going on in our heads without our being aware of it and without our being able to control it directly, since it is unavailable to our reason, our common sense. Like a stomach or a spine, a mind may have to be treated as if it has a certain amount of autonomy, even though it is indisputably part of us. We have to learn what foods affect our stomachs in which ways, and for our own health respect that knowledge. We have to learn what our emotional responses to certain situations are and for our own comfort respect that knowledge, even if we dislike it. We may know that if we bend in a certain way it brings on backache, but we may still find ourselves doing it. We have to allow for a certain amount of automatic functioning on the part of our minds and bodies, in a sense, when it comes to everyday behaviour. The better we take note of these aspects of ourselves, the more we can learn to behave in such a way that they do not cause too much trouble. We cannot just 'pull ourselves together' three weeks after the death of someone we love; if we try to, or seem to, this can only be because some part of ourselves has been temporarily lost so completely that it is apparently not missed. Later we may weep for no apparent reason; we may turn against sexual relations; we may get our own back on someone who did not understand our deadness as fear of mourning. If we understand ourselves better, we may instead decide to weep sooner rather than later; to withdraw from the world for a time early on, the better to retake our place in it later. We cannot just decide not to be jealous any more without perhaps losing also the ability to love; we cannot choose to be a perfect parent or an ideal child. We have to learn to accommodate ourselves; to give ourselves what we need and to control our greed. What we can do is to learn to see ourselves and others as we are, and to find ways of changing or living with ourselves which are possible.

Change

Let us look now at some of the problems involved in trying to change ourselves or others, and in taking more responsibility for the way we are.

In the first place, many people are actually unaware that there are different, more comfortable ways of functioning. Some people seem to believe that life has to feel gloomy and dismal and depressing all the time. A friend of mine thought that everyone went around with their packet of suicide pills ready in case the world did become too much. Some people seem to think that all husbands have to be demanding and violent and derogatory towards women; if their husbands are like this it may seem a fact of life which has to be accepted. John Donne, the poet, seemed to believe that all women were unfaithful; if this were so, being continually let down by women would be nothing to do with the man concerned, and there would be no point in him seeking help.

Many people who are unhappy about the way they are seem quite frightened of seeking help; as if they were afraid that they would receive only confirmation that nothing could be done, that their problems are too great or too small, that the doctor would be overwhelmed or would scoff, or that confessing to being unable to solve all their own problems would imply they were unfit for their present job. Many people seem to feel that glorious independence is the only honourable way to live: asking for help would seem like a total failure to such people. (The fact that in their lives they are far from independent may be overlooked, as if they can do nothing about this; but they can express their 'independence' by refusing to ask for help which might make them face their actual dependence.) Other people seem to think that there must be a magic pill which would make everything all right without any work: even the work of having to attend regular sessions with a marriage guidance counsellor, for example, may seem too much – it makes them indignant that such a demand could be made of them. The implications of seeking help from psychiatrists who may offer ECT, new drugs or lobotomies, and perhaps all kinds of social disadvantages, such as being labelled 'in need of psychiatric help', are also amongst the more realistic reasons why people do hesitate to explore their own uneasiness and to seek out ways of changing.

Even if a decision to seek help has been reached, there may really be little around. Many people seem to find help in their love relationships so that as they grow older they do become wiser and more loving themselves. Others find help in therapies of various kinds, or in their work. It may really be the case that our parents could not help us with some of our anxieties because they did not know how to, and the same may apply to those around us now. Our culture is seriously lacking in some kinds of understanding, such as understanding the processes of mourning and of dying. Our tolerance level for other people's misery does seem at times very low; we undervalue 'being there' to suffer with people, and feel that if we cannot 'do' anything, there is no point in waiting around for a situation to change of itself. The value of listening with attention, or remaining with someone in silence, is recognized, it seems, only in certain sections of our society.

Sometimes, what help there is may be made unusable, once again, by us in a way we made it unusable before. If we seek always for an improvement in our lover, just as we sought always to change our parents, we may not be able to use and enjoy the love they can offer us now. If we demand too much of ourselves, we may be unable to gain much satisfaction from the work and parenting we actually do. We may interpret our children's confused attempts to make us see something just as we interpreted those of our parents – as no more than attacks and demands that we prostrate ourselves and confess total guilt for the sins of the whole world. Advice offered by colleagues may be seen as attempts to put us down; their attempts to share their problems may be greeted by us with impatient derision; offers of help may be rejected as implying that we cannot manage on our own as we feel we should, or could if only things were different. We may feel so envious of someone else's calm that we cannot use it to nourish ourselves, but must try to destroy it in some way.

There is a real problem in changing phantasies which cause us trouble. What to one person is quite clearly an exaggeration is to the sufferer simply reality. We believe our assumptions so much that it is often extremely difficult to think about them. Our very processes of thought, which in principle could sort out truth from falsehood – real ability to hurt people from exaggerations of this, for example; real loving feelings from the tangle of conflicting and spoiling feelings – these processes seem to be so caught up in the phantasies that we never dare to ask the important questions, or, even if we do, we may too quickly dismiss them. While we still believe that wishing someone dead is the same as killing them it may be very difficult to allow ourselves to feel anger – and so to allow ourselves to move on from the anger to the more loving and caring longings which are buried by the anger. While we are convinced that another person's success means not only our failure, but also our smashing them to pieces in a jealous rage, we may find it very hard to allow someone else to help us successfully. It is not until we are able to *think* about this process that we can question our conviction and perhaps find that it is not entirely true.

All the primitive phantasies which made it hard for us to develop differently as children, and leave us with a knot of anxiety in the stomach now, or a feeling of being watched, on trial, a failure, a mess inside – all the real problems of our culture and environment which fed into our deepest phantasies may still be there making things harder. We still use much the same mechanisms for getting rid of pain that we used throughout childhood; we may still see pain as a sign that we are dying or being terribly punished and may be unable to bear it long enough to find out that this is not true; we may even 'kill off' part of ourselves in order to get away from this pain, and so in a way make the phantasy seem more true than it needs to. (People sometimes seem to do this with their feelings of dependence when they cause too much pain; they 'kill off' the dependent parts of the self and feel as a result 'dead' inside; at which point they may really be unable to feel much pain – or life.) We still keep parts of our minds in separate boxes so that one part can neither contaminate nor modify another. We are still struggling with assumptions about other people's perfection or gifts, or value, which idealize them and raise in us a furious envy or jealousy, so that we turn from them in defensive contempt. If we looked long enough at what we thus affect to despise, we would see that our anger and the pain of not-having-it are both derived from these unrealistic assumptions about what they mean. We are still faced with daily conflicts and problems which have to be dealt with and may be dealt with in ways we have used for years, and which contribute to our problems while seeming to protect us from them.

We have, I think, to admit that we must accept being the way we are without necessarily being able to change it, except under certain circumstances. I have to accept that I have brown hair; I can curl it or bleach it, but the more I accept the kind of hair it is, the more my dealings with it will be successful. (It does of course have an 'innate' tendency to grow long: but as with many innate tendencies there are things we can do about that relatively easily.) Responsibility for the way we *became* as we are, and often for what we *do* too, must also be shared between ourselves and our environment; just as responsibility for the quality of my present hairstyle depends not only on what happens to grow on my head, but also on the hair preparations on the market, the quality of the scissors or hairdresser that I use, and so on. What I did with my hair last year in particular will be playing a part too.

I would like to look briefly once again at the way we develop the 'automatic' ways of thinking and experiencing and behaving, the way we develop the phantasies which structure our world for us, to draw attention to the interplay between self and others, internal and external world, so that it is clear how I see this shared responsibility. We cannot claim innocence; we cannot claim total guilt; we cannot assume that this is the way we are and will stay for ever; we cannot assume that what we do is either irrelevant or absolutely decisive for other people.

Sorting out the world as a baby: the interaction between baby and environment

Let us look at the way a small baby develops its ability to sort out the world.

As with an adult, a lot of the baby's experience is going on without the baby being quite aware of it. In some obvious ways this makes sense; we take in so many 'bits' of sense data that, unless we had a vast unconscious, automatic capacity to sort them and to 'present' them to our consciousness as already organized perceptions, we would never be able to cope. Focusing our eyes, sorting out the sound waves that hit our eardrums into words – a baby's cry, an aeroplane flying overhead or a thunderstorm – goes on largely automatically for an adult; at some point these sounds must have been allowed into consciousness and in some way a decision made to reject them when they are not needed. It is as if information is fed from one part of the mind to another, and the adult or the baby simply makes the choice of where to consider the information.

(A teenager going out with one boy, but with her eye on another, was haunted by the song with the words 'If I catch you talking to that boy again I'm going to let you down, and leave you flat ...' It was as if one part of her mind at that point were considering the consequences of being unfaithful, and another part of her not wanting to know. The song could be understood as a kind of 'message' from one part of the mind to another; a way of bringing the unwanted thoughts to awareness in a way which could be recognized or ignored. The song actually became conscious before the thought of being unfaithful.)

Like an adult, a baby has a certain amount of choice about what it notices and what it does not choose to know, what it leaves to be dealt with by the automatic system and what it leaves on the edge of awareness and does not choose to think about.

A baby lying in its mother's arms, watching her face and copying her mouth movements, may hear a noise from outside the door which heralds the appearance of a noisy three-year-old, or the mother's friend. The baby may seem to start slightly, and then to continue with its conversation with its mother, but with a certain tenseness detectable in its limbs, as if to fend off the expected interruption. Another baby might break off communication with the mother immediately and seem to wait in expectation – anxious or hopeful – for the newcomer to contribute to the situation. The baby may turn its head to the door or struggle to move in that direction, even if it has as yet not enough control over its body to do that. This may be accompanied by looks of rejection or regret towards the mother, or by ignoring her; the baby may be holding on to her hair or clothing tightly perhaps, or pushing her away, or by some combination of signals be expressing a conflict between these different attitudes.

In this situation we can see different reactions to an apparently similar perception: one which seems to 'put it away' or put off an evil moment, and another which reacts immediately with some kind of attention to the new event. The turn from the old to the new can be made in different ways, and these differences may be very important. Just as an adult or teenager may turn from an old lover to a new one, rejecting the old, persecuting and pouring scorn on them (in their inner world or the external one), or with care and love for the previous lover, so can the baby. The results of repeated experiences of such shifts will feed into the phantasies which control them. A failure to take notice of a troublesome brother, for example, may lead to a blissful phantasy of unity with the mother being very rudely destroyed; turning too quickly and in too placatory a fashion to the troublesome older sibling may hinder the process of building up a firm belief in a safe relationship with a solid and good adult. Such weaknesses in the phantasy world are going to affect the amount of belief the child has in its ability to be and do what it wants, and how much conviction it has in its ability to love fully and deeply without too much anxiety and fear.

How the baby does turn from mother to newcomer, how the old situation is given up for the new, under what emotions and what phantasies, will depend on the mother and the interrupting visitor and also on the baby itself – its history, which creates expectations and gives strengths and fears to greet them with, and its physical state.

The mother may try to 'bring the baby round' gradually, altering her conversation to bring in awareness of the interruption. She may help the baby to feel that the conversation with her will now change, but will not be completely destroyed. She may help the baby to name its tenseness or its expectations, so that the baby can place them and localize them and so feel less overwhelmed by them. Once named, these feelings can take up less of the baby's attention; this means the baby is better able to keep its attention on more pleasurable aspects of the situation and does not have to lose them. If the mother shows the baby she understands what the tenseness is, the baby no longer has to translate it into physical tenseness, but may be able to relax and feel again. The mother may be able to name their mutual regret at having to give up the conversation, and a hope that it will be resumed again in the future, or that the new person can themselves add to the conversation without spoiling it. She may turn her own attention in an anxious or angry way to the interrupting person. In the way she shifts her own attention she may be able to make the baby feel her own enjoyment, annoyance, regret, anger, disappointment or excitement. Some of these will reflect what the baby is feeling, some will add to or conflict with the baby's feelings. While mother and child are still at the phantasy stage of being utterly 'wrapped up in' each other, the mother's emotions will be highly significant for the baby. Not only do they show the baby a kind of mirror to its own emotions, but they also provide a kind of 'container' for those emotions, which actually changes them.

(Let me recapitulate what I described in Chapter 5 about containers like this. When the baby screams in pain, it seems that part of the phantasy is that the pain is being thrust out of the baby – though at first the concept of 'outside' and 'inside' is not fully distinguished. When the mother (or someone else) comes along and soothes the child, the phantasy seems to be that there now exists something which can take the pain away; which can take in pain and give out pleasure. The mother or her breast act as a kind of container which takes in bits of agony and gives out peace and good food; she takes in confusion and gives back understanding; takes in lumps of faeces and gives back good milk. It is the mother, her breast, her presence, which seem to the baby to act as a kind of transformer of badness into goodness. A father and others may of course also function as this kind of container. What is important is the idea of the existence of a container for pain which transforms it into love and food and understanding; which cares for the baby. This container works too in situations of less emotional terror. It seems to be the basis for phantasies of the existence of something which is 'not me'; which is the source of all goodness and hope; and which underlies our passionate seeking out of people and things in the outside world. In particular of course it enters into our phantasies about our lovers – into whom we put things and take them back changed, in phantasy and perhaps in reality too. Some of the deepest anxieties we have are about the possibility that our badness might be so bad that it can destroy this container; the one we have inside ourselves or the representatives of it outside. Our feelings about words in particular, too, are deeply connected with their ability to function as a container like this. Misusing them, or using them in good ways, can give us a deep sense of guilt or satisfaction, partly because of this link.)

The mother's responses to the noise of someone coming to interrupt her conversation with the baby, then, will be important for many reasons. Her body signals and her voice may fit together, and give deep, resonant meaning to the words she uses; or they may contradict each other, giving a sense to the baby that words are something quite separate from bodily sensations. Gestures may encapsulate some of the emotions, where another mother would use words; a hand laid on the baby's head might serve to 'hold' a particular sense of togetherness, while the conversation drifts away from the baby. In such ways, contradictory and complex messages will be passed from baby to mother and back again, and the baby will be picking up some of the enormously varied ways we have of expressing ourselves and keeping hold of passing emotions. The baby's own confusion or clarity will be influenced by the mother's and by the contribution of the newcomer.

The baby has some kind of choice as to which of the many signals it notices, which it allows into consciousness, which it dismisses. Those which 'fit' its own experience best will be of most interest to the baby, since they may be felt to provide a container for that experience. If the baby has a stomach ache, or is feeling generally tense and miserable, how it reacts to the changes around will be different from the way it will react when there is a general feeling of benevolence towards the world. A lot of this must depend on the chance and hereditary influences on the child's body – the state of its digestion and lungs, for example – as well as on the influences on the mother's state of mind. The economic and emotional climate of the household will have an effect on the mother's ability to help her child bear and modify some of its worst anxieties, its confusions and despair, and also its wildest hopes. Another factor, as I will discuss in Chapter 7, is the alternative sources of support for the baby and the mother. Where they are too much alone, or she is responsible for too much, the anxieties and fears generated between them can lead to an overloading. The effect of such an overloading, of being overwhelmed by something which is too much to deal with, is to lead to a shutdown of some phantasies. Attention can only be given to so much at once, and withdrawing attention from some phantasies may have unfortunate consequences. Denial is far more likely to be brought into action where there is a sense of something being too much. The effect of other people in helping to dilute these extreme and frightening phantasies for the mother and the child can be enormous. Where more than one person has a close and understanding, familiar relationship with the baby too, the baby can find other sources of strength both inside and outside itself.

The baby can make some choices: to give in or to fight; to placate or to ignore; to enjoy the enjoyable parts of life or to 'see' only the unpleasant ones. Some of these choices will affect the build-up of helpful or frightening phantasies inside the child, and will affect future 'automatic' choices. How long the baby tries to satisfy itself, how soon it demands or asks for help, how much pain it tolerates before making a fuss, and how much and how it tries to protect its mother or a phantasy that an ideal live breast is there, before succumbing to a feeling that it has gone for ever, may all relate to choices made quite early on under the influence of both internal and external troubles. How much hope the baby can maintain that losing an ideal of some kind is not a total disaster, but can lead to a rebuilding of some more reliable and long-lasting good phantasy, will be dependent upon the amount of help it has had compared with the amount of difficulty it has had to face, from both internal and external sources. Once established, a phantasy world with good firm, strong, resistant, internal 'people' may be proof against all kinds of external knocks.

The baby must also have some kind of effect on its environment. How the mother feels and behaves towards the baby depends partly on her own ready-made phantasy world, and partly on the ways the baby actively influences this. Not only is the baby going to be affected by the mother's phantasies of, say, a relative the baby resembles, but it is also going to be affected by how much it lets the mother get away with, for example. How much the baby forces the mother to respond to him or her, how much the baby works to get the mother's attention and to make her feel things for the baby, will actually bring about changes in the mother's phantasy world. Her sensitivity to the baby's demands and projections, her own strength to stand up to the baby and to know her own limitations too, will all contribute to the baby's environment, to the satisfying of the baby's needs and controlling of its greed.

It seems that some babies feel overwhelmed very much more easily than others, and may be able to make their mothers experience this feeling too. Most babies do not close down certain kinds of contact with the external world in the first weeks of life, though perhaps this is what happens to autistic children and to those who will later develop schizophrenia or some kind of psychosis. There is a chance later to modify the child's overwhelming terrors and to help it to regain a hope that the external world can offer reassurance and something worth having. But how easy it is to get and to use this help must depend on the way the baby has picked out which phantasies to follow; real choices made in the very early days. A very suspicious baby will be less able to use what love and help there is; a more trusting baby in a helpful environment may be more able to grow with the good parts of the surroundings, and give up less realistic phantasies more easily. A baby which manages to influence the environment so strongly that it can get what it needs without breaking its phantasy of being totally united with the world-mother – again, this in an extreme form seems to characterize the relationship between autistic children and adults – may continue to hang on to its unrealistic phantasies – blissful and terrifying – far longer than a child which for internal or external reasons has a different effect on the feelings and behaviour of adults. Responsibility for the baby's state of mind must clearly be shared between the environment and the individual, and the interaction between them.

The pressures exerted by some children on their environment are extremely difficult for many adults to withstand, just as the pressures exerted by some adults are extremely difficult for many children to withstand. There is no 'right' way of bringing up a child which can be guaranteed to do away with conflict and misery.

This idea, which may be distasteful to people who like to see babies or themselves as helpless victims of a rotten world does actually seem to me a very hopeful one. It does offer the hope of change being possible; it also returns some of the responsibility to each of us to make the best we can of our own lives and those of our children. It recognizes that baby and mother and the rest of the world do have some control, some effect on each other, but that this is a two-way process, and that change can take place from both, or all, sides. We can perhaps make things easier for our children, but we can also make things easier for ourselves – and perhaps even for our parents – given sufficient help.

Difficulties in changing behaviour

This way of looking at people also makes it clear how hard it is to bring about change. It is not easy to alter patterns of behaviour which are based on very early decisions, made under the influence of quite overwhelming and terrifying or passionate feelings, to close down some areas of perception. The schizophrenias, where the closing down took place extremely early, and where parts of the ability to perceive were disowned and in phantasy thrust into other people, are very hard to affect. Work has to be done on the whole set of phantasies which control knowledge of perception and knowledge of where one person begins and another ends. Work has to done on the very processes of giving meaning to words and to objects in the world around, if a schizophrenic is to gain relief from terrifying phantasies. Psychopaths seem to have closed off all perception of their own guilt, which means that it lives on in a very primitive form and cannot be reached by any 'normal' conversational means. Work with such people is extremely difficult because the psychopath has no perception of lacking anything, or of any kind of discomfort except what comes from outside. But for less disturbed people too there may be quite a lot of gaps in perception – denials – which make life hard for them or for those around them, and which at the same time make it very hard for them to seek or to use help.

The fantasies which once led to the choice to become fat, say, and have now become unconscious phantasies, may not be easy to pinpoint. They lead to particular kinds of behaviour which can make it very hard to begin looking. Some phantasies, like these, tend to increase guilt enormously, and this makes it seem more frightening to seek out the underlying causes of the guilt which led to the behaviour which now increases the guilt. Once these were conscious decisions, but part of the effect of them was to make it harder to remake them.

We can see it perhaps in analogy. Some phantasies, such as those which lead to being fat or being pathologically thin, or being permanently angry or drinking too much, say, can be likened to the contents of a book. For some people there is little problem in reading the book and in rewriting sections of it. Such people can relatively easily choose when to express anger and when to store it up; when to give up something and when to hang on to it; they can choose which of two phantasies, which of two situations they would rather have and accept the loss of a contradictory one. Such people can decide not to smoke, or not to clean the house when something else would be more appropriate. They may be able to accept guilt or help where appropriate and reject what does not fit with relatively little difficulty. They can face internal pain and witnessing some external pains, without feeling taken over by the experience. But other people have decided to keep the book shut. The struggles they have will then be fundamentally influenced by this decision. The fantasies which have become ossified in the book retain their terror and cannot be altered. Such people cannot pull themselves together since they cannot bear to recognize whole parts of themselves. They cannot simply decide to lose some symptom, not to jump over the cracks on the pavement or to stop eating so much. The decision they have to make, which nobody around may realize, is to open the book in the first place. But the difficulty is that while the contents of the book are expected to jump off the page and eat up you and everyone you love, it is extremely hard to work up the courage to open it.

Not only is there a difficulty with the terror attached to primitive phantasies, but there is a difficulty in finding out what the book looks like. It may not be obvious that compulsive activities or phobias, say, are connected with feelings about one's parents or about sexuality. It may seem ludicrous to suggest that thinking about conflicts in one's normal daily life may be a way to affect something which seems totally unconnected, such as the need to polish the bathroom three times a day or to spend literally hours choosing which kind of milk or bread to buy. The idea that what were once fantasies about your parents' sex life might affect, say, a spider phobia or an inability to ride on trains or aeroplanes or to leave the house at all or to have good sex with your partner, may seem crazy. Opening these 'books' may be thoroughly rejected on all kinds of sensible grounds. 'My mother is depressed because she has had post-natal depression for thirty years – what is the point in stirring up all the conflicts and troubles she had as a child too?' It may seem very difficult to believe that listening to someone who never stops talking, or that asking someone if they have ever considered suicide, say, could be worthwhile things to do – the fear is that these things would only make everything worse. Our impulse, trained by years of a particular culture, may be to shut the book and to sit on it hard.

It is this kind of decision we make every day which affects our state of health as much as anything our mothers did or did not do for us. It is our own lack of information, lack of knowledge about the way the mind works, plus our own lack of courage to do something we know we have to do, or to listen to our own inner 'voices', which keep us stuck where we are. Most of the time we decide 'better the devil we know ...' and we continue with our denials, with avoiding tasks and people we dislike in spite of a gradual shrinking of our contacts and our world, perhaps, and even a gradual increase in anxiety, rather than daring to sit down and consider other ways of treating ourselves. There comes a point when we could choose to ask for help – from a parent, a friend, a lover, a relation, a therapist or counsellor; instead we may choose to battle on alone and keep trying to change something we cannot change alone. We may tell ourselves that all we have to do is to stop eating so much, or to find another job, or another boyfriend; then everything will be all right. The fact that we have been trying all these things for ten years and they have still not helped may still be seen as something blameworthy, rather than as a sign of needing help. The decision to ask for help may not be something we think we need worry about.

Helping

The responsibility for asking for help may be our own, but people can sometimes help each other with this kind of problem, from birth on. Let us look at this side of it for a moment.

How other people accept what is put on them by you, as a baby or as an adult, can affect your willingness to accept responsibility for parts of yourself you do not like or are afraid of. The adult who can stay with the baby or adult while they are suffering may in the primitive phantasy physically share the pain. By surviving the pain in a way which shows the baby that the pain is felt, and which at the same time shows that it is not overwhelming or unbearable, the adult can feed back to the baby a new phantasy of a container for pain which is not destroyed by it. In adult life we see this process going on: 'a trouble shared is a trouble halved' has some real sense to it. Many women report that the pain of childbearing is considerably reduced by the simple presence of someone they love, be it the father or a friend or a mother. Much of the work of counselling agencies consists in providing an ear and attention; the problems which seem overwhelming when they are just inside the head 'look different' when they have been 'poured out' to a sympathetic listener, even if there is nothing they can do about them. Sometimes the value of the listener may lie particularly in their inability to do anything; the fears are compounded by the anxiety that they might actually spill out into behaviour and lead to some kind of action which would be regretted.

Part of this process of sharing anxieties involves the other person's full recognition of how bad they are. Watching – even in the theatre or on television – nasty things happening to children, in particular, we tend to have a very physical reaction: we *do* feel the pain. This mechanism, it seems, is very important for our development of means of communication. Full and feeling recognition of something in us seems to be terribly important, partly as a means of combating the feelings of loneliness which go with knowledge of our separateness from others. Too much idealization on the part of the listener leaves the troubled person, child or adult, unable to find a 'container' for the parts which are being left out. A child whose mother only sees the best in them may well be left alone with a secret and guilty burden, carrying the 'bad' parts alone. I described this before when I was describing how adults could 'hold' fears and phantasies and guilt for others, as the people in my seminar did for me when I was being accused of being aggressive.

The kind of 'soft' social worker who tries to tell a beleaguered foster-mother that the difficult child is simply asking for love, when that child is in fact tearing up the sofa, breaking cups and strangling the cat, is perhaps just as unhelpful to the child and foster-parent as someone who says the child is wicked and needs to be beaten. Both views have picked up some elements in the situation and ignored others. Recognition of the destructiveness, of the attempt to spoil everything and to rouse the fury of the adults, perhaps, would be more realistic and might enable both foster-parents and child to feel that their anxieties and their conflicts had been engaged with, and could therefore be looked at and modified. Talking with a child – or adult – about its desire to mess things up can be done in a sympathetic way which does not imply that it is permissible to *do* the destruction.

Where something is denied – as the child's destructiveness might be by the social worker here – it tends to keep on until it is recognized; if it cannot find a straightforward outlet it will keep going until it has engaged with the outside world in some form or other. Not until the anxiety has been sufficiently closely identified can it give way to something different. The child who wants something it cannot name may go on asking for something it can name – food, money, presents, attention – until something happens to make the unnameable nameable, or until the child loses hope in ever finding it and turns to destroying everything in sight. The child who sees its mother preoccupied with the new baby may ask for all kinds of practical things, none of which seem to satisfy unless, in the giving, the mother and child manage to connect with the feelings underlying the requests or demands: a feeling of wanting to be the new baby, or to have a new baby themselves; a feeling of being left out of the relationship, or of wanting or fearing to spoil the relationship – whatever is uppermost in the child's consciousness at the time. Some mothers can do this relatively easily most of the time; others may be so full of their own guilt about having a new baby too soon and 'ruining' the life of the older one that they cannot even allow the child to express its longings and anxieties in a way which could show mother and child that they are not as enormous and unforgivable as both feared. As a result, the hidden feelings do remain at a relatively unrealistic pitch, and may in fact be expressed later in a way which shows them up as quite enormous and dangerous, as any feeling originating in a two-year-old might appear if expressed directly by a ten-year-old, say.

Difficulties in helping others may be affected too by the 'nonsense' reaction, which makes out that babies and children do not suffer from anxieties, that you can see in a week or two that a child has not been affected by something, such as a death in the family, or that an undemanding child is 'of course' a very happy child. Anxieties are not always obvious at the time, although closer observation might reveal them sooner, particularly if we know the kinds of reaction which lead to long-term benefits, and those which are potentially trouble-causing. We often do not make connections which we might make if we knew to look out for them. If we know that distress at parting is to be expected in a small child and is easier faced with the mother there, say, we may be less likely to disappear without telling our infants that we are going out for a while, leaving them to face the disappearance and the fears – become the worse for being discovered too late – on their own or only with someone they do not care for in the same way. If we know these things, we may be better able not only to observe our own baby or child, see how distressed they actually are and how they deal with this, but may also be more able to avoid forcing the child into heavy denial as a result of putting too much in the way of emotional demands on them. But we may well have to struggle with other people claiming that this is nonsense, that a child does not suffer, that a small baby does not know the difference between its mother and someone else, or that it is better to lie to a child 'for everyone's sake' because it spares the adult temporary pain.

Summary

Let me now summarize what I have been saying in this chapter.

We can use psychoanalytical insights to reassess blame, responsibility and intention. Often – but not always – blame may be used to deny responsibility and to excuse a desire to punish someone which arises from other sources. Pinpointing guilt and ascribing responsibility in a realistic way, refusing to allow the self or someone else to deny realistic guilt, can however make it easier to avoid repetition of some unwanted event. This is often hindered by great fears about retribution owed and owing, but if these fears can be faced the punishment often fails to materialize. Forgiving others and the self, grieving and being sorry and sad without attacking or feeling attacked, may be possible.

Accepting responsibility, shared with others, for the way we are may in itself be hard. It may or may not mean we can change. We may be able to discover ways we are ill-treating others and ourselves and begin treating them better, but without some kind of help this may be extremely difficult. Help may consist of simply helping to bear the pain – the pain of guilt, or the pain of being responsible, for example – and so enabling it to fade realistically without having to be cut short, swallowed whole and kept as a dangerous 'foreign body' in the psyche. Sometimes people claim to accept the responsibility for being the way they are as a way of fending off any attempts to make or help them change.

A realistic view of responsibility for our own state and that of others – mental and physical – must include a check on feeling *too* responsible and a check on denial of responsibility. It must allow for natural processes such as mourning, or the distorting effects of childhood on perception, or the anger of children towards their parents for being older, for having babies or for dying or being ill. It must allow for these processes to take their course and be dealt with over time. It must allow for fallibility without condoning it or using it as an excuse for avoiding work which could prevent repetition of a serious injury. It must also include taking responsibility for 'unintentional' behaviour such as forgetting, at times, but not exaggerating our power to affect the environment with our phantasies alone.

One of the main points I have tried to make in this chapter is that we are, to a much greater extent than some people believe, responsible for the way we are and for maintaining our own discomfort and that of other people. Our society is seriously deficient and so were our families; we can try to change both society and our own families; we can also try to change ourselves. But a lot of the ways we suffer are determined by what have become 'automatic' ways of seeing things. Our envy of other people's love and creativity, for example, may be so automatic that we no longer recognize anything good in those very things we most desperately longed for, and in some way still long for. Such automatic ways of destroying our world cannot be changed easily, as we might decide to change our clothes, for example. The process is more like deciding to learn to play the piano. First we have to find our piano and then time to spend on it. And there are very few people who can make their own pianos from scratch; we do need the help of other people.

Correspondingly, I think we can help other people rather more than is commonly supposed, once we discover better ways of listening, for example. The kind of person who can listen and appreciate and understand without giving advice, or minimizing what is involved, can be of enormous help to those around. As with many skills, our society has tended to devalue listening because it is generally not paid and is often done by women. But we do not need to accept this devaluation.

If we can help each other, we can also make things harder for each other. A lot of our social interactions seem to encourage the use of particular phantasy systems which tend to make things worse in one way or another. Our culture seems at times to be bent on making people into enemies when they could be learning to work together; to encourage idealization and devaluation of others when it could encourage constructive and supportive interactions; to encourage greed and destructive competitiveness when it could encourage concern that everyone has enough. These more positive aspects of cultural life do of course also appear in places; discovering the 'good' aspects of our society and helping them not to be overwhelmed by the 'bad' aspects seems to me a worthwhile task.

SEVEN

PHANTASIES RELATED TO FAMILY LIFE

In this chapter I shall put together some of the phantasies which seem to help make sense of the events around birth and death, and relations between parents and children at various stages of the life cycle. It is very incomplete: I say little, for example, about adolescence and sexuality, although these are very important in relations between parents and children. It is really a collection of insights which have proved helpful to me and to people I know in their dealings with family and friends.

Memories in feeling

A theme which runs through this chapter is the way memories and phantasies can be stirred by some event or situation in everyday life. Seeing someone else going through something you once went through; seeing your children reach an age at which something painful or significant happened to you; experiencing something which seems in any way a repetition of some earlier experience – all may evoke memories. We can look on these memories as having two components. One is a verbal or intellectual component: we remember what happened to us, what we said or thought at the time. The other is a non-verbal component: phantasies are re-experienced without naming and conceptualizing them in quite the same way. Feelings we perhaps did not experience fully in the past, but were frozen into some phantasy of the time that we could not bear to acknowledge, we may experience now as for the first time. Or the phantasy may be evoked again and once again have to be dealt with in a way which prevents the feelings being felt.

What often happens is that the verbal component of the memory is correctly attributed to the past, but the non-verbal part, experiences and phantasies which were not felt directly at the time, may be incorrectly attributed to something in the present. They may be treated now in much the same way as they were in the past – denied, attributed to someone else, evoked in someone else, or whatever – or they may be treated differently this time round. Some change in you or the circumstances may have made them more bearable, and the new experience may be used to modify memories and phantasies which belong to them.

Memories in feeling about death

A typical example involves feelings which are triggered by the death of a parent. Many of the phantasies which come up at the time may be so frightening that they are not acknowledged. These may include, for example, the phantasy that your parent's death means that they did not love you enough, and/or that you have not loved them enough. The conviction with which this is believed may be so strong that it cannot be verbalized: it seems so true that it simply does not arise in words to be tested against good sense. As a phantasy it may then lurk not far from consciousness after the death. When something happens which reminds you of the death, the loss, it may emerge attributed to someone else.

Sonya's father died when she was five; when her own daughter reached five she became convinced, quite without good reason, that her husband no longer loved her. One of the dangers of this situation is that it can become a self-fulfilling prophecy. I have known occasions when this feeling of not being loved enough, or not loving enough, was attributed to sons and daughters, as well as to husbands and wives. Putting the feeling back where it belongs with the dead or deserting parent often leads to relief as well as grief; and to guilt which can be felt and allowed to pass, rather than hidden petrified guilt of a much more powerful kind.

Memories in feeling about birth

A lot of the feelings which are around at the time of a birth can be attributed to some form of memories in feeling. Let me begin by giving an example.

When a close friend of Mary's was having a baby, Mary offered to go and help when she came out of hospital, just as Mary's mother had come to help her with her second child. The offer was gratefully accepted and Mary set out, leaving her own family behind. On the way there she developed a terrible headache and terrible anxieties about whether she was just bringing flu and trouble; whether she was greatly exaggerating her ability to help; whether she would be able to feed them properly; or whether they would really all be much better off without her. She worried about the fact that she was by no means a perfect mother, and whether she was going to spoil her friend's chances of being a better mother than she was. For a while all these worries seemed terribly real; they utterly overwhelmed the realization that, for a few days, after coming out of hospital into a house often mistaken for a deserted building site the friends would be grateful for *any* food and help.

Some of these fears – and the headache – went immediately Mary arrived and found she could do enough of the things she wanted to do for her friends. But late that night she had a totally unexpected and unrealistic emotional reaction. She suddenly felt a great loneliness and longing, not just for her husband and children, but for her own mother too. In fact it would have been extremely awkward if her mother had arrived just then and, although she lived on the other side of the world, Mary did not often experience such feelings of inadequacy and longing for her; certainly not as intensely as that night.

The next day it became clear what was happening. Mary's own experience of having babies was being evoked as well as remembered. Talking with her friends about her own experiences, especially with her first – it was their first baby – Mary had remembered her own enormous and unrealistic self-confidence. *Then* she had had no conscious doubts at all about being able to feed the baby, as many mothers do have. What she was experiencing *now* was anxieties about being able to feed those she loved – but attributed to feeding her friends rather than to feeding her own baby. Her self-confidence then was not grounded in reality; it was dependent upon a need to cover up and hide the opposite fears from herself as much as from anyone else. But having successfully fed the child, Mary was able to feel the anxiety this time round, and even to test it against the reality.

Equally, Mary's longing for her mother was also a memory in feeling. When her first child was born, relations with her parents were difficult and it had been impossible for various reasons for Mary's mother to do more than pay a flying visit on her way abroad. At the time, Mary did not want to be aware of the great longing for her mother which was stirred by becoming a mother herself. It was these feelings which made sense, in a way that they did not make sense in the present situation.

As she realized this, Mary suddenly also realized that such memories in feeling must be common, and that they might also have been responsible for some of the difficulties her mother and she had had when her mother had come to help while Mary had her second child. Mary's mother's own childbirth experiences must also have been evoked by looking after her daughter in childbirth; Mary remembered her mother had mentioned feeling lonely and missing her father. Mary now suspected that perhaps her mother too was going through similar memories in feeling, experiencing feeling for her own mother too perhaps, which she too had not felt earlier. Just as looking after her friend stirred in Mary quite conscious feelings of great gratitude towards her mother for what she had done for her, so her mother must have felt towards her mother. But her mother was by then dead. Mary had been aware that her mother was upset at times and had assumed that it was her fault; she now realized that this upset may well have been largely independent of her. The consequent reduction in her own guilt enabled Mary to write to her mother and ask her about it, and she made all kinds of discoveries about what had been going on for her. Her own generalized guilt about not being a good enough daughter for her mother when she was looking after her changed into a much less painful specific guilt, that she had underestimated the difficulties of her mother's situation. Her mother too, it turned out, in spite of an extremely confident exterior, had been beset with doubts about being 'good with children' because she had been unable to get on well with Mary's first child. This had upset and shocked her considerably and had contributed to a quarrel between Mary and her mother.

Many of the difficulties between mothers and daughters, and mothers-in-law too, may well have some factors in common with this. Many daughters feel so generally guilty towards their mothers or mothers-in-law that they become quite insensitive, and as a result may be actually cruel. In particular, relations between them are changed when a baby is born, especially if it is the first grandchild or the first child. Many anxieties from the grandparent's own experiences must surface and in some way influence the present-day relationship. A mother who was very anxious and guilt-ridden when her own child was born, or very angry with her husband for not suffering like she was, or furious with everyone for being free when she was trapped, may feel that these feelings were so dangerous and guilty that she had better not mention them even if she does remember them, and so in a roundabout way she may even perhaps encourage similar guilt in the new mother who is allowed to think 'It was easy for her; why is it so hard for me?'

In this example we see the birth of a child triggering specific phantasies in mothers who are around: phantasies about being able to feed and care for people, and phantasies of revenge or longing towards other adults. But during such a time everyone involved is also having other phantasies evoked directly by the baby. These phantasies can have a serious effect on what is and is not perceived: on how much anxiety feels safe and how much seems to be quite terrifying; on which feelings can be experienced and which feelings cannot be.

Phantasies evoked by identification with a new baby

When people have new babies they may seem for a while to behave in extreme ways. They may be excessively over-confident, as Mary and probably her mother too were, or excessively nervous; totally absorbed in the baby perhaps, or totally rejecting it; extremely happy or extremely depressed. They may experience a lot of feelings of being persecuted. The world seems too much; visits no longer offer anything except dread, tiredness, a sense of duty and a burden; it is difficult to get enough to eat and drink; enough sleep and peace and enough time and understanding from or for your husband or wife. Anything other people say may be felt as an attack, even if, to an outsider, it looks as if it was intended as a reassurance or an offer of help or sympathy. The housekeeping may seem a terrible burden but others who are perfectly competent may be totally untrusted to do it properly. Any failure in them may seem too much; a dirty kitchen felt to be a sign of total collapse of all order and safety; unwashed nappies a sign that no one can care for the baby properly.

At the same time the mother in particular may experience a sense of enormous gratitude towards some people who do understand. Someone who gives her a drink before she asks for it; who takes the baby when it is screaming and manages to calm it without making the mother feel inadequate; who offers to look after an older child or do the shopping in the 'right' way at the right time. The mother, like the baby, is enormously dependent upon other people; even fathers may suddenly become aware of their own dependence, and for many men, perhaps partly for cultural reasons, dependence in themselves or their wives may be an extremely difficult thing to cope with. Memory, time sense and the ability to think and to organize existence may seem to go completely for a while and only very gradually be regained over the next few years. 'Now' really does seem like 'forever' for very new parents.

Many of these experiences seem to recall very directly Melanie Klein's observations and deductions about the way a new baby sees the world. It makes sense that it should; parents have to empathize and identify with their new baby in order to know what to do, what to offer. The exaggeration of the feelings for all concerned – the desperation, the huge anxiety, the distortion or loss of a sense of time passing, the enormous self-confidence – relates partly to the fact that the situation is one which does involve life-threatening dangers. And this sense is increased by the parent's own infantile phantasies being evoked. These phantasies cannot so simply be remembered verbally since words were not part of the experience then, except as comforting or scaring noises.

(Very quickly words, including their meaning, become part of the baby's experience, in their ability to give form and boundaries to sense impressions. Talking to a baby while changing it or while holding it even in the first few weeks produces a clear 'listening' response in the baby. I have seen adults and babies 'holding a conversation' in the first two or three weeks. The baby moves its mouth and eyes, and the adult copies it; the baby then seems to copy the adult's facial movements; and the noises both make, to the great pleasure of the other, have a definite element of responding, giving and receiving 'gifts' of sound and attention, the parent continually modifying the child's sound into one which fits within the range of sounds in the adult's language. I think that individual words are actually understood by babies much earlier than most people think, too. Certainly the sense and intention of words can contribute to the baby's state of mind from very early on, as the baby responds to the body language accompanying the words.)

Idealization of mothering: the phantasy of the perfect mother

One common phantasy which seems to be played out by adults around a new baby is the phantasy that there exists a perfect mother *somewhere*. When Mary was looking after her friends, sometimes she felt she was or had to be this perfect mother; sometimes it was located in a grandmother somewhere; sometimes in other women in hospital; sometimes in 'working-class women' (Mary and her friends being 'middle class') or 'women in Africa'. All of these other mothers were supposed to be able to cope better than the actual mother and, by their coping, to leave the mother feeling inadequate by comparison. Idealizations, as I have said before, often work in this way; some picture held up initially perhaps partly as a means of not losing hope entirely – since if nobody knows what to do with a baby, how will it survive at all? – becomes very quickly persecutory, as the actual state of affairs is compared with the ideal and some blame attached somewhere for the 'failure'. I think the phantasies of the baby might be involved in this too; the baby part of the adult feels that there must be someone who can do it, and is ready to panic and fall to pieces if that belief is lost.

The pressure to play out this image of the Perfect Mother seems to be strong. For the first day or two of looking after her friends Mary tended to keep up a front of being totally competent and totally in command of everything she was trying to do. Consciously she was trying to keep the pressure off her friends, and not to load her problems and failures on to them. This I think was partly responsible for her sense of exhaustion and misery at night. She felt she was giving them the wrong impression – she knew she was not really so competent; why was she trying to show them she was? This is a dilemma which arises often in such situations where one person is dependent upon another; the feeling is that you must show them how strong you can be; that any expression of your own weakness would just upset them and might actually be dangerous for them; after all, if someone is not fully in control, what hope is there?

But as I pointed out earlier, this 'showing' behaviour can have the opposite effect from the one intended. If Mary had gone on playing 'supermum' to her friend, the friend would have felt more hopeless about herself. What they had to do was to discover together that it was all right for Mary as well as her friend to be in a bit of a state at times. The idealization of motherhood had to be reduced to more normal proportions, otherwise it could make life even harder. Mary had to hand back to her friend her own competence which for a while Mary carried for her; she had to keep reminding her friend that her state was temporary and that the feelings of being unable to do anything ever again were not in fact permanent ones. For a time Mary seemed to 'hold' her friend's memory, her good sense, her reason, her ability to think about anything except the baby, and in particular her ability to care for herself. But Mary had to beware that her anxieties did not make her take over in such a way that the friend felt even more depleted and empty, or as if she carried Mary's terrifying incompetence and anxiety as well. I have known for a long time that the role of 'mothering the mother' is important; Mary made me realize how difficult it is.

Cultural influences on the phantasy of the perfect mother

The idealization of mothering is perhaps partly related to problems we have as small children when we long to be mothers ourselves but are as yet too small. It often seems to me that people have in general extremely infantile views of mothering: assumptions about it which perhaps fit better with a view of a mother which a two- or three-year-old child might have. Perhaps it is not coincidence that this is the age at which boys seem to discover that they cannot have babies themselves. (This is an observation made on small children; adults often have no recollection of when they found out, or they put the date quite improbably early or late.) Our culture may well encourage small boys to deal with this loss – for it is experienced as a loss of a belief, a hope, a conviction – by denial. Many a small boy is actively encouraged to despise girls and women, and to deny any desire whatsoever that he should be like her or have what she had – at least the potential for breasts and a womb. The feeling that he could only have these things by giving up his penis may enable him to feel that he has after all got something worth having, and he may turn this to his advantage in an attempt to get rid of a hopeless longing to be a mother by arousing in girls a hopeless longing to be a boy. Little girls also have to deal with the discovery that they cannot be a woman yet, and they too may deny their feelings about this. Where these feelings seem too powerfully destructive, as a girl grows into a woman she may be unable to allow herself to have children since this would release the floodgates of longing her denial has been holding back. (For many girls and women their attitude to the male role in child-making may also smack of heavy denial; they may attempt to maintain a belief that having babies is something they can do on their own. This can contribute to difficulties they have with fathers, and which fathers have with them.) One of the consequences of denial of infantile feelings about mothers is that the wonderful, omnipotent, ever-present kind of mother that the child wanted to be before discovering that it was not possible – yet or ever – remains as a static phantasy, frozen in time, as a result of being suddenly cut off from the free passage of emotions, phantasies and perceptions to and from it. In order to avoid arousing again those feelings of wanting to be something he can never be, as well as in order to avoid his schoolfriends' mockery, the small boy in particular may refuse to think about or play at being a mother again, and so his picture of motherhood does not develop as he grows up. This image, then, formed at around the age of two or three, may remain as a view of women as they should be; women as they are may well become not much more than the carriers of the envious and jealous feelings the small boy felt towards them.

Unrealistic expectations of mothers

This culturally supported denial may well account for the horror with which some men greet the idea of their wife not being home for them whenever they require her; as if they were still a helpless two-year-old and she were such a big, all-powerful mother. It may account for the denial of the importance of other people to mothers; the two-year-old seems often to want to think that she needs no one except him or her. It may affect the way some men treat their wives with great cruelty; if she *is* this huge mother, she can take all kinds of attacks and demands without *really* suffering, since her power is quite enormous compared with the child's. Equally, her ability to give in such a phantasy is enormous; anything she does not give may be seen as being deliberately withheld out of malice, so she is just 'asking for' punishment. Such an age-related phantasy may account too for some of the despair some men feel when faced with marriage: as if they had to satisfy such a large mother sexually, when they are so small themselves. Such despair may well lead to running away – in reality or metaphorically, in their minds – from being married. Or it may lead to desperate attempts to 'prove' superiority, or to 'looking big', which have a hopelessness about them and may easily be seen as stemming from feeling small and inferior.

Such phantasies may also contribute to the very common assumption that the baby when it is born needs *only* breast-feeding, as if anything a man can do for the child is no more than second best, substituting for the 'better' care of the mother. Both men and women may join in these phantasies. The fear of the demands the child can put on the mother, seen through such early, unrealistic phantasies, can also hurry her back to work in such a way that she has no time to enjoy the experience of more realistic caring which involves surviving the terrible experience of saying 'no' to a child.

Self-criticism by parents

In their attempts to live up to a very infantile picture of parenthood both parents may easily feel vulnerable to criticism. And each may also attack the other or other outsiders for showing signs of being critical in the way they themselves felt enormously critical of their mothers. They may still be working on the assumption that their mother really could have been so much better; that all she had to give in their phantasy did exist, but was going to someone else whenever they did not get it themselves. The pressure to give it to their own child, to actually be this impossible self-sacrificing and all-powerful mother, who can take away all pain, produce home-made cakes at the drop of a hat (though children often do not seem to appreciate them as the mother thinks they should), allow limitless television watching and make absolutely no demands on the child, for example, may be enormous. Expecting their child to feel the same fury they felt at being thwarted, some parents find it hard to see their children's anger in more realistic terms. To them, this anger still feels world-shattering, and they have never realized that actually, from the point of view of an adult, a small child's anger is a relatively puny thing. Some parents respond to all this by withdrawing from the attempt to satisfy the child at all, treating the child as if it were the child of their phantasy and trying not to see what the real child is like. It is no wonder that some mothers face depression as they contemplate their own reality compared with their fantasies of how it would be; they may be forced to reassess a lot of their feelings about their mothers and about their whole perception of the world. The guilt and sorrow they then feel, realizing how they have misunderstood their own mother's behaviour, may alternate at times with feelings of being persecuted by the baby (and by their own 'mother inside their heads' too, perhaps) when they do not admit their fault. Resentment left over from real or phantasy 'failures' of their own mother can make it very difficult to ask for or receive any real help from their mother in the present.

Idealization of mothering: passionate love gained and lost

The phantasy of a mother which sets at the age of two or so can also give rise to enormous love; a love which knows no other; a love which spreads through the whole body and feeds a total devotion and hope and excitement and peace. Feeling attached to such a huge person – in the present-day form of a wife, a husband, a religion or a job too, perhaps – there may be a sense of tremendous power; everything is possible for the mother of a two-year-old, and for that child supported by such a mother. Falling in love with someone who represents this loved mother, and who can 'be' her in a way the real mother could never be her, may be a wonderful experience. And the birth of a baby may be felt to interrupt and take away *this* experience, as the magic of the lover relationship is replaced with a different set of phantasies governing a parent relationship. Lovers can be exclusive in their love in a way a parent or fellow parent cannot be. Feelings of jealousy towards the new baby pick up phantasies arising when this relationship with the mother was broken by awareness of her love for and dependence upon other people, especially for sexual satisfactions. This, I think, is part of the problem which can disturb sexual relationships after the birth of a child. The two-year-old's jealousy of the mother's sexual relationships may somewhere influence the powerful hold Christianity can have too. A virgin mother would solve the problem of to the fact of life which small children – and many adults ...rd: that somebody had sex with their mother. The way ...ently gets mixed up with feelings about dirt and mess may ...ected with this feeling that sex means jealousy and envy; for ... must discover that adults can give each other things the child cann...give at a time when the child is too small to be able to give them. The longing to feed and love the mother like an adult man can may be very strong and may emerge in deeply loving relationships later in life, both for women and for men. But in order to be able to want to do this the caring and the sexual relationships must have been kept as valuable and not too deeply spoiled by the child's envy or jealousy.

Difficulties of dealing with bad feelings towards a baby

The idealization of motherhood is one means we use to fight off the hidden bad feelings we have towards being a mother. There are also many bad feelings towards the baby which have to be dealt with somehow, by mothers and by everyone else around. One of the sources of these bad feelings, as so often, can be envy. Even the mother – and certainly other people – may at times feel (secretly or openly) furious with the child because the child seems to have it all its own way. The child is being totally cared for, and can simply lie there and eat and sleep – which is exactly what the mother would like to do and cannot unless she is very lucky. Other adults too may feel like this; the new father may want to be cared for like the baby is and like the mother is, and yet nobody offers him anything except huge demands on his time. (This may contribute to his seeking a lover at this time, to give him the loving attention his wife and the baby seem to be getting – and also to punish them perhaps by depriving them of some of his devotion.) The new grandmother too may feel this envy, and suddenly begin to make more demands herself, or to interfere in some subtle way with the baby's or the mother's satisfaction, for envy destroys the very thing you long for and cannot have. New mothers and fathers often feel the most overwhelming feelings of hatred or anger for the child; this may then be compounded with guilt, and with the belief that the child must be innocent and the parent who cannot love the child in a totally self-sacrificing way, guilty. Feelings of envy bring their own guilt, since the desire to destroy your baby's or husband's or wife's comfort is quite reasonably felt to be a guilty desire. Where these feelings cannot be tolerated long enough to realize that they are mitigated by real love, there may be over-compensation, and the attempt to martyr the self out of penance. (But martyrs die, and so would a mother who totally ignored her own needs; this is quite an effective way of spoiling the pleasure of those around too.)

Social contributions to difficulties

Social attitudes and organization contribute in many ways to the difficulties parents have dealing with their bad feelings. Often there is little help when the bad and dangerous emotions do threaten. The daily isolation of single adults with babies is I think a dangerous aspect of our society. People certainly need some time to be alone with their baby or their spouse or on their own entirely, but too much of this can have significant consequences on the mental and physical state of the next generation. Where feelings become very intense and frightening they may be cut off; baby and mother can both become so terrified of their feelings that they can never let them out in small doses throughout the day. There can be a build-up of frustration and despair which encourages the all-or-nothing aspect of primitive phantasies. Where other people are around to help take the pressure off such overpowering feelings, to reduce frustration, to come between mother and child when things get too much, more gentle and reasonable phantasies can develop more easily. Grief, loss, separation and closeness may all be borne more easily if the adult has a supportive relationship themselves and somewhere to turn to for help when things begin to feel too much like the very primitive and total phantasy situations. Another adult may be vital if the mother is not to lose all sense of being an adult herself, of having good parts to her which are only temporarily overwhelmed and which can be regained. A father left alone too much with a child can suffer in the same way.

Mixed feelings: jealousy and siblings

It seems that jealousy is unavoidable for a child or baby. In order for the mother or father to look after themselves properly they must turn to other adults for help and sustenance of various kinds. This is bound to make the baby jealous: the baby or small child seems to want to be *the* supplier of the mother's needs. But this jealousy, even though it is painful, gives at the same time relief. Very quickly the child may find it is glad that someone else can share the burden of looking after the mother (or whoever else is the child's primary love object). The presence of a father or siblings or other people who have a significant relationship with the mother and arouse the infant's jealousy can be extremely helpful to the child in many ways. Firstly, of course, they can offer the child love and care themselves so that, if anything really happens to the mother, the child is not so totally abandoned to a strange world as it would be if no one else was a close friend. But they can also arouse enormous gratitude and love for their help in protecting and supporting the loved object – be it the mother's breast (very early on) or the whole mother, or, later, the father or siblings themselves. (Close friends and nurses, or anyone else, can play the role of primary love object – and occasionally do – or, more often, that of a supporting figure for the mother; I expect the reader to make the necessary translations to fit their own experience.) The anger and the attacks which a rival for love receives are made greater by anger and attacks deflected from the loved and longed-for person. For example, by blaming your brother for taking your mother away from you, the attack is deflected not only from her, perhaps, but also from your father who takes her away in a quite different way. This can protect your relationship with your father, making it easier to love him. But this also serves to bind you to your brother in a way which sheer indifference could never do. The sibling who is a rival can also be extremely helpful in sharing the guilt of wanting to attack the parents, so reducing the weight of the guilt. Siblings in particular can share the burden of wanting to keep the parents safe and whole; something which can at times seem a huge and impossible burden for an only child, or for an eldest whose treatment of the younger ones has relegated them to the position of enemies or weaklings. A favourite child carries a similar burden, as I showed with the example of Alice in Chapter 5. Jealousy, then, can provide a means of dealing with bad feelings which allows good ones to be kept and new relationships to be developed too.

New babies become aware of other children very quickly, and seem often to take a more direct interest in them than in adults. They may very early develop a desire to take the other child's place, either to get rid of the other child or to be loved exclusively by the sibling as well as by the mother and father – separately. The child's attempts to overcome its jealousy and to keep hold of love for both parents and for siblings may be very useful lessons which can make marriages later on easier to maintain, it seems. Recognizing the realities and the pain of being jealous helps to keep it from remaining at a very primitive level, where the desire to destroy the rival seems so powerful that it is possible to do it. This feeling, of the effectiveness of wishing ill on someone, arises from a time when thought and deed were not clearly distinguished, and can be extremely important later in inhibiting some people from getting into any situation where jealousy is possible. It may be so bad, for example, that marriage is impossible because it might lead to jealousy of the lover's parents; or having children is impossible because it might lead to jealousy of the baby.

Siblings and other people who share the love of the person who knows and cares for the baby best are very much a mixed blessing for the baby. Where an older child is very close in age to the new baby there may be serious problems for both children in sorting out where one of them ends and the other begins. The identification between them can be extremely strong if the older child has not separated itself out from its mother sufficiently, in phantasy and probably in terms of behaviour. The strong identification can of course involve great love between the children, but often it may also contribute to 'identity crises', where one has to disentangle itself forcibly from the other in phantasy, and may act it out in aggressive or secretly attacking behaviour.

Jealousy and sibling rivalry as memories in feeling

In adults old feelings of jealousy and sibling rivalry not perceived at the time often seem to be evoked by the birth and upbringing of their own children. Adults who have not managed to accept their own jealousy of siblings or parents, but have condemned it out of hand and tried to deny it (because it seemed too life-threatening), may get into complications with their own children. Jealousy between their own children may be provoked, partly in order to play out in the external world a set of phantasies which are too frightening to keep inside. In this way reassurance and revenge may be sought concurrently. One or more children may be 'identified' with a particular sibling of the parents and then treated as if the child were the sibling. If Martha's brother rejected her (by dying or leaving home or by preferring another child to her) she may see him in her son and this time round make sure that 'he' does not leave her at all. Or she may punish 'him' for wanting to leave her (when the real child does not actually want to go) and so create in the child a real desire to leave home and mother as soon as possible. The child Martha may also be invested in another child, perhaps, and this child made to feel similarly rejected. How this child then responds to such feelings may be of great significance to the mother; Martha may in fact discover that it is not so bad to be rejected herself now; that this time she has a husband and other people to keep her going and she is not alone.

In general, how much an individual child is prepared to be manipulated like this, or will add to or modify such attempts on the part of the mother or father, will depend on the child concerned and on various other factors too. A child who was different from Joel might have demonstrated other of Peter's feelings on being left – feelings of helpless misery perhaps, or actually of being lost (see Chapter 4). Children can also manipulate their parents too, of course, again in attempts to receive help with very painful feelings as well as in attempts to deny these feelings. Where the parents are too easily manipulated, the child may lose hope in the adults being able to understand and withstand them and to provide the 'extra bit': that part of the adult which is bigger and better than the child, which refuses to be destroyed by the child and which can enable the child to grow. Similarly, the resistance of other people in adulthood to being manipulated into playing out past scenarios can be of major importance for the modification of memories in feeling.

Sibling rivalry may often manifest itself in adulthood when one member of the family has children, or when friends have children, and old feelings of 'they've got something I haven't got' emerge again. Brothers and sisters of the new parents may shift their alliances; they may turn against the new parent, citing the reasonable grounds of 'having nothing in common any more' to give respectability to more unreasonable and undiagnosed feelings of jealousy. Several childless friends of ours accidentally hurt our eldest son when he was small, or they totally ignored him as if he were not there at all. In such cases clearly there can be envy and jealousy on both sides; the new parents may long for the freedom of non-parent friends, just as the friends may long for children and either the parents or the friends can deny this longing and try to spoil what they cannot have. It is also realistically hard to give up a close, mutually attention-giving adult relationship; and yet the sudden presence of a new baby may require that such a relationship has to change. Both parents, as well as their friends, can fight off this realization. I can also think of good reasons why I might have found a certain satisfaction in seeing my rather demanding son being disciplined harshly by somebody else.

Conflicts between parents and their own parents as memories in feeling

As the child grows, problems arising between the child and the parents may reflect hidden conflicts between the parents and their own parents, especially where the conscious, verbal memory is very different from the hidden, secret feelings which the parent as a child could not verbalize and tolerate. Loving feelings towards the parents may be evoked where the conscious memory was made up mainly of angry fights; similarly, angry or bitter feelings towards the parents, seen in the children, may arise where the memory was mainly of a good and happy home. This may perhaps explain the rather odd fact that I have heard more than one parent complaining bitterly about being sent to a convent school when they were small, and saying how much they hated it, and yet these same parents were sending their own children, for no apparently good reason, to a very similar school. It seemed almost as if the child was to suffer as they did; or as if the child was to stand for the cruel parent and be punished in this way, perhaps as the parent had also felt punished.

Very often people almost consciously treat their children as if they were their parents: Jean Renvoize, in her book *Web of Violence* (p. 136) describes one mother saying how she came to hit her baby. 'It was my mother's voice again, yelling at me I was no good, I couldn't do nothing right, exactly her voice just as though she was there. It wasn't a baby I hit, it was my mum. I hit her right in the mouth with my fist, just like I always wanted to when I was a kid and I couldn't. I don't expect you to believe that but it's the truth. It wasn't my baby I hit at all.' In its loving form, this sense of bringing up one's own parents in the form of one's own children can also be a source of happiness and delight, and give the sense of restoring the world in a more hopeful way. The delight of having a child who will be more like your mother than you are yourself – who will be able to make pastry like she can, or sew or be an artist perhaps – in a way you failed her, can be very powerful. In this sense children can also be seen as 'gifts' to the parents, making up to them for some of the trouble and misery you caused them. Where this works, a good relationship between grandchildren and grandparents can be a source of deep satisfaction for the parents – even if they are at times the target of an alliance against them.

The way children can evoke their parents' parents may also contribute to the surprisingly lasting and repetitive nature of some extremely unpleasant relationships. Where child and parent have 'carried' some intolerable parts of each other, such as a violent or clinging part, neither gains a conviction of being a whole person and the child, like its parent before, may choose a lover who seems prepared to represent this part of the self, allied with the parent. The difficulties of breaking away from a violent husband or a destructive wife may include the problem that a parent was just like them and never enabled the child to integrate that part of the self. Hanging on to the violent spouse may then feel like hanging on to a part of the self (which is violent but *alive*) to such an extent that separation is extremely difficult. And a parent who feels so much like a half-person may develop a relationship with their child in which the child is allowed to feel that it is no more than the other half of a person.

Discipline problems as the child leaves babyhood may be related clearly to the ways your parents treated you. You may have to learn to accept your own hated 'bossy' or controlling self, in order to be able to control your children at all. Controlling parts of yourself which you put into your parents when you were small will have to be taken back in order to be a parent yourself. You can no longer claim that your parents were simply making life difficult by demanding that you wash your hands or get ready to go out half an hour before it was time to go. Suddenly there may seem good sense in having that dreadful routine. Life without boundaries no longer seems as attractive as perhaps it did in adolescence; in order to keep a three-year-old reasonably content regular mealtimes may be essential. Or the unbearable mess – or tidiness – in your parents' home may have to be accepted now as part of your own response to the pressures of having children. You may find yourself doing precisely those things which you so resented in your parents. As a result, your relationship with them may change considerably; you may find you have more sympathy for them, and you may even turn utterly against 'you' as you were then – seen now in your children.

In the conflicts between parents and children, repeated over the generations, the child may at times stand for the parent's parents, and at times for parts of the self, with the parent identifying with their own parents. This issue may emerge in particular when the children make friends outside the home and when they finally leave. Depending on the parent's experiences of being left and leaving, the children's behaviour will be interpreted in various ways, some of which will be extremely painful and may lead to very destructive or frightening behaviour on the part of the parent or the child, such as beatings, or 'accidents' on the road. Just as my son's friend Peter managed to make my son play out the role of being left in such a way that Joel – who has no fear of his anger – became extremely angry, so a parent can provoke their children into leaving in anger or jealousy, and so relive and relieve some of the parent's deepest anxieties.

Partly as a result of these conflicts, the relationship between grand-children and grandparents may flourish. Parts of the child which are unrecognized by or unacceptable to the parents may be affirmed by the grandparents. The two may unite against a common enemy – the parents. Grandparents may be able to play out old conflicts between themselves and their parents, or between themselves and their siblings, by provoking or enjoying conflicts between grandchildren and their parents or siblings. Or they may be able to express gratitude, in phantasy, towards their own parents or grandparents, for what they were able to give, by giving a grandchild or its parents something to be grateful for in the way of really loving and sympathetic support. This of course depends upon the support being acceptable. A grandmother described to me once, in a very moving way, how her grandfather used to give her sweets from his pocket every time she saw him, and how she had looked forward to doing this for her grandchildren. Unfortunately their mother said that sweets were bad for them – and the grandmother was devastated, in a way which went far beyond any 'reasonable' response. She had somehow felt, I think, that, by acting as her grandfather had, she could keep him alive, or bring him back to life as a helpful and loving person in her; her daughter-in-law's prohibition then meant to her that her grandfather was once more pushed into his grave by ingratitude.

Restoration of sanity as children grow up

It is interesting how the phantasies affecting mothering seem very often to change considerably around the time the youngest child in the family reaches three. Parents often seem to 'come alive' again at this time. The interrelation between the family and the outside world and the phantasies of all concerned is of course complex. It is always hard to sort out how much of what is going on is directly the result of the realities of life, and how much is affected by emotional influences from other sources. But the sense of time may seem to return to the family; the memory and hope that things can change in the future. The hopelessness about ever working or thinking again in a less baby-oriented way, which may seem to have dominated those years (though with the occasional let-up perhaps), seems to fade. What affects this is not only the real opportunities for sending the child to nursery and for the parents to spend more time on more adult pursuits (either of which may or may not be there). But there is also something about the way the child demands a different kind of emotional involvement and has itself a developing reason and memory which can affect all those around. The parents' own memory and reason seem to be liberated once again, and a different kind of creativity returns. The child's need for and ability to use the help of other people in many ways seem to free the parents from the fears of enormous dependence in the child. Here again, the parents' own experiences are going to be evoked. What happened to them when they were two or three will have left its traces in phantasies which are now evoked. Some modified form of the most frightening of these phantasies may be in some way created in the children, or in the parents' relationships. Losses, in particular, may have to be mourned or relived once again; these include not only losses of people or pets, but also feelings of loss connected with moving house, with illnesses in people who were loved, and of course with discoveries about the realities of life, such as your own potentials and your own lack of potential not only sexually but also in other fields too. Girls facing the fact that they are not boys; boys facing the fact that they are not going to be mothers; the unmusical facing the fact that they will never be able to sing like the rest of the family; the clumsy facing the fact that they are not sylph-like and elegant movers; any of these facts of life, together with the unrealistic aspects of them, may have to be lived with once again as one's own children go through them. This time round of course they may change; some of the unrealistic aspects may be shed. The discovery that you are not the most beautiful person in the world, made at the age of three or seven, seems different when it is remembered as an adult. The emotional force of memories in feeling which stem from older childhood has a far more reasonable air about it than that which stems from babyhood; even in connection with the death of a parent, the later the event in the child's life, the less fundamental will be the effect on the phantasies and the structure of the phantasy world of the child as it grows to be an adult.

Family events affecting friends and relations

Friends and relatives become involved in many ways in what is happening to each other. This is particularly clear when the event is a birth or a separation, either of which will sometimes evoke a huge response which may surprise the main protagonists. Other people's lives, even if miles away, may be affected quite seriously. Decisions to have a baby may be triggered by the news of someone else in the wider family circle having one. Decisions to break up a marriage may be similarly affected. Not only are other people in the family and amongst family friends carrying all kinds of parts of the self and of earlier loved people for their friends and relatives, but they may all have their own memories and phantasies stirred by what happens in a very direct way. Deaths and illnesses, as well as marriages, births and divorces, may have a much greater effect on the 'internal economy' of those even distantly related than could be explained by simple concern for others, or ties of affection, though these may of course be involved too.

Aunty Meg, who had an illegitimate child and ran away from home; Uncle Sam, who went bankrupt and drank himself to death; Cousin Mathilda, who never married but stayed at home looking after her parents until they died; Cousin George's children, who have turned out much better than anyone expected, considering his past; the Smith cousins, who were so much more beautiful and well behaved than you were, but who have all turned out badly – all such relatives may stand for parts of the self, ones which are felt to be unsafe, tempting, threatening or hopeful. What happens to them may reflect upon the self. They may be taken as models not only for your own children, who remind you of them in one way or another, but also for what you might have been or might yet become. If the 'happily married couple', whose presence in the family myth is a constant reminder that marriage can work even if your own is thoroughly shaky at the moment, openly quarrel and separate, the upset they cause can be considerably greater than concern for their welfare would warrant. The desire to punish them for upsetting you may be very strong. If the cousin or sister or mother of your friend, who seemed to be a perfect mother, suddenly leaves home or dies, for a while all your belief in the possibility of being a perfect mother may die with her – bringing about a reappraisal of your idealizing phantasies, or leading to a loss of hope. If your dog, for you a symbol of, say, your rebellion against your parents, dies, what has died is more than a friend. Either you will have to take back the part of you which rebels against your parents and show it in some other way, integrated with the previous 'you' which was less rebellious (since you can't be blamed if the dog growls at people, but your own growling is a different matter), or you may feel that rebelling is far too dangerous and give up all attempts to stand up for yourself in case you too die of it. Cousins and friends can equally stand for such rebelliousness; their living through a period of bad relations with their parents can affect feelings about such conflicts considerably, making it easier or harder for those who follow them.

Adult children and older parents

Phantasies where the children take the place of parents in the phantasy world seem to play a large part sometimes as the parents grow older and the children become adults. One woman was extremely upset about her daughter being involved in 'political activities' – in fact, helping Chilean refugees in London. Her panic was quite directly traceable to her own and her parents' experience of 'political activities' when she was a child in Nazi Germany.

As your own children become parents themselves it becomes even easier to relate to them as if they were your own parents. They may be seen as just as rejecting, ungrateful, independent and/or loving and caring as your parents were; where illness or old age reverses the role of dependence there may be a reversion to very childish ways of behaving in which the people who look after you – or fail to – are treated like parents. Someone who worked in an old people's home told me that it was common for some of the old people to get confused, saying 'My mum just came to see me' when in fact it was their daughter. Childish ways of relating to people may emerge partly because they are natural ways of relating to people when you are dependent on them, and partly because dependence revives old feelings which were not worked through at the time. Anger, envy and complaints, as well as love and gratitude, may be directed at the 'working generation' now, as they were at the working generation when you were small. As helplessness and frustration increase, where dependence cannot be accepted easily and kept realistic, some people find they allow themselves more freedom to say things they previously would have kept quiet about; or they may resort to direct action for getting attention where their childhood taught them they would never get it any other way. Sometimes old people who wander are looking for someone they have lost: in phantasy this may not be only a loved parent or friend, say, but also a lost part of themselves – a more alive, younger self, or a vigorous angry part which their lives smothered. Sometimes they may be looking for death to come and take them away to peace; conversely, a new fear of open windows or burglars may be a disguised form of fear of death personified, coming to get them.

My grandfather at the age of ninety told me every time I visited him that his grandson (a father himself), who looked after him, came in every evening to make sure he was all right for the night. The meaning of this for him was evidently powerful; I suspect that in some way it recreated for him the feeling of being cared for and loved as a child by his mother; being protected from harm seemed to be an important part of this.

It can happen, of course, that grandchildren and children carry split-off aspects of attitudes to the parents, one being seen as excessively good, carrying loving feelings towards the parents, and one being seen as excessively bad, carrying more destructive feelings. Where this split attitude to the world is still strong in old age, there may be strong feelings of being persecuted by everything around, and related strong criticism of the younger generation. One of the common difficulties of looking after some old people is the problem that the near person is often seen as the 'baddy' and the further ones as the 'goodies'. Where this does occur – and it is certainly not universal – it can seem most unfair for the person doing the bulk of the hard work.

Envy of younger people, as well as jealousy of them, may be reflected in parental attitudes at any age of course. I am reminded of the son who said bitterly: 'I didn't have an adolescence: my father had it for me.' His father felt the accusation was justified. The lucky people are those who do not suffer too much from envy or jealousy and can enjoy their own pleasures and those of the people around them. This applies at any age, but younger people may be able to compensate for hidden envy by exaggerating their possessions, or keep it down by working hard themselves and so feeling there is some good in themselves, or by planning for happiness in the future, or by creating envy or jealousy in others. Such people will suffer all the more in old age if they can no longer make these mechanisms work. For very envious people, death in particular may seem excessively frightening since it is likely to mean to them the destruction of the whole world, including all the goodness in it, as they cannot bear to conceive of the existence of goodness they do not control or own.

Phantasies about death and dying

Phantasies around death can be very disturbing. We tend to treat death and dying as if they were truly horrifying and unspeakable, to be denied if possible, rather than as something which is part of life and which can be made more or less comfortable, more or less lonely, more or less frightening, for example. Part of the discomfort arises probably from the fact that we are only able to represent the state of being dead with frightening phantasies of being alive. We may see death as agonizing disintegration, of the kind we feared and seemed to experience as tiny babies, for example. We may think and talk little about it, and so maintain unrealistic assumptions, which prevent us from helping each other much when someone dies, and so contribute to our general level of anxiety and guilt and denial on the subject.

One old lady was convinced, quite without recognizing it, that when she died she would be roasted on a spit, like a martyr in a picture she had seen as a child. Another old man saw death as a state of permanent starvation, which he had suffered as a child. He was considerably helped in his seventies by analysis which he undertook because he had a mental breakdown on retirement. Just before he died, ten years later, he asked for a glass of milk and a bun. Having eaten them he died peacefully in his sleep, with a full stomach. This old man also went through what is very common: a process of 'placing' the people he knew and loved, relatives in particular, just before he went to bed that night. This process can be connected with making peace with them too. Sometimes the fears around death include the fear that it does mean the loss of everyone and everything we have worked for in our lives; that they cannot survive after our death. Partly this arises from a fear that our anger, or envy, is so powerful that it can destroy everything. The 'placing' process, which reassures the dying person that loved people will go on after their death, can then be understood in terms of making sure that their love is stronger than their destructiveness. Those around can sometimes help with this process (provided they can cope with their own anxieties about wanting the person to die) by helping them to see that much as they are loved, the world and life can go on without them. This can be difficult for many people; the conflict between holding on to and letting go of those you love is one which must be struggled with throughout life and especially at death. Where any parting is felt as a rejection it may be hard to allow someone to die when they are ready for it.

When I worked in a mental hospital one old lady used to ask all the nurses as they went by: 'When am I going, dear?' or 'Where am I going, dear?' There were of course many possible interpretations to be put on these questions, but when I once gave a minute to ask her if she was worried where she would go when she died, and when she was going to die, the response was quite startling. For a while she seemed to become sane and she looked at me with a new expression, as if she really saw me for the first time. But it frightened me: I was very young and inexperienced and I was suddenly afraid she might make huge demands on me for something I could not give. I was also afraid the other nurses would notice that I had done something. I went back to sorting clothes and making beds, but determined to find a way in the future to deal with the anxieties both of old ladies like this one, and of myself and nurses like me.

Hanna Segal, who analysed the old man who was afraid of starving, has suggested that possibly much of senile dementia may be related to fears of dying which interact with physical changes. There may be, for example, phantasies of punishing those who will stay alive after the self is dead, or getting your own back in advance for the triumph they are supposed to feel. (It is extremely common, and often very disturbing, for people to react to a death, even of a very loved person, with a temporary state of triumph: 'Hah! At last I've got my own back on you!' This is usually so upsetting that no one mentions feeling it. It can lead to disturbances in behaviour: not only laughing at the funeral, but also a sense of horror and guilt so strong that all contact with others or with the feelings is cut off.)

Melanie Klein's paper 'Mourning and its relation to manic-depressive states' describes in great detail some of the reactions of a woman to the sudden death of her son. She describes very movingly the struggle to stay alive rather than follow her son to death, and the changes which took place in this relatively 'normal' mourning process. Where the death is expected there is more time to prepare; more time to separate the self from the loved person and to establish a sense of being able to look after the self even when the dying person is a parent. It seems, not surprisingly, that parents represent, *par excellence*, the part of the self which does 'look after' the self. Illness or death of the parent may seem to threaten this ability to keep going; it is only after a week or so of actually continuing to live that the bereaved person can believe that they are not in fact dead themselves. This is especially true if the separation between the real parents and the 'internal parents' – the 'parents in your head' who are there throughout life and are always a potential support or a potential criticizer – has not been substantially made before.

It can be extremely painful to watch your parents growing old. Not only may old insults and anger, swallowed in a lifetime of caring for others perhaps, suddenly be expressed in no uncertain terms, terrifying the child who must now see their parent in a totally new light, but perhaps even more painful, old sorrows may be felt and expressed. Fits of weeping, fears of being left alone, self-recriminations, fears of being unloved and uncared for and wished out of the way may all emerge and have extremely upsetting meaning for the child of whatever age who must watch and bear it. This can often be exaggerated by the tendency people have to believe that all their parents' unhappiness and sorrow was somehow their fault. This kind of unrealistic guilt, as well as anger with parents for not keeping quiet and putting a good face on it, may make it very difficult for their children to tolerate their misery and complaints. Where they are being criticized – and they may be criticized for 'sins' committed not by them at all, but by someone else in the parent's past – the child may easily be tempted to reject the parent or refuse to listen in some way. The child may in fact quite easily be pushed into responding like this, in just the same way perhaps that the old person's parents themselves responded – which is perhaps one reason why the particular complaints and misery have survived so long unchanged.

Summary

In this chapter I have looked at some situations where earlier phantasies re-emerge and are interpreted in the light of the present day. Here I have concentrated on aspects of situations such as childbirth, the growing up of children, old age and dying, which seem to be accompanied by deeply disturbing phantasies of an all-or-nothing kind, and which raise anxieties about the ability of good to overcome evil, life to overcome death, in the self and in the world around. Where these anxieties are very strong, the world can seem for a while to be very black; people and situations and images of the self can be very split into excessively good or excessively bad. Ordinary work is hard because a good relation with reality requires that good and bad come together and are integrated without destroying each other. Where work situations can be maintained to some extent through-out family crises, as long as they do not prevent the work of mourning from taking place, this fact may help restore a more balanced and hopeful view of the world which mitigates anxieties and helps feelings of depression to pass. But as a general rule of thumb in my counselling work I have found that two years is needed to recover from any gross shock to the internal world, such as a death, a divorce, a birth or a marriage. In that time, a considerable amount of restructuring of the expectations and assumptions with which the world is greeted must be undertaken; where this mourning process does not take place, where depression is not allowed in but is denied, some contact with reality will have been lost, and there may be a later depression or family crisis brought about quite directly by 'delayed mourning'.

Verbalized experiences from the past may be remembered; unverbalized feelings and experiences may be evoked, 'remembered in feelings' and mistakenly attributed to the present day. To the 'realistic' reactions to what is happening in the world around is added a whole set of 'unrealistic' reactions, deriving from such evoked phantasies. In the new situation these memories may be treated once again just as they were before: denied, seen in others, terribly feared, for example; or kept away from people in order to protect them. Or they may be treated differently this time round. The different responses of the people who are involved this time, together with new abilities and knowledge in the adult self which make childhood feelings perhaps recognizable, forgivable and thereby bearable enough to test against adult reality may enable old phantasies to be actually modified. This time round they may not be cut off in their terrifying form, allowed into behaviour only and not into thought, but may be allowed to run their course in interaction with others and so reach a different, more satisfactory conclusion. Fears that love is too weak for the destructiveness of the self and the world around may this time be not hidden and believed, but convincingly refuted.

In the next chapter I look at some of the phantasies involved in situations outside the family, where the issues are less likely to be so disturbing, though they may be. On the whole, I suspect, relationships at work can be enjoyed or hated in a way which is slightly less fraught than love relationships with parents or with sexual partners. Work may give people the opportunity to work through some of their anxieties in a way which is easier for being further removed from the very infantile ones evoked so often in families. Perhaps this is one reason why analysts tend to discuss such relationships less; they seem in many ways less fundamental and less disturbing than the more primitive phantasies involved in the family.

EIGHT

PHANTASIES ABOUT WORK

In this chapter I want to look at some phantasies which come into operation in connection with paid work of various kinds. There is always a problem when it comes to writing about the relationship between people and their work. It is often implied that there are only two choices: either someone is in favour of changing society to fit people, or they are in favour of changing people to fit society, however bad that society is. Psychoanalysts are often assumed to belong to the second category.

In fact, of course, the two processes cannot be separated like this. Change in society and change in individuals and their personalities always go hand in hand. There are two obvious ways in which psychoanalysts can be seen to contribute to changing society. One is through the means of therapy. The increase in hope and clear-sightedness which a good psychoanalysis may give can free individuals to use their energy to help change the society they belong to, at home, at work and in other areas too. One member of the family, the office or the residential children's home who has had the support of a good psychoanalysis can have a considerable effect on the ability of others around to work well and in a satisfying manner. Often this will include making decisions to change some aspect of the situation and being able to carry out these decisions. (Problems arise, it must be admitted, when the analysis or other form of therapy has been less than good; sometimes people do seem to emerge from a course of therapy with a sense of their own importance and self-righteousness which are obviously exaggerated, for example. 'Having been in therapy', it seems, is not enough; what matters is what happened there and how it is being used in the present.)

Change in society can also perhaps be influenced by the spread of new ideas. The work of Bowlby and the Robertsons in making available to the public some insights from psychoanalysis helped bring about changes in the way the child–mother relationship was regarded and treated in our society. In spite of the many shortcomings of this work and the many justifiable criticisms of it, some of the effects it has had, such as freer visiting hours for children in hospitals, are quite clearly worth having. Similarly, attitudes to children's play have changed over the years under the influence in particular of the work of Susan Isaacs, an analyst colleague of Melanie Klein who set up the Malting House School in Cambridge. Schools have changed as a result so that the experiences, and probably the personalities too, of children brought up in our society have been affected. The changes in schools and hospitals may actually have had an influence not only on pupils and patients, but also on teachers and nurses and doctors, affecting the personalities of those who take up the work and those who stay in it.

There is another way, too, in which psychoanalytical insights have been used directly to help in the process of changing organizational structures. One analyst who has strongly influenced my thinking is Isobel Menzies, whose work as a management consultant for NHS hospitals and social services departments has had very far-reaching effects in humanizing some institutions. Not only has her work shown that psychoanalytical insights can be used to bring about difficult and valuable organizational change, but it also clearly demonstrates some of the links between personality and organizational structure.

Sometimes people assume that what is wrong at work is merely a matter of personalities, their own or someone else's. Looking at the details of the relationships and at the demands of the structure, both practical and emotional, on those involved sometimes makes it clear that the personalities are strongly affected by the place or role they occupy. Sometimes this close observation enables the role or place to be changed, and with it the personality of the person holding it may appear to change. This, I think, is what Menzies did, and what I would like to try to help readers to do if they want to.

Menzies was called in to help solve an organizational problem for a hospital in the 1950s. In the process she interviewed nurses at all levels of the hierarchy. In her paper she describes the relation between the anxieties experienced by the nurses (which arose both from their tasks and from the pressure of the hierarchy) and the way the hospital was organized. Both of these were related in turn to the difficulties the staff experienced in getting their jobs done as they felt they should be. A crucial part in all the difficulties was the way in which senior nurses saw the junior ones as irresponsible, while the junior nurses saw the senior ones as all-powerful – either as wise and good and able to give enormous amounts of help if only the junior nurses could get it from them, or as severe and cruel sources of blame and punishment. These 'personalities' appear in Menzies's study as dependent upon the way in which the hospital was organized and on the way in which the nurses tried to deal with the anxieties facing them every day. The enormous changes which have taken place in hospitals since her paper was written seem to me to bear out many of Menzies's conclusions. New ways of dealing with the anxieties have enabled the nursing profession to become more 'human', and as a result both nurses and patients have benefited. (Unfortunately, many people working in the NHS today are seeing the effects of the cuts and the general uncertainty eroding this more 'human' atmosphere. Any increase in anxiety must make it harder to deal with anxieties in a human way. I take up this point later in this chapter.)

Where non-Marxists will sometimes blame personalities exclusively, Marxists and other people with an interest in structures sometimes feel that personalities are irrelevant and that economic and historical and political considerations are of overriding importance in determining conditions of work. My own view is that psychoanalytically informed analyses of work should add to other forms of analysis, rather than replace them. Studying the role of anxieties arising from the organization, from the task and from members' personal histories can contribute an understanding of emotional forces which may themselves significantly interact with economic and other factors; but I by no means wish to imply that these other factors are unimportant. It seems to me that it could be useful to look at the way phantasies are shaped and moulded by the conditions of work, as one mechanism which links economic, social, historical, social-psychological and ideological aspects of society and the individual: a mechanism Marx knew existed when he wrote about the conditions of production determining the ideology of society, but which he himself did not elaborate much.

In this chapter I am strongly aware of two motivations and two audiences. One is academic: to suggest ways we can understand the world around us in an intellectual manner and to point to ways others could use such ideas for more detailed research into means of improving working conditions. The other is more immediately practical: I would like to be helpful to the many readers who will be experiencing problems to do with work which could be alleviated by a better understanding of some of the phantasies involved.

Relationship with the work task

Each individual comes to their work with their own history, their own phantasies. But there are common concerns which may emerge, faced with a common task. It seems that a general common concern which is related to paid work is connected with the hope that old phantasy situations can be put right; that terrible things done in phantasy, as a child or as an adult, can be made better. It seems that we all 'know' that we have done wrong; through work we feel we can make some kind of reparation or restitution which puts our internal phantasy world – as well as the external, real one, with any luck – into better shape than it was before. Phantasies evoked by work may in fact enable us to face damage we have done, in reality or in phantasy, and reassure ourselves that we can do and be something good as well.

Let us have some examples.

Marion had an older brother who was mentally subnormal and never learnt to read. Their father used to torture the brother with questions which he could never answer, and Marion would sit there in agony, longing desperately to take out her own brain and put it into her brother, *giving* him the ability to answer. In later life Marion became a teacher for adolescents who could not read, and in this way attempted to make up for what she felt was her failure as a child to make things all right for her brother. Her job, I think, was made harder because she so desperately wanted to give these adolescents her own ability: she was not aware that she could also perhaps help them to bear the difficulties of not knowing how to read. For Marion, the world in general – and work in particular – seemed to contain only people who misused their superior positions or brain power to torture others, and those like her brother who were victims, weak and helpless but loving and deserving. She herself still often felt much as she had as a child: able to see what was going on and know the answers, but utterly impotent against those in power over her. Her feelings about the 'victims' were compounded by her guilty secret feelings that she had out of envy and jealousy stolen her brother's brain in the first place – and that was why the brother could not read. These feelings sometimes made it difficult for her to get on with people at work.

Marion's feelings about her work were made up of many 'realistic' present-day feelings, and many which directly connected with her childhood. Jill, a mental nurse, was two when her father 'went mad'; in her phantasy it was clear that she was convinced that it was her fault. Working as a mental nurse helped her to face real madness and to reassure herself about its causes and consequences. Both Marion and Jill brought their burning desires to *do* something, fuelled by these anxieties, to their work. For both of them, these anxieties contributed to the rewards and difficulties of their jobs. The sense that they were playing out a past scenario affected their whole relation with their work, and at times prevented them from seeing people they worked with in a realistic way.

It is quite probable that such past histories will have their counterpart in the lives of many mental nurses, teachers or social workers. Anxieties about past behaviour may influence the choice of job in the first place or be evoked – out of many possible ones – by the job which is undertaken. Being surrounded by suicidal patients or by angry adolescents may easily bring out phantasies about death and suicide or angry adolescence which would otherwise have remained dormant. Similarly, being thrust into a position of responsibility can bring out the ability to be responsible, or a fear of it, which perhaps was previously never suspected. When I was on jury service I saw startling changes taking place, particularly amongst the women: it looked very much as if being asked for their opinions in a situation where it really mattered had significantly changed the self-image of some of the people there. But a friend of mine left her job because she was 'threatened' with promotion.

The work task, then, can bring out hidden anxieties, or can engage with more conscious ones, and can enable some of them to be evoked and significantly changed. Equally, some people find they can no longer tolerate their job because it brings up in them some aspect of their character they cannot bear: their authoritarian side, for example, or, as Menzies found in some nurses, anxieties about illness and death derived from infantile phantasies which were too strong. The very fears which drive some people into particular jobs may prove to be too strong to enable the job to function as a defuser of the fears. Someone who takes on a job of nursing or childcare as a means of taking care of a needy or child part of themselves, may be able to satisfy this desire, or may find that the child part of them gets too confused with the real children in care, and causes problems of jealousy and envy. Seeing children now getting something you felt you never had may be extremely satisfying, or it may arouse fury and a desire to take it away from them too. Where conditions are good, the job can be an enormous relief and reassurance in both the external-reality and internal-reality worlds.

Where tasks are directed towards people it may be fairly clear that an element of reassurance about having done dreadful things to people – or having failed to act effectively – in the (phantasy) past may be involved.

However, it is possible that more primitive phantasies may also be involved, and that these may show themselves in other jobs too.

If we consider any kind of job which involves working on cars, or buying or selling them, we may quickly see that such jobs could well arouse or help to settle phantasies about sexual performance. (Advertisers use, rather than create, connections on the level of phantasy between cars and sexuality; Melanie Klein's work with children makes this very clear.) Many people feel very personally about their car; as if it were an extension of themselves or a representative of someone they loved and cared very much about. Many women feel that the men in their lives relate to their cars more as lovers than as vehicles; women, too, can have strong feelings of power and satisfaction from owning a car. (The phantasies involved on a deep level include not only phantasies developed around penises, but also around the mother's breast and body; something enormously powerful you can get inside and control and be controlled by in phantasy.)

One car salesman I knew behaved as if he very much wanted to be admired by and to seduce his customers. When I first knew him he was married and was also looking after the cars he sold. Gradually this side of his personality gave way to one which moved on continually to new pastures; selling became more of a passion with him and he neglected the other side of his business, leaving it to others. His marriage broke up and his sexual relationships of the one-night stand variety continued. A woman customer criticized work his garage had done on her car once, and he flattened her against a window, threatening her in what seemed a very sexual way, just as if she had questioned his virility and he was showing her that he was capable of raping her if he wished. For him, I suspect, as with many people with sexual difficulties, sex and violence were strongly linked to the exclusion of more caring and reciprocal elements. 'Conquests' and admiration seemed more important to him, both as a salesman and as a lover, and in the process he isolated himself more and more from really caring relationships and people.

Clearly this man is a particular kind of car salesman, whose sexual anxieties have apparently not been reassured through his work, but possibly made worse: perhaps by bad workmanship, perhaps by selling in a way which left him feeling he had conned people, and that he was therefore vulnerable to their getting their own back, perhaps by greed on his part, which overcame his more caring characteristics and relationships. This is of course by no means the only way in which working with vehicles may be related to sexual anxieties. Many of the garage men I have dealt with have been impressive in their honesty, their conviction that they have a real skill which they offer at a reasonable price, and their ability to deal with customers as equals without attempting to seduce them. On the whole they seem to be older; these are individuals who have presumably been able to use their work in a more satisfying and less anxiety-provoking way. I would expect them to be more happily married, and to feel about their sexuality in a somewhat similar way to the way they feel about their ability to care for cars. But such mature and serene people are less likely to bring their private lives to my notice, and I can only guess about them.

Buildings too have deep significance in phantasy. Small children's fascination with the inside and outside of the bodies of people around them can develop into a fascination with the working parts of machinery, or with the inside of books; with biology or physics, astronomy or archaeology (distance in time and space are often identified in our phantasy worlds); and perhaps always into concern for the buildings they live in or work in. The building itself, as well as the 'body' of workers to which people belong, can easily evoke phantasies related to early situations of looking after and being looked after by an enormous mother upon whom we rely. The fabric of the building, what state it is in, how clean and tidy, how well looked after, how safe, who it belongs to, may all have not only realistic significance but also deeply infantile significance which at times may obscure or give emotional force to the more obvious mundane issues. Working to mend or build such a building, installing furniture, keeping it clean or simply being dependent upon others doing all this can all connect with quite primitive phantasies, in particular about the body of the mother who looked after us at a time when she appeared more like the whole world, or a piece of furniture, than a real person. The way people inside the building live and move about may relate to phantasies about our fathers, siblings and other people who happened to be important to us in infancy and who seemed to us to be moving about inside our mother's body. Such phantasies may sometimes explain apparently irrational, deeply emotional involvement with other people and objects or structures at work.

Our own impotence in the face of an apparently immovable and insensitive work organization may directly pick up phantasies about our impotence to care for or influence an equally – or more – important world when we were small and everyone around was so much bigger. Our feelings of being utterly indispensable, too, may be related to such infantile phantasies of omnipotence more than to the real world of today. Where we have left-over excitement and fears arising from such very early times, real people (such as our real mother now) may be unable to come close enough to the primitive perception of her embodied in such phantasies. If we want to change some of these phantasies, we may try to do it in the context of the wider world which seems as important now as she did then. This may give us the energy necessary to 'move mountains'; as long as we are sufficiently in touch with reality at the same time, these infantile motivations can be extremely socially useful. Erin Pizzey and her work with battered women and men is an example of someone whose enormous energy in this field seems quite clearly, from her own report, to arise from her own childhood experiences. The strengths and weaknesses of such pioneers, the enormous good they do and the enormous hostility they both arouse and survive, can both perhaps be attributed to the infantile origin of their passions. For other people the task of changing the world seems too enormous; they may curl up in a corner at work, shut off as far as possible from others, trying to defend themselves from the onslaught and the demands of the outside world in a safe haven of their own, much as they might have done as a child when they perhaps fled to a corner of the room, a box, or a 'den' which brought the world down to a manageable size, when they were small and life seemed too much.

Let me give an example of the link between the inside of one's own body and the place of work – in this case the home. (As babies, as I have said before, we are not always entirely clear about the distinction between our own and our mother's bodies; phantasies about the one are very closely intertwined with phantasies about the other.)

Christine came for counselling because she was afraid of giving birth – for perfectly realistic reasons. I was unable to help much with the realistic reasons of course, but together we enabled her to feel much happier, and more able to deal with them, by looking at unrealistic fears she had as well which were being reinforced by her circumstances. Quite quickly she told me how she felt strongly that the inside of her body was a safe place, and the outside world was full of threatening and nasty people and situations. As we discussed this she began to see that she was keeping the good and the bad totally separate so that the one could not threaten the other. Unfortunately this also meant that neither could mitigate the other. The good place inside was felt to be wonderfully good; the bad outside was terrifyingly bad, and not at all a fit place for a baby. She kept her external appearance deliberately unkempt partly in order to show her contempt of people who could not see through to the pure goodness inside. Gradually she came to have a less split view of herself and her world. She came to allow some goodness into her own external appearance and into her view of the world. She came to realize that she hung on to the idea of her wonderful inside partly because she was secretly also terrified that it was all bad. Allowing a little of the goodness into her view of the external world, she was able to allow herself to see more realistically the badness in her own interior. This felt much more secure. She was able to tolerate her own faults as well as those of others, and to see real virtues too. As a result she no longer felt so beleaguered and vulnerable. The relevant point in this connection is that she came back near the end of her work with me saying that she had suddenly realized that she had always treated her house in the same way as she treated her own body. One room – her bedroom – was always kept clean and extremely tidy: she would spend hours keeping it like that. The rest of the house she had always neglected: she had not cared whether it was clean or dirty; she had never spent any time on it. Now she was feeling so much better about herself, more able to allow good and bad to mix together without destroying each other, she had begun to take more care of the rest of the house, and the garden too, and to stop devoting such unreasonable amounts of time to her bedroom. Living in less uncared-for surroundings, she no longer needed such an extremely cut-off haven. She also lost her fear of bringing her child into the outside world, and found a satisfactory way of dealing with her realistic fears.

For Christine, her feelings about her house reflected her feelings about her body in a quite direct and obvious way. It seems that this is a common phenomenon which may contribute to strong feelings of affection and safety attached to the building in which people work, be it offices or hospital, factory or town hall. These feelings can also contribute to feelings of loss and mourning when people leave their jobs, move to new premises or move house. The settling-in period brings up huge resentments and upsets derived from feelings of being pushed out into the cold, being unwanted and replaced by someone new, which are fed by past feelings of losing your mother as a place of security. Working on a building in any capacity, as a caretaker, a plumber, a carpenter, architect or organizer may evoke and modify old feelings towards one's own and one's mother's body which are left over from early childhood.

In a work situation, whatever it is, old phantasies are evoked and worked through again. This time round the adult self is there to help. Other sources of support in the people around, new kinds of adult strength, clearer perceptions, greater knowledge, may all contribute to the old phantasies being brought to a more satisfactory conclusion this time. The first time a new task is undertaken there may be enormous fears about it, some of which will be reassured by successfully – or even unsuccessfully

– completing it. The second time gives a second chance; gradually the anxieties may change as some of them are tested out. Fears of what it means to fail – that it means being totally annihilated, ground into the earth by triumphant colleagues, or a past father-figure perhaps, who have been just waiting to show you up as a disaster, for example – may be lessened by the actual experience of failing. When you are no longer so afraid of it failure may become less likely as nervousness and panic recede. Fears of what it means to succeed, too, may be faced or forever avoided. Some people seem to be so sure that they would trample everyone else to the ground in their triumphant war-dance of success that they can never allow themselves actually to succeed in anything they set out to do. Other people may be scared of the envy others would feel towards them, or be afraid of being utterly alone at the top of the heap, having pushed away everyone else the minute they seemed to 'prove' they could 'do it alone'. 'Succeeding', and finding out that the world is not noticeably changed by the fact, may be a sad but reassuring lesson to learn.

Actually testing your ability to make things happen can be a significant part of the effect of working. Trying to make changes and discovering how hard they are may modify phantasies of total omnipotence which were left over from childhood. Discovering that people are not just putty in your hands, nor can be knocked down with a feather, may be chastening but also a relief. Challenging people and finding that they do not respond by rejecting you entirely may surprise and modify expectations. Being shouted at and finding the world has not ended as a result may be quite an unexpected experience for some people.

Equally, work situations must modify unrealistic hopes. The hope, for example, that 'if I love them enough' anything is possible may be tested by nurses, doctors, social workers, teachers, priests or even prison warders as well as foster-parents. Such hopes may be quickly or more slowly dashed and replaced by total cynicism or a more realistic assessment of the role of love and the ability of the self to love 'properly'. This in turn may then enable new assessments to be made of childhood memories of times when you failed to love 'properly'. Real abilities to make things better for real people can be enormously reassuring for those who feared that they were fundamentally lacking in strong love.

Phantasies around being paid

With many work phantasies the issue of caring is important. Earning money enables people to care for those they love and those towards whom they feel a sense of responsibility. This is true on a practical level, and also on a phantasy level where the money may take on a larger-than-life significance. It is remarkable how different people, in apparently similar situations, feel very different about the money they receive or do not receive. What is even more remarkable is how changeable this is. During counselling I often find that people whose financial situation has not changed at all simply feel more able to cope with it, or actually able for the first time to do something to change it, by the end of the counselling. In the middle there is often a period of panic about being unable to pay at all. There are real effects of having too little money, and these cannot be ignored. There are also real effects of phantasies which load the money with huge emotional significance which lead to its being used as a symbol for something else which might be better separated from it.

Andrew worked many hours of overtime partly because he felt he needed huge amounts of money to satisfy a very demanding wife. He was very surprised when he eventually allowed himself to see that his real wife did not want so much money: what she did want was to be able to go out to work herself. This man's conviction seemed to be derived from a feeling he had as a child when he was the only male in a houseful of women and felt he had to 'be the man' for all these adult women. He was still trying to satisfy such impossible needs now, as a man. In the process he was pushing his wife into feeling the dependence and the impotent rage and depression brought on by the kind of dependence and responsibility he as a child had suffered.

Sandra was unable to feel that she deserved any money at all for herself: she felt she should only allow herself to exist if she devoted herself entirely to the needs – and greed – of others around her. Any need or demand on her own part was understood by her as destructive greed which she must abolish or deny, but never satisfy. She kept herself in a permanent state of poverty, partly also as a mute reproach towards the people around her who she felt were so much richer in all senses than she was. She was afraid that if she allowed herself to be active and demanding in any way she would simply attack and destroy the rich people she knew: as a result she never allowed herself to come alive – except under the influence of alcohol when she sometimes did become destructive. It was partly her fear of such destructive, envious attacks from others which prevented her from taking any steps to improve her own financial position.

Money is often felt to be a source of power which draws such envious attacks from others – and from the self. It may be coveted and feared as a means of defence and a means of attack, and this symbolic meaning (derived in part from realistic considerations) may swallow up more neutral or loving meanings which would allow reasonable amounts of money to be spent on the self or on the family or on work. The feeling that payment reflects assessment of the value of the work done and of the person who does it may on the one hand add to the effectiveness of work in warding off depression, or mitigating it, after life crises, for example, and may on the other hand lead to great rivalries, anger and frustration as a consequence of being 'valued' in a way which seems unjust. Sometimes it is sought as a means of becoming totally independent of others and so invulnerable to the pains of being dependent; equally it may be feared in case such independence should become possible, with the result that others would then disappear, be lost or rejected, leaving the self with money but no loving relationships at all.

People who are overpaid often suffer hidden anxieties about money, though they may be unaware of such a factor in their problems. This is something which Elliott Jaques uncovered and described. It may be hard to feel terribly sympathetic towards such problems; most people are more likely to suffer from the opposite anxieties about not getting enough. But there is a real importance in such anxieties amongst the overpaid, in that their position of relative power may enable them to offload their discomfort on to others. Quarrels with unions, for example, may be exacerbated by such emotional factors, whereby union members are seen as no more than representatives of the greedy self which has enough but cannot feel satisfied or comfortable with that. There may be guilty fears about having stolen the money (and other things which it stands for, such as power and glory) from those who are receiving less. This can add to mutual distrust, defensiveness and aggressiveness, and interpreting other people's motives in the light of quite angry and deprived phantasies. I have been told that the income structure of some South American countries has a very clearly disturbing effect on the state of mind of the richer classes, in spite of their conscious acceptance of the enormous inequities of their systems. (One assumes, of course, that the effect on the poorer classes is worse, but it may be less obvious that the rich are also observably unhappy under such economic conditions.)

Overpayment can contribute to feelings of being put on a pedestal and to the pressures to live up to such an image of the self. There may be terribly unrealistic fears about the dangers of being pulled off that pedestal, which can work towards encouraging increasingly desperate attempts to maintain or justify being so high up. Sometimes there is a strong desire to jump off the pedestal in some way; to have a less ideal self recognized by the idealizing people or person. If this cannot be done in a 'reasonable' way it may be done in an 'unreasonable' one. A teacher idealized by her head, a manager idealized by his subordinates or his boss may struggle hard to be accepted as a more 'real' person, while at the same time being frightened of the consequences. If they do not succeed in gaining the more secure recognition of themselves as they are, the response may be for the 'wonderful', 'excellent' member of staff to throw up the job entirely, a course of action which those around find quite inexplicable. There are many reasons why senior executives may decide to retire early; the desire to relieve themselves of the burden of deserving their income or their status is just one I have come across.

Relations to other people at work

It seems that we relate to other people in our work environment in many ways; they are all grist to the mill of our phantasies. Many people find themselves in situations which bear a strong resemblance to childhood scenarios of sibling rivalry, or rivalry with a parent, and find that their adult self temporarily disappears under the onslaught of infantile behaviour and feelings. A frown from a 'superior' may temporarily put you back into feeling like a small child faced with the headmaster; an overbearing customer may touch a chord from a time when you were sixteen or six, and your behaviour may then become more understandable in terms of the sixteen-year-old you than in terms of the adult you now are.

Specifically, we may often use other people at work to stand for different parts of ourselves. Obstinate, rude, controlling and bossy parts, as well as greedy and destructive parts, of the self may be feared and disowned; they may be separated off from the more pliant, polite and caring parts and 'seen' in other people at work. These people may then be treated as if they were no more than 'part people', like cartoon characters with one characteristic and no more. They may be treated in a very high-handed way, tightly controlled, cruelly misused and overloaded with quite unrealistic expectations. Because we see them as separated from the more mitigating aspects of ourselves (kept in ourselves perhaps, or someone far away) we may perceive them in a more pure state and so fear and attack them in a more pure way. Our treatment of them then loses some of the mercy and concern for the 'whole' person which it would otherwise have: we start behaving as if *we* were no more than cartoon characters with the precise characteristic we are attacking in them. People treated in this way frequently respond too in such a way as to confirm the fear and rejection felt towards the characteristic they are 'representing'. I come back to this aspect of things later.

Seeing people as merely parts of ourselves, or as carrying parts of ourselves, we can ignore the part of them which is different. People do not of course always do this. Other people may be allowed to add their own contributions to the phantasies of others. This can be difficult but rewarding. A more experienced person or a newcomer who is allowed to do their job in a way which is not excessively controlled or interfered with by others may be able to teach the others something. They may be able to deal with a problem which was insoluble before, or show a new way of dealing with it. This can only happen if those around are able to take the risks involved. Some people are frightened of finding, say, that they are no longer needed, or that they actually have nothing to contribute themselves. Some people are scared that they *should* know already all there is to know; being involved in any learning process for such people may simply 'mean' that they are small and insignificant and of no value at all. The frustration of having to learn slowly, of not being able to just open their mouths and swallow other people's knowledge immediately, whole, may make them so angry that they will do almost anything to avoid the learning situation. Matthew was so desperate, at the age of four, to play the piano 'just like Daddy can' that he gave up piano lessons. He could not bear the frustration of seeing his own incompetence. He wanted to be too big, too quickly, and so could not bear to learn or be taught.

This is a situation which may often arise at work, and it may cause friction between those who want to teach, to offer what they do know or to show that they are now 'big' compared with the newcomer, and the newcomer who may idealize the knowledge the other has and at the same time devalue the time and work necessary to learn it. The 'teacher' may have to struggle with feelings of being rejected and devalued, as well as being usurped and threatened in their role, and also perhaps worrying realistically about the consequences of the newcomer's refusal to take advice. The 'learner' may have to struggle to tolerate the knowledge that there is something to be learnt and the frustration of having to learn it. It is usually only too easy to find fault and failings in the teacher and to use these to bolster a spurious sense of superiority which leads to mutual rejection and failure to learn in the fastest manner. Both may have to struggle to determine how much supervision is necessary and how much must be learnt by experience: decisions on such matters may be seriously influenced by the fact that they trigger old phantasies about growing up and becoming independent.

Where people are allowed to be different from and to teach each other there may be a chance for a reworking of old teaching relationships which were less satisfactory once – or many times – before. Someone who was unable to learn at school, perhaps because of disruptive home events, or because of bad teaching or social class problems, may be able to learn in the new circumstances of work. In the process fears raised by the failure of the earlier teaching situation may be stilled. 'Can I learn at all?' 'Was the school at fault or was it, as they said, just me?' 'Am I guilty, or foolish, or seriously lacking in something important?' – all of these fears may be evoked and at times calmed at work. On a deeper level, as for Marion and Jill, fears to do with relations with one's parents may also be touched by these processes. 'Will I ever be as big as daddy – and would I then be as cruel or as mad as him?' or 'Will I ever be able to impress my mother?' may also be questions which, unstated, underlie anxieties about work. A person who can be treated as a 'mummy' or 'daddy' at work may be a very helpful counter to the original model, enabling old secret feelings towards parents to be allowed out and changed.

How other people fulfil their roles at work may have important implications for the ways we use them as models for the self and for expectations of others. Whether it is possible to be strong and good, for example, or whether power and cruelty always go together, as Marion feared, may be 'proved' or questioned by the way power is wielded at work. Some people seem to test the benevolence of the powerful so much that they force others into very polarized and threatening relationships. A girl living in a hostel I worked with used to behave in a very provoking manner towards those responsible for running it. In a typical incident she brought into the office a half-bottle of wine, showing it to the member of staff on duty. The rules were such that she knew she could be sent back to a mental hospital for bringing alcohol on to the premises; she could easily have finished the bottle before coming in or without showing the staff member. She seemed to be testing those in power over her to see how they wielded it and how much control she had. Because of the way she did such things she seemed to be likely to get the answer that those in power were cruel and unreasonable, but could also be kept in a state of frozen indecision much of the time. It would take many such incidents before she would finally be sent away again, having 'proved' her own power and theirs to destroy her own comfort.

Other people can never challenge those in authority over them, as if they are convinced that all authority is by its nature pure and good. I came across this attitude in a clerk in a German council office. I was supposed to inform the authorities that I was leaving my place of abode and in passing I expressed some feelings about such invasion of privacy on the part of the state. The clerk was truly horrified. 'If the state wanted to do it, it *must* be right!' was the sole content of his response. My son, now five, has a similar idea; if the teacher says it, it must be right, desirable and true. Terrible anxiety seems to be attached to any questioning of this attitude: in a five-year-old we can accept this and expect him to grow out of it. Five-year-olds perhaps reasonably cannot trust their own judgement and must depend on more knowledgeable people around them; questioning what adults said would seem to leave them with more responsibility than they can be expected to bear at this age.

If Authority cannot and *must* not be questioned still as an adult, where it is being misused such adults are likely to seek the fault in themselves and may go to considerable lengths to twist their own beliefs to fit those of the authority, in the face of real contradictions. This kind of internal twisting can of course have serious consequences for the individual and for those around them. In an obvious way, stifling your conscience, your own judgement of what you are doing, can allow you to commit terrible atrocities on other people. Yet the ability to suspend judgement and to act under orders can also be life-saving at times, such as when a frightened child who obeys an adult in a house fire may be rescued whereas one who disobeys may die. People are faced with real problems and dilemmas about the benevolence of the authority they are supposed to trust when they are asked to refuse or perform an abortion, or administer ECT, and there may be times when a decision simply to obey seems wisest. But the consequences of subordinating your own conflicting opinions to those of others over a long period of time may include quite serious illnesses. Internal conflicts, especially ones which are denied or ignored rather than acknowledged, cause stress on the body which can emerge in various physical illnesses. It is as if the body may express the conflict by fighting part of itself: phantasies can have physical instead of mental expression. Sometimes depression seems to be caused by the turning inwards of attacks which other people would turn outwards. It has even been suggested that cancer can be linked with such hidden, internal conflicts. In Menzies's study it was generally agreed in the hospital that the more 'mature' nurses left: these were ones who would not subordinate themselves to obviously foolish and counter-productive rules. Those who stayed were frequently ill: repeated short-term illnesses can often be understood – as in the army they are taken as a measure of morale – as a means of protest which stops short of open challenge or leaving the job. These nurses also seemed to become less able to relate to patients as whole people, and to behave as if straightening the blankets was more important than the patient's comfort. Obedience to the authority had been achieved at the cost of losing the more caring and satisfying aspects of the nurses' behaviour towards the patients.

Special problems of dealing with disturbed people

In any job where the task involves dealing with people, the phantasies of the 'staff' will be affected by those of their 'clients'. The phantasies of prison warders are affected by those of their prisoners; the phantasies of nurses by those of their patients; and the phantasies of teachers by those of their pupils. Relatives, colleagues, superiors and the general public may also contribute to the phantasies involved of course. Where anyone involved has particularly troublesome phantasies, problems are compounded.

Let me give an example of an interaction in a school where this process – amongst others – can be seen.

A headteacher of a school for disturbed children told me of an incident at her school. One of the teachers was new and was feeling that the job was too much for her. She was getting more and more bogged down when one child finally made her so angry and despairing that she sent him to the head, feeling that she was totally incompetent to deal with him. The child had made a mistake in his sums and had scribbled over the whole page 'SHIT'. The headteacher had been discussing in my seminars the way children (and adults) can want desperately to produce something wonderful and be afraid that they are just producing 'shit'; one mistake can then 'mean' that their worst fears have come true. With this in mind she was able to say to the child, 'Come on, let's make it not just shit.' Together they rubbed out the marks and redid the sums. The child – perhaps also stunned by the head's ability to use the word without dropping dead – apparently went back to the class and caused no more trouble. In her tone of voice, it seemed, the head had managed to convey her acknowledgement of the attack on the school and the teacher, and to accept it as something which was painful, real but also bearable.

It seems that the child's hopelessness about his ability to produce good work had fed into the new teacher's similar sense of helplessness. Being new, she was unable to contain his fears: first, her own had to be contained by the head. The children's fears that one mistake meant disaster brought up similar fears in her; for a while she completely forgot that she was a good teacher in her previous school. There is a danger in such situations that the head too has no hope of actually bringing about improvement in the new teacher or the child; in such a case the head may give an underlying message: 'Your teacher is incompetent and bad; I am clever and good and your ally against her.' The 'badness' remains, simply being relocated from the child to the teacher. This particular head was aware of her own failings and her own need for help at times; of her ability to use such help and to deal with her own mistakes. She did not need to make others feel worse than they already did. Her confidence could feed back into the system: the child be calmed without making him feel triumphant or punitive towards the teacher. Punishment of the child would have been felt by the teacher, on one level at least, I think, as unfair: it did seem that it was her lack of experience which was contributing to the child's bad behaviour. Equally a firm 'talking to' would have failed to get in touch with the child's and the teacher's desire to do good work together; it could have compounded the child's sense of despair and fear that all that could be expected from the outside world was punishment, verbal or physical. By helping the child to put its mistakes right the head was giving the child and the teacher back some hope of a mutually rewarding relationship. By using the word 'shit' the head was showing, I think, that she acknowledged the attack on the teacher and its origins in the child's feeling that its own work could never be more than shit. In this way the despair was defused rather than sat upon or denied in some way.

Some teachers and social workers, police and prison officers must face a similar kind of despair – a sense that inside and outside the self there is only 'shit' – in the people they deal with daily. Sometimes they can acknowledge and deal with it, as the head did; sometimes they can also get help from more experienced colleagues – or from fresh, less cynical ones. The social worker and the teacher, as well as other workers 'with people', must have plenty of anxieties arising from their own past, including ones about their own goodness and its strength. Some such workers may be tempted to encourage their clients to fight those in power in order to satisfy hidden phantasies derived from the worker's own past dealings with parents, teachers or priests for example. They may idealize themselves or their charges, setting them up as 'the good ones' against others as 'the bad ones' for reasons which derive from the worker's own past history and their present-day relations with other people. Such temptations can cause the worker anxiety as well as arise from anxiety. But what is probably even more disturbing is the way the worker must deal every day with people trying to get rid of their own even greater anxieties by handing them over to the worker in various subtle and less subtle ways. The more sadistic and cruel the phantasies expressed in the behaviour and words of the person concerned, the more powerful will be the pressure on those working with them simply to join in such terrifying phantasies. A class of 'maladjusted' children, governed by extremely disturbing phantasies themselves, can put enormous strain on the teacher to respond in violent and cruel ways. The teacher's own infantile and sadistic impulses may be powerfully evoked by the children's, and the power of less destructive methods of dealing with them may seem insufficient.

(Children who are classified as 'maladjusted' tend to be dominated by what are known as psychotic processes which I discuss further at the end of this chapter. In general the phantasies concerned include heavy use of denial and splitting, and lead as a result to an escalation of anxiety in the long term. Sadism, punishment and cruelty are intimately bound up with them. Reality is split into separate 'bundles'. There may be extremely accurate perception within each of these bundles, but very little memory or time sense which would link them together. The teacher may be powerfully and extremely perceptively attacked one minute, with a wonderful awareness of the most painful and sensitive spots; the next minute the same teacher may be the subject of passionate affection of a kind which seems equally perceptive. The link between the two states of mind may seem to be totally lacking.)

People who come into contact with the social services, with the police or the prison service, very often have good, realistic reasons to feel hopeless and destroyed, unloved and unlovable themselves. Where such feelings are unmanageable, a natural way of dealing with them may be to make someone else feel them, if possible *instead of* the sufferer, rather than *as well as*. Social workers, police officers and prison officers may all find themselves prime targets for such feelings. A powerful sense of guilt and of deserving punishment, probably totally unconscious since it is too strong to bear consciously, may be a motivation for arousing powerful attacks from those who are in a position to administer them. Police and prisoner may each find themselves playing out the parts in a very violent and destructive phantasy world, each externalizing an internal fight, whereby the only possible roles are victim or aggressor, much as they were in Marion's phantasy described at the beginning of this chapter. Where there has been violence in the family such left-over phantasies of mutual attack can be very frightening. The policeman from a violent background is extremely vulnerable to provocation from a member of the public who is also from a violent background. Each has a ready-made pattern into which the other will fit. Each may have great difficulty in hanging on to more hopeful and gentle-yet-strong phantasies or roles.

A common scenario for social workers and their clients may also reflect internal fears. An initial period of hope and euphoria, the sense that at last Superman has arrived, may be followed sooner or later with bitter disappointment. Such a scenario may be a reflection of the client's life history which has slotted into the social worker's phantasies about cure and rescue, which are based more on childhood magical hopes than on knowledge of the intractability of some human problems. Sometimes ordinary social work help is virtually impossible to give because the perception of the social worker 'succeeding' makes the client feel too bad and small and angry in comparison; where this cannot be recognized and dealt with on a verbal level it is likely to emerge as some kind of sabotage.

It is important to note that not all clients have such an attacking and potentially destructive effect on social workers. Some clients do manage to use what the social worker offers them in a constructive and anxiety-reducing way. Some clients do sort themselves and their lives out with help from the workers; some do take themselves off the books in a way which is satisfactory to all concerned. These clients contribute not only to the satisfactions of the job but also to the growth of the social worker too at times. But there are some clients in every social work department who cause more trouble than all the others put together.

Where there is a fear that no one can help in an utterly damaged and persecuting world, where any attempts to 'get through' are experienced as a violent attack, help itself may be warded off violently. Where communication is predominantly on the level of behaviour, where words are used more to hide or cover things up than to contain and modify reality, relations between staff themselves may often be disrupted by a process of 'reflection' from the client's phantasy world. Some of the books published by the Tavistock Institute of Human Relations describe this process. It can take place in schools and mental hospitals, prisons and police stations, wherever severe emotional difficulties are experienced by 'inmates' and/or staff.

Let me give an example of such a process. Two members of staff at a residential hostel for ex-prisoners and mental patients seemed to be playing out parts in the phantasy world of a resident. The ability of the staff to care for and help each other was severely attacked in the process: help of a secure and stable kind was under great threat, just as it probably was in the phantasy of the resident. Her past history made it very likely that she had no hope whatsoever of being cared for in a stable manner. She managed to get the staff to experience both their own lack of care for each other, and the sense of being uncared for and unjustifiably attacked. These feelings, I would imagine, were related to her anxieties about herself and those who had cared for her in the past. One of the members of staff told me of a terrible battle between himself and another member of staff over whether this particular girl should be asked to leave or allowed to stay. It seemed that her behaviour was becoming intolerable, yet she was also making progress in some ways. These two members of staff felt very strongly indeed about her, and it seemed they could scarcely discuss the issue without becoming abusive towards each other, though it was obvious that such behaviour was not likely to be in the best interests of anyone involved. I wondered aloud if the two members of staff were in some way playing out two aspects of her: one which despaired of ever getting help and ever changing, and one which felt she could improve so much that she would become the counsellor for all of the staff, and would solve all their problems with her amazing insight. (I had picked this up from something joking my informant had said about the girl.) It seemed that these two phantasies coexisted without actually tolerating each other: one would have to throw the other right out, just as the two members of staff felt they wanted to throw the other member out of the hostel, with or without the girl. The exaggeration of both views suddenly became clear to my informant and after this the two members of staff were able to come to an agreement which took both into account.

The technique of considering whether quarrels between staff could sometimes be deeply influenced by internal conflicts in the patients or inmates or clients, depending where they take place, seems to be a powerful one. It is important not to deny the fact of personal disagreements between staff, but looking at such disagreements as *also* picking up something in the client often produces a good result. Personal difficulties between staff can often regain a more realistic level where they can be dealt with by friendly banter, for example. The differences of opinion are still there, but they have lost their exaggerated importance and their ability to destroy any caring in the people concerned. Each may be able once again to value the other's sensitivity to different aspects of the situation, their different insights, their different responsiveness to, say, the attacking and the 'asking-for-help' elements in the behaviour under consideration. Each can feel that their own contribution is taken seriously rather than denied by the others. Partly, I suspect, the process works because it simply takes away some of the guilt which is making each staff member more and more defensive and aggressive. Instead of a sense of 'how awful to be fighting like this', a new sense of hope that the fight can be understood and attributed to something not entirely within everyone's conscious control may emerge. Putting it outside the self in this way, and making sense of it, can reduce the fear of it and enable more constructive methods to be employed.

In such situations it is important to bear in mind and discuss alternative underlying causes for staff quarrels, such as the possibility that this particular client is being used as a pawn in a power struggle between two conflicting definitions of the role of staff and client, or as a representative or container for troublesome phantasies of the staff in some other way. Or perhaps a situation of rivalry between the members of staff has other far-reaching causes and effects. This side to the question may at times be more important and at times less important than the role of the subject of the quarrel. Usually both are involved; clients pick on real conflicts in the world 'out there' as vehicles for their own internal conflicts. It is extremely important that the staff try not to offload their own guilt as they mentally 'hand back' the client's. Some horrific stories are told of perfectly justifiable complaints against members of staff being persistently defined as 'acting out' or as products of the phantasy of the person who is criticizing. I know from experience that this is an extremely frustrating situation to be in, and it is one reason I try to emphasize the importance of the fact that people always project on to something which is already there. It is extremely important to take an accusation seriously as well as wondering if it might be arising mainly from the client's phantasies. And this does not mean just *pretending* to take it seriously, or saying 'I accept what you say but ...': both of these strategies are sometimes used by people in positions of power to duck a more sincere acknowledgement of their own part in the problems which could lead to real change. When a client complains to me that I am ignoring the good sides of their personality, for example, I have to take this complaint as a possible reflection of the truth as well as wondering if it is a reflection of the client's tendency to ignore the good (or the bad) sides of their personality.

The effect of being in a group

Almost any work situation involves being in a group at some time: for training, for staff meetings, for union meetings or for carrying out the actual job, be it coalmining or working in a shop. The group may actually meet as a group or it may be defined simply in terms of working for the same organization, where other members of the group are not met face to face but have some kind of existence and importance as a factor in work conditions. It seems that the very fact of belonging to a group can bring into operation certain psychic mechanisms which then have their effect upon the group. A typical example of this is the way people sometimes feel they have 'lost their identity' or lost the ability to 'be themselves' as a member of the group. They may be saddled with unwelcome expectations or may be almost forced into behaving in ways they dislike. This can happen at parties, where alcohol and the presence of many people brings out a side to people's characters which they regret terribly the next day. Teachers sometimes get annoyed at the way they find themselves 'putting on a face' for the children which is quite different from the one they have at home: with single children a quite different aspect of their personality may emerge, which responds to the particular child; the whole class of children has to be treated differently, with less sensitivity to each individual. For other people the group offers an identity which seems to serve instead of one of their own. A certain type of personality, for example, enables someone to function very well in the army, but 'goes to pieces' in a less structured, defined situation. To a lesser extent, anyone losing their job, and the sense of belonging to a group defined in this way, is bound to feel a certain loss of identity, at least for a while.

Perhaps it is worth looking briefly at some of the ways this group effect can work.

In a group there seems to be a potential for a 'multiplying' effect. Any particular cause for anxiety in one or more members of the group can affect the general anxiety level and help determine which particular set of phantasies will be used. Where anxiety is high it is more likely that it will be fought off by the short-term means of splitting and denial, both of which can often work in a very powerful way in a group and can contribute to raising the level of anxiety even further. Where the group culture works in this way, various other anxiety-reducing mechanisms may be discouraged. A desire to belong and to conform may encourage some people to submerge their own dissent, thereby contributing to a set of collusive idealizing phantasies which can then encourage others to conform in a similar way. The hard work of opposing such a group culture may be avoided.

If it is felt that to be a successful businessman depends upon rejecting any 'softness', this softness may be firmly defined as 'womanish' and – along with many women – be despised. A member of a group of businessmen who believe in such a view may find himself under great pressure to avoid any sign of such softness; if he does show it he may be used as a scapegoat and rejected by the group. Where this process is based on denial of softness in the self, rather than a more secure grasp of the need to behave at times in ways which are not quite ruthless but are firm, it will fail. What it means to be soft and not to be soft will remain at an idealized level, as it is in the *Beano* comic, for example.

In many groups it seems that individuals or groups can come to stand for particular aspects or characteristics of the others. One of the important ways in which working in groups seems to satisfy us is by giving us the opportunity to share out different aspects of our selves. We are no longer totally responsible for all the things we feel need doing, either practically or in phantasy. Our better as well as our worse impulses can gain strength and legitimacy or be controlled by interaction with other people who have similar impulses. This can give us great relief from guilt and anxiety, as well as enabling us to work more effectively and satisfactorily. Sometimes reorganization of work can be strongly resisted because of a hidden, unrecognized set of collusive phantasies which perform an important function for us in this sense. For example, we may resist moves to get rid of the hierarchy because of the emotional significance it has for us, rather than because it gets the work done well. Any change at work will set in motion serious changes in our phantasy worlds which will involve hard work and temporary increase in anxiety as old mechanisms of dealing with anxieties are taken away and new ones have not yet been worked out. Sometimes changes are made ineffective because the underlying emotional collusive phantasies have not been changed sufficiently.

Delegating others to act for parts of ourselves at work can be extremely useful, both for emotional purposes and for enabling work to be done. Jaques describes a situation in a factory in which a group of workers elected representatives to a management–worker committee. Not only the practical negotiations with management but also the other workers' suspicions of management seemed to have been delegated to these worker representatives. Partly because this process worked well, normal day-to-day relations with individual managers were good; suspicions and hostility could be felt to be dealt with adequately by the representatives and could be ignored normally. The use of the subgroup of representatives to represent troublesome or disturbing phantasies or feelings enabled the group to work effectively at its task, at least for a while.

Jaques had some interesting insights into the equivalent process for the managers too. He found that there was a certain amount of unconscious feeling amongst the managers that their authority was destructive and omnipotent and actually damaging to the workers 'under' them. This manifested itself in the committee in placatory attitudes towards the workers who were idealized as a defence against this fear of having damaged them. This placation and idealization in fact worked to increase the suspicions of the workers, quite reasonably. Both sides seemed to contain these feelings in the negotiating situation and were thus able to work together well outside it. While negotiating, the managers were seen as 'bad' and felt themselves to be bad; while working together, the same managers were perceived by the workers and themselves as much less bad, and could get on well together.

In the hospital Menzies studied, the splitting up of aspects of the self like this was far more obviously troublesome, though it caused trouble in Jaques's factory too. In the hospital the nurses higher up in the hierarchy were endowed with an excessive sense of responsibility and those lower down with an excessive sense of irresponsibility. As a result, those higher up were overburdened and ineffective and those below were given too little responsibility and with it, opportunity for work satisfaction. This was all in an attempt, it seemed, to deal with the enormous anxieties involved in the nursing task itself.

All of these processes, it seems, are group ones in the sense that no single individual can be pinpointed as the prime mover; individuals in the organization may come or go and the organizational structure remain substantially the same. However, individuals can at times influence the structure, provided the rest of the group is sufficiently motivated to allow this. The interaction between individual and group is extremely complex and I can only touch on some relatively simple aspects here.

It seems as if the expression of one idea or emotion or characteristic in a group can either produce the expression of its opposite by the other members, or act to 'allow' others to express a similar idea or emotion. Let us look at an example.

When the organization moved to a new building, everyone went round saying how wonderful it was, and what an improvement on the old one. Janet alone, it seemed, felt upset about the move; it seemed there was suddenly no place for her to eat her sandwiches; the secretaries' office where she had eaten them before was now too small and full of furniture for there to be room for her. She felt pushed out and unwanted and miserable. Talking of this with a group of other people who worked there, it seemed suddenly as if their delight in the new building was also mixed, though until Janet had said something they had not been aware of this. Janet was in turn quite hesitant in saying anything, partly because she did not want to pour cold water on the celebrations, and partly because she did not want the secretary who had organized the move to have the added burden of being criticized by ungrateful members of staff.

In this case, Janet's feelings did not lead to her being made a scapegoat; the other members of staff were able to express their own mixed feelings and even laugh about the unrealistic emotional side to them. The problem remained, but some room was made in the secretaries' office, and the feelings of being unwanted turned out to be partly brought on by the secretaries' feelings of being overwhelmed and having to keep people out of their space; these feelings could be seen as temporary results of the move, and a hope about the future restored.

Whether an emotion or an idea or a characteristic will produce the relieved expression of it in others, or whether it will give rise to 'scape-goating', to being ignored or being rejected, depends it seems on many factors. One factor, perhaps, is whether it includes total rejection of the existing ideas; Janet was careful to acknowledge the good things about the move while remarking on her unhappiness with it. She did not tell the other people they were stupid to be thinking that the move was good at all, and she was careful to express her fear and guilt that she might be spoiling these good feelings.

Another factor involved must be the security and maturity of those in the group; their desire to be conforming or rebellious or creative members of it, and by pressures on them from outside as well as from their own psyche. Any group under pressure, such as an evangelical church, for example, may strongly reject certain opposing ideas in order to maintain the cohesion and identity of the group for its members.

The kind of idea which is involved must also have an effect. An idea or piece of behaviour (such as being emotional, being 'honest', or being polite) which touches on unwelcome facts will be harder to get accepted than one which touches on more welcome ones; the truth or 'reasonable-ness' of the new behaviour or idea may be at certain times less important than this factor. Ideas about racial differences, for example, may be rapidly embraced by certain sections of society for whom these ideas are welcome, and rejected forcefully by those to whom they are unwelcome. The context, again, is important; a policeman on his own with a sympathetic listener may admit that there is a problem of racism in the police force, while the same policeman in a group of his friends or in an interview with the newspaper might deny such an unwelcome thought.

It is not only the actual idea itself which matters of course, so much as what it stands for, very often; similarly with behaviour and feelings. If homosexual feelings 'mean' homosexual behaviour, and this in turn 'means' the epitome of evil, any suggestion of love or even affection for anyone of the same sex will be severely rejected. If asking after someone's health 'means' a desire to get inside their head and take their lives over, or 'means' being nosy and intrusive and likely to lead to mockery by other people around, the group culture may severely restrict the kinds of inquiries people make, and any attempt to show concern for each other in this way.

It seems that sometimes the group has to reject a non-conformist. Some kinds of phantasy worlds have a very disturbing effect on those around and expression of them may not be appropriate for a particular group. One psychotic child in a class can cause enormous problems in all those around, evoking cruelty and viciousness in other children and in the members of staff. Removing such a child is not the same as 'scapegoating' as long as the child is not blamed for everything. The adult who recognizes their own fear of their own violence, and asks for such a provoking child to be taken away in order to protect both the child and the rest of the class, will not hope by removing the child to actually get rid of their own violent impulses or self. The adult will hope only to be able to contain such impulses once again – though it may have been a shock to discover them in the self – and prevent them being too often aroused. The decision to end a relationship for such reasons may sometimes be taken in a divorce, and in some cases where an employee has to be asked to leave. I have learnt through experience to deal fast with severely disruptive members of my evening classes in order to keep other members of the class and to enable work to be done. The difficulty of distinguishing between a disruption which can and should be contained, and one which will not lead to creative discussion, but only to the prevention of any creative thought in the class, is always there. Making the decision as to which kind of disruption the person offers involves hard thinking and observation and is never easy.

Groups, then, throw up problems which can be extremely difficult to deal with. We are faced in groups with phantasies about taking in and rejecting, being accepted and being ignored, manipulated, used by others, influenced and shaken up. We are faced with phantasies in which we are totally responsible for all these things being done to us, and phantasies in which we are totally innocent victims. All of these link back with our earliest passionate relationships, whereby we took in and were taken in, in phantasy, and were fed, loved, ignored or actively acknowledged in reality too. We may respond to the group in much the same way as we did as infants faced with a body which was so much larger than us and which had so much that we wanted for ourselves. We may be suspicious or trusting, angry and feeling deprived, jealous or envious of others in the group and at times, too, enormously uplifted, loving and warm in a way which is far less common in a two-person adult relationship. One feeling or phantasy in someone in the group can play into and exaggerate or stifle or evoke another. This can be experienced as extremely powerful and may be used to enable people to feel safe enough to explore and calm some deep anxieties, or to push them into closing up and making real some quite frightening and destructive phantasies left over from an infantile experience of being utterly at risk and in danger of eternal punishment.

The work culture and organization

The organization of work may be seen as a way of attempting to deal with the group situation. Tasks must be shared out, and so must responsibility and anxiety, as well as rewards. How this is done will seriously affect the load each person must carry, their willingness to do it, their chances of doing their job satisfactorily, and the effect their work has on their emotions and their phantasy world, and on the phantasy world of those around them. Rather than concentrating on different ways of organizing work I shall look at the culture or attitudes which determine how this organization takes place. But it is important to remember that the practical organization will be interpreted as representing a particular set of attitudes – which might conflict with conscious, official ones – and that this symbolic meaning will then influence which particular phantasies are available for use in the organization. What we do influences our phantasies as well as vice versa; and this is true in organizations as well as for individuals.

Melanie Klein used the terms 'paranoid-schizoid position' and 'depressive position' to describe two different ways of dealing with anxiety in the individual psyche. Paranoid-schizoid mechanisms come into action when anxiety is high; they provide a kind of 'first aid'; in particular, by separating out goodness from badness, they function to 'protect' the goodness. If left in action for too long, however, they add to anxiety rather than defusing it. They allow us to put off work we have to do to sort out ourselves – or an organization or group – but they do not substitute for that work. Reduction of anxiety in the long term depends on 'depressive' mechanisms, but these cannot come into action in states of terror or panic. If we use Melanie Klein's work, which is based on analysis of individuals, as a guide to mechanisms which can be observed in organizations or groups of people, we find some interesting links appearing. It has been suggested that some forms of organization encourage more of one of these sets of mechanisms to come into operation, and some encourage more of the other. The level of anxiety and stress in an organization will be linked directly with whichever of these 'positions' is dominant in the work culture at the time, and what has happened to the other set of phantasies which is not dominant.

Paranoid-schizoid mechanisms work by splitting things up in phantasy. The aim is to deny the existence of trouble and conflict, especially within the self; in the case of organizations, to deny conflict within sections of the organization or the whole organization, or in individuals with power within it. So, for example, 'trouble-makers' may be seen as having their base outside the organization, and may be quickly ejected – even if it means promoting them. The myth is that everyone inside would be perfectly happy if only they were left alone by the outside world. 'Selling the company's products would be easy if it weren't for the unfair competition of other firms.' 'The prison system would work perfectly if only do-gooders did not keep interfering.' Clearly, this attempt to split good from bad leaves both idealized. The good is seen in unrealistic, conflict-free terms, and the bad is fiercely attacked. The fact that the attack comes from the supposedly good insider is covered over by blaming the intolerable nature of the bad outsider. Competitors in the market may be seen as having no morals and 'therefore' it is perfectly justifiable to use immoral methods against them. Trade unionists may be seen as extremely greedy and restrictive, and the employers' or government's own behaviour may, in attempts to deal with them, come very close to what an outsider might call being greedy and restrictive. In this type of splitting, real needs and greed are likely to be confused, both in the self and in others. Such splitting adds to the chances that the feared behaviour will be created in the others and other, less feared kinds of behaviour stifled. Where all firms are being immoral, standing out against immorality becomes harder. Where employers are being greedy and restrictive, the unions may have to fight back.

In such cultures the 'good' is seen as very vulnerable. Goodness tends to be perceived as merely fending off the bad, which is seen as far more powerful; as a result, there may be a feeling that somebody should be punished. The punishment is felt to be necessary to bolster up the defensive goodness, but, in anything but the very short term of course, it actually destroys it from within. The kind of company, for example, which frequently dismisses people as a punishment for trivial offences may well arouse increasing suspicion, fear and consequent lack of loyalty in those working for it. The kind of headmaster who maintains his powerful status by getting rid of those who challenge him in any way may feel he is doing it simply in order to protect his school and his way of teaching; but, however good he is as a teacher, this high-handedness is going to undermine morale and eventually bring down the level of teaching of those under him.

Related to this is the fate of mistakes. Where paranoid-schizoid mechanisms are predominant it may be very hard to ask for help which would prevent mistakes or catch them early enough to make them salvable. Mistakes are likely to be seen only in terms of maliciousness or total and irredeemable incompetence, or an attempt to destroy the reputation of the department, for example, and to be punished as a means of distancing the person who punishes from the deed. As a result, mistakes are likely to be hidden as long as possible and, when they are discovered, are likely to confirm the phantasy that they are totally unacceptable. Cover-ups may come into operation, compounding mistakes and adding to the belief that goodness can only consist of fending off horror and destruction.

All of these mechanisms can be seen to feed into each other. People and groups of them are seen as part people; denial of internal conflicts and of mistakes accompanies punishment, projection and denial of realistic guilt. Unreal hopes and unreal fears tend to intermingle in such a way that fears are more likely to be confirmed than the hopes. The world is split into goodies and baddies, and a great distance kept between them, in perception if not in fact. The roles can reverse very rapidly, so there is no security in being a 'goody'; the next minute the goody may become a baddy. In order to deal with these anxieties, work is likely to be controlled very tightly so that individual initiative and work satisfaction are severely limited in attempts to avoid the dangers of mistakes, conflicts and badness. Tasks may be defined in such a way that they are either impossible or utterly unrewarding. Power seems to be misused and to overwhelm those who have it, and to have been stolen or taken unfairly from those who are defined as incompetent to wield it. Caring and concern is separated from power, just as the social work role was gradually removed from the police, leaving them to be far more an instrument of punishment than they were when their power was mitigated by the task of caring in a more obvious way.

The predominance of paranoid-schizoid phantasies in a work culture is more likely to occur under conditions of stress and anxiety where the people concerned have little faith in their own and others' ability to cope.

Where the organization is run in such a way as to confirm such phantasies, work relations tend to deteriorate and the work task may suffer. Typically, there will be tight and rigid hierarchical roles, involving, on the one hand, closely controlled tasks which have been stripped of any need to make any but the most elementary decision, and, on the other, tasks which are impossible since they assume a level of control over and responsibility for other people's work which cannot be realistically fulfilled. Where the work organization is not normally run like this, periods of stress, such as a move to a new building or the advent of a new head of some kind, may temporarily give rise to increased attempts at such control, which fade away as conditions improve with familiarity.

Let me give an example of a temporary case of paranoid-schizoid mechanisms being used.

A new teacher may deal with her great anxieties about teaching by making huge demands on the children in the class. The pupils may be seen as perfectly able to organize themselves and to be in no need of control – all control being defined as authoritarian. As a result, such an idealizing teacher gives the children little sense of limits and boundaries, and the children's anxiety may be raised while they test out where these boundaries begin. The experiment is likely to make trouble. The children have been set a task which is beyond their capacity at the time, and the teacher has to learn the lesson of beginning more firmly, and then 'letting up' from a position of security later. The need children have for adults to 'hold the boundaries', especially in a new situation, to give some measure of protection against their own unruly and unrealistic impulses and those of the other children around them, can be then recognized and worked with. The child's own sense of safety and self-control can be developed more gradually in a way which does not leave the child vulnerable to terrifying fears of its own ability to destroy safety and security. This kind of idealizing approach to children may be based on placation; the new teacher is often secretly terrified of children's violent feelings towards those who are in power and towards those who know something they do not know. These feelings are ones which may be evoked in any teachers who suffered as pupils from a strong desire to be better than the teachers, and from anger and rage towards teachers who made them feel their smallness. Such past feelings, not recognized at the time, may be seen in the pupils and an attempt made to placate them by pretending to be a friend rather than a teacher. It is only later, with experience, that such a teacher is able to feel more able to bear the difference in position and role and power, and to help the children bear it without attacking it. Once this stage has been reached, the teacher's anxiety may be lower and the children may be allowed more freedom within boundaries which feel safe for the children and the teacher. Some teachers never resolve such anxieties, and simply use their pupils to carry feelings of being small and inadequate which have never been resolved in the teacher.

Where there is less anxiety and/or more hope of dealing with it effectively, 'depressive' mechanisms can come into operation more easily. These involve the bringing together of perceptions in such a way that real caring goes along with honest guilt; guilt is not made worse than it need be, but is recognized without being denied. There is less idealization of either the good or the bad; goodness seems less brittle and defensive, and more like a sponge, capable of absorbing quantities of badness and being changed but not destroyed by it, just as the water added to a dry sponge changes but does not destroy it. Whereas 'paranoid-schizoid' cultures tend to maintain the belief that there should be jam tomorrow to make up for the fact that someone has cruelly deprived us of jam today, a more 'depressive' culture depends on the equivalent of making the effort to get good bread today, and enjoying it with or without jam. Getting on with the person at the next desk or in the next room is not put off in the hope that their successor will be a wonderful improvement.

Where depressive mechanisms are predominant, people are perceived less as goodies and baddies, though good and bad can be applied to actions and behaviour. Good actions can be more appreciated without the feeling that they are hollow, or just signs of 'being a creep', or covering up badness in some way, or making others or the self feel blamed or unrealistically small. Bad actions can be the subject of disapproval without its being necessary to reject the person who does them. When rejections or dismissals have to take place, guilt is bound to be involved, but there is more hope that the people being rejected or dismissed are cared for and not simply abandoned, and more of a sense that the organization is worth protecting or improving in this way.

In such cultures, punishment is less likely than help; the real consequences of one's actions cannot be avoided, but they are not increased by a desperate need others have to get rid of their own guilt or bad feelings. Conflict within the group and within the self is recognized and permitted. Where there is division of labour, tasks shared out are more manageable and allow more realistic levels of responsibility, initiative and satisfaction. Where responsibility, power or money are handed over, the process feels less like theft or rape and more like a grateful sharing of the troubles and rewards of life, neither devalued nor idealized. (Handing over the responsibility for cleaning up after you, or for keeping an eye on spending limits, or for checking the quality of the work done, for example, may be done in recognition of the real task taken on by the other person, and the lightening of the others' burden may result. In this case it is less likely to be made harder, as it might be by someone who completely ignores the need for these tasks to be done and recognizes no sense of responsibility for them. This sense of responsibility and mutual gratitude is very dependent upon the work culture and upon perceptions of how fair the organization is. It is more evident in an organization in which depressive mechanisms are dominant, and in which people are as a result seen as whole people, feel cared for, and are given tasks they can manage with sufficient satisfaction.)

Where such a culture rules, past mistakes and losses can also be grieved over rather than denied or turned into punishments; as a result, what is lost is not compounded by the loss of the ability to feel at all, or the ability to take a risk. (When a young carpenter spilled paint over my carpet his immediate response was to say he would never paint anything for anyone else indoors ever again; all he needed to do really was to admit that he had not bothered to prepare the job properly. Restricting his future so severely was actually unnecessary.)

Where depressive mechanisms are available for use at least some of the time, people will relate to each other in such a way that anxiety is dealt with rather than shelved. There will be less need to worry for a long time about other people's opinion of your work; asking is easier and support available. As a result, more energy can be released for considering the worries of other people, and perhaps for interpreting their behaviour in a less persecuting, accusing light. Occasional fits of bad temper on the part of colleagues or bosses may be taken less personally and so perhaps be treated sympathetically rather than defensively. General chat and gossip may be used to understand each other better as people, and so to interpret people's motives in a more constructive way. In this way, people are more able to make use of their strengths and tolerate their own and others' weaknesses; not only are personal relations better, but the work is likely to benefit too.

Summary

In this chapter I have tried to look briefly at some aspects of work and phantasy. I am very aware that it is no more than suggestive.

What I have tried to do is to pick out some of the phantasies which can influence the satisfactions of work. I have suggested that different people have different phantasies which give them anxiety, and that these may lead them into one kind of work rather than another. Any work situation evokes early phantasies and allows them to be worked through in a new situation by applying them to the present day. This process may at times give a new hope of a more realistic kind where past phantasies were dominated by a child's perception and child's sense of guilt and fear. Work can thus be a maturing process which enables people to feel generally more secure about themselves and less afraid of other people. Old ideali-zations may be destroyed but they may be replaced by new, more realistic convictions.

Where the culture at work is less favourable, anxiety may be increased. To ancient, infantile anxieties are added those from the present day caused by inadequate or persecutory phantasies built in to the organization of the work and perhaps arising from the work task too. Old phantasies of being inadequate or undeserving may be evoked and 'confirmed' by low pay or lack of respect at work. Old phantasies of being deprived may be evoked by new real deprivations. Resentment and anger from the past may be compounded by new reasons for resentment and anger in the present. Realistic causes for grievance often include a sense of not being allowed to do the job properly; this grievance goes very deep, for satisfaction at work can be a powerful means of attaining inner peace. The examples of Marion and Jill at the beginning of this chapter, illustrate some of the powerful motivations which drive people to work, and the anxieties which might be aroused by being deprived of the chance to do something about them. An organization of the economy which prevents many people from gaining satisfaction from work is seriously depriving people in more ways than the obvious ones. Where anxiety levels remain high in individuals or societies, the chances of people fearing and attacking, punishing and depriving each other may grow. People are likely to be seen less as whole people, with their own internal checks on greed and malice and aggression, and more as split off and feared dangerous parts of the self. The social consequences of such a culture can be counted in terms of high crime rates, illnesses, violence and discontent.

The significance of work for individuals and society of course goes far beyond anything I have mentioned. Many other phantasies and other factors too are important. Being able to get out of the house, to separate one's life into discrete areas – home, work, travel from one to the other, for example – may be important for many people and in fact affect the whole organization of their phantasies and personalities. Work as a means of defining one's identity – as a Real Man, More than Just a Housewife, a Manager, a Caretaker, a Mother, for example – has many levels of significance and symbolism. Work, it seems, can function in many ways similarly to a lover, giving similar satisfactions, challenging, bringing out and developing unexpected parts of the personality which would otherwise have remained dormant, while forcing the loss of others and taking away attention from other areas of life which may be more disturbing or more taken for granted.

NINE

EVIDENCE: (1) IN THE CONSULTING ROOM

In this chapter and the next I want to pick up some of the more thorny and difficult questions which I have ignored so far. The question of evidence is one of these. How do we know our minds work in these peculiar ways? How can we say that someone suffers from guilt when they say they do not? What about the role of the observer: the problems of bias and suggestion and the self-fulfilling prophecy? I shall be looking at ways the observer can and cannot influence what is observed in the context of analysis, baby observations of an academic kind, family observations and friendships. My main point is that we have to be aware of many possible sources of error, and we must admit to a large degree of uncertainty. We cannot be sure our observations are accurate, nor our interpretations completely justified. In some situations we have more evidence to back up our interpretations; in normal family life interpretations are likely to depend far more on our own internal world than on the evidence in front of us. Even in counselling or once-a-week therapy this may be the case, and any interpretations we make of other people's feelings or behaviour can only be offered as possible ones, in the certain knowledge that they are both partial and probably inaccurate in quite significant ways.

This uncertainty is not quite total: we may be able to be quite convinced about some of the outer limits involved, and about the kinds of distortion which are involved, in a way which allows us to use our observations. In some situations we may find ourselves having to behave as if something were true when we cannot prove it, simply because the consequences of any alternative would be so disastrous if it did turn out to be true, and this possibility can also not be ruled out. The possibility that babies care very much about being left with strangers may be difficult to prove; but if we act as if we needed to take care over who we leave them with, how we hand them over and take them back, we are at worst erring on the safe side. It may be difficult to prove that a baby is crying because it is in pain or terror, and not just because it is 'exercising its lungs', but for most people the safest assumption will be that the cry does mean distress. The fact that psychologists are now actually testing the effects of responding to such cries in different ways makes little difference as long as we have erred on the safe side all the way along.

It is in psychoanalysis that extremely close observation, followed by careful testing out of hypotheses, has led to the formulation of the concept of unconscious phantasy. It is in psychoanalysis that many unexpected phantasies, deriving from babyhood as well as from later, have been uncovered. It is in the relationship between patient and analyst that we can most easily see phantasies being expressed and having a powerful effect. Once they have been observed there we can approach everyday life with new eyes. Using modifications of psychoanalytic techniques in psychotherapy, we can observe many of the same phenomena there too.

Many readers will know of analysis only from the media, where the images presented are in general not much like the methods practised in Britain by members of the Institute of Psychoanalysis. Many people do not realize that psychiatrists are on the whole quite ignorant of psychoanalysis; that the two trainings are quite separate and few psychiatrists are trained as psychotherapists of any kind, let alone as psychoanalysts. Many people do not realize that a psychotherapist can have any kind of training or – at present – none at all; that psychotherapy may be totally different from psychoanalysis or very similar, the two perhaps differing mainly in that analysis is undertaken five times a week, and psychotherapy generally used to describe anything much less than that. There are many misconceptions about psychoanalysis, some of which I hope to tackle in this chapter.

The psychoanalytical relationship

Many people are confused about what a psychoanalyst is. Here I am referring primarily to members of the British (or other countries') Psychoanalytical Society; though there may be some differences of opinion, on the whole there is broad agreement about how to work.

In an analytical relationship the analyst is paid by the patient to help sort out what the patient feels are his or her psychic problems. The analyst, note, is in this way under the control of the patient in that the patient can stop coming and stop paying: unless both patient and analyst remain convinced that the relationship is worth money, time, hard work and some discomfort, it will end. A psychoanalyst cannot and will not take on a patient who does not sincerely want to cooperate as far as the analyst can judge. Sometimes, with children, both child and analyst want to continue the work, but the parents are paying and they may feel that enough has been done to solve their problem; this can be frustrating.

At this point already many emotional difficulties arise. Even after the difficult decision to find the money for the analysis has been made, difficulties arising from the fact that the patient is showing the analyst that the analyst's work is worth something when the patient may be feeling totally worthless may have to be dealt with throughout the analysis. Difficulties of dealing with dependence and with competitiveness may make the financial relationship, and the fact that the analyst has something which the patient wants, very hard to bear. The analyst will not pretend to be in precisely the same situation as the patient is; the analyst has a kind of independence and also a kind of dependence upon the patient: many of the accusations made against the analytical 'power relations' arise from failure to recognize this, or from anger that this is the case.

For the sake of simplicity I shall refer to the analyst as female and the patient as male; there are of course male analysts and female patients too.

The normal way of working is by 'free association'; that is, the patient agrees to say anything and everything that comes into his mind, regardless of what it is. The analyst then interprets when she considers that an interpretation would be appropriate for the task in hand. (Analysts may disagree with each other over the kinds of intervention they feel are appropriate, and with the timing of them: different kinds of interpretation will affect the phantasies which are elucidated by the process.)

As the patient enters the room, lies down on the couch with the analyst behind his head, and begins to speak and to listen, there are many levels of communication which can be observed. Here I shall try to describe three of them, the third in rather more detail than the other two.

Level one

On one level we can look at the most obvious meaning attached to the patient's words. Let us suppose that the patient has said 'It's cold outside.' Then, on level one, the statement is about the weather.

Level two

On what I am calling level two, there is another possible kind of meaning. This is a level of symbolism which is fairly commonly recognized, in poetry or literature or everyday metaphor. *Wuthering Heights* and *Macbeth* come to mind as works in which the state of the weather is used to create a certain atmosphere which is paralleled by the state of mind of the actors. In real life, too, our perception of the weather depends upon and influences our state of mind at times. In this case the patient may be expressing something to do with how cold he feels emotionally as well as physically, for example.

Our use of symbols like this is enormously complex and subtle: there are within this second level numerous different meanings overlaid upon each other. Unless this statement about the weather does express more than the superficial meaning it is unlikely to be made. After all, why pay a lot of money to talk about the weather? There are so many different things we could choose to say about the kind of day it is that we are likely to choose one which says something else for us too. 'It's cold outside' might refer simultaneously to a wage freeze in a cold economic climate, a fear of another cold war beginning, a place inside the self which is felt to be always cold and unloving, a feeling of being left out in the cold by the rest of the family, and a series of sensations concentrated in the feet, the face, the hands, the shoulders which are associated with memories of being cold in childhood and have metaphorical meanings too. Without further elaboration by the patient, the analyst would not interpret such a statement since the possibilities are so many. It is also worth noting that the different meanings or interpretations may be like different proofs for the same fact in mathematics: they can harmonize and illuminate each other, rather than being mutually exclusive. We may notice the coldness of the weather or the economic climate more when we feel that we ourselves are being cold shouldered by someone we love, and when we are afraid that their coldness is simply caused by our own internal coldness and inability to love them.

An important aspect of 'level two' observations lies in how the patient seems to be feeling about the analyst. The statement about the outside may be in contrast with, or the same as (or both, contradictorily and simultaneously), the way the patient feels about the inside of the analyst's room and person. He may feel she is offering him a touch of warmth or a freezing glance. In order to discover some of the underlying phantasies affecting the patient's feelings and behaviour the analyst would consider the whole context of everything he was saying, what had gone on in previous sessions, how the patient looked and moved, and also perhaps anything in the outside world which seemed likely to be relevant to the patient's inner world. A public assassination, a declaration of war or local rioting, for example, might well be expected to affect certain patients, and whether it was directly mentioned or not, the analyst might use her knowledge in some way to help her make sense of what is happening to the patient. Since it is the patient's phantasies which are being explored, the analyst will avoid giving information about herself, including facial expressions: this is why the analyst sits where the patient cannot see her. In this way, it becomes easier to sort out phantasies from reality; if the patient is convinced that the analyst is disgusted or frightened or angry it may be very important that the patient can also become convinced, where appropriate, that this perception arises from their own inner world rather than from the analyst's actual expression.

Level three

There is also a third level of observation which is important for the understanding of the patient's phantasies, especially of the most primitive ones. It merges into the second level of observation but is also something distinct.

On this third level the focus of attention is on the way the patient uses what he and the analyst say. On this level we can look at words as elements in a relationship in the way that cards are elements in a game. The face value of the cards is sometimes less important and sometimes more important, and so it is with the meaning of words.

We can use words as if we were having 'verbal diarrhoea', where the content seems less relevant than the fact that we keep talking. We can use them to stop the other person getting a word in edgeways, or to prevent them thinking at all, or to relieve ourselves of a guilty secret, not caring who is listening. We can use words for extremely complex and full communication between adults, or for the pretence of such communication. We can use them as if they were magic, like children might say 'sorry' to ward off a punishment; we can use them as a distraction from what we are doing or to accompany and make sense of what we are doing – like a stage magician's patter, or a small child talking itself through tying a bow. We can use words to arouse emotions in others, to seduce or to annoy, to show what we are feeling or to hide it. We can use them to blame or forgive, to pick out the useless or attacking parts in someone's statement, or to pick out the loving and helpful parts; to attack or defend ourselves, to make excuses or to complain.

It can be very illuminating for a patient to discover that he is experiencing his own and the analyst's words in one or other of these ways, especially when the conscious intention seemed to be different. Often we interpret other people's words as an attack when they could just as easily be interpreted in another way, perhaps more usefully. If someone points out a misunderstanding I have made, I might feel they are blaming me or trying to show me up, or I might be able to feel they are trying to help me. My interpretation will depend on me as much as, or more than, on them. It may simply never have occurred to me that there was another way of interpreting it. A patient might discover, for example, that their whole behaviour seemed to be aimed at placating an analyst who was assumed to be waiting to attack, or at seducing an analyst who might otherwise have been seen as independent of the patient. Or they might have been trying desperately to show the analyst that they can do without analysis, without help, or seem afraid that no help is going to be available.

Difficulties at this level of analysis can affect the whole relationship in such a way that everything the analyst does is in some way 'messed up' by the patient, and cannot be used straightforwardly for the avowed purpose of the analysis. Of course, the way the patient does manage to mess up or spoil what he is offered becomes itself a very useful focus of the analysis, provided it can be actually looked at.

One client of mine (in psychotherapy, but it happens in analysis too) continually turned my words into magic talismans which would solve his problem without him having to do anything about it. He tried to remember the precise words I spoke, and in the process totally failed to 'take in' the meaning and make use of it. Analysis of the content of what he said was far less effective than elucidating this particular mechanism he used.

There are two important threads to be picked up here. One is the way the relationship between patient and analyst is affected by the patient's treatment of the analyst's offered interpretation, and the other is the significance of this for some of the most important and primitive phantasies which control our lives. It is this level of interpretation which not only tends to have the greatest effect on patients, but which also gives us insight into some of the earliest phantasies developed around speech, thought, love and dependence, as well as eating and drinking, breathing, feeling and defecating.

Let us look at these two threads in another psychotherapy case.

Mike was an attractive and intelligent man in his late thirties with a rather challenging manner. He had been quite successful in his working life but had been married three times and had left behind the children of his first marriage, breaking off all contact with them in order to 'spare them the pain of being torn between two sets of parents'. His own parents had been separated and he had spent his childhood with each alternately: both had loved him dearly and had made much happier second marriages. He had come for help mainly because he was very much afraid that his third marriage was now, after ten years, also breaking up, and he was feeling that there must be something very wrong with him.

During the course of his therapy it emerged that his relationship with his wife was still very important to him. He was suffering from inexplicable fits of weeping and was feeling desperately guilty about having to choose between his wife and his lover. It seemed that as he had left his previous wives and children he had in phantasy left in them feelings which belonged more realistically to him. He had never consciously felt sad about leaving them; it was his children or his wives who were to feel sad, not him. There had always been someone new who wanted him and was pleased to see him; his wives and children, not him, were to feel they had lost something. Guilt he could feel, but never loss or sorrow. As a child, going from one set of parents to another, he had felt guilty about any betrayal of longing for the parent he had left behind; there was always a new parent who wanted him and would not have liked him to share this feeling of loss of the other parent, he felt.

During the course of his therapy he had broken with his lover and decided to stay with his wife when he became – predictably – very depressed. He was aware that he was facing feelings of sadness and regret at losing someone – in this case the lover – which he had managed to avoid before throughout his life. What was unusual for him was that he actually appeared at his session extremely miserable and weeping. He arrived at the next session saying that he was sure that the therapist was going to say that he was a hopeless case after the last time, and that she was going to send him away. He also thought the therapist might feel 'suicidal' after such a session.

The therapist interpreted that he seemed to feel that his depression and misery were too much for anyone to bear: too much not only for himself but for all the people round him. His sorrow seemed to be world-shattering; not only did it make him feel dreadful and hopeless about himself, but it also seemed to threaten the life and sanity of the person he was asking to help him. He was afraid to be miserable in front of the therapist because he was afraid it would literally kill her.

In this particular case, Mike was able to use the insight. He was really surprised that the therapist had not thought of sending him away, and was able to think about other situations where his assumption had been the same. He talked about his parents' attitude to mess and misery and how it was quite impossible to talk to them about, say, his troubles at work or in his marriage. He eventually saw, too, that his relationship with his wife had seemed superficial because he was attempting to protect her from this terrible, dangerous 'mess' inside him. He saw how he had withdrawn into a protective shell whenever he felt miserable, to keep the mess in, making her feel rejected and in fact making more likely the separation he was so desperate to avoid. He was also able to remember occasions when she too had not in fact sent him away, but had been able to share his sadness and continue to love him.

Here the patient has taken up what the therapist suggested: he has been able to 'digest' it and make it his own. He was able to make links in his own mind between what he did and what the therapist had pointed out.

Attacks on the interpretation or the analyst

Not all analytical interpretations produce such results. Even where the interpretation is close enough to the truth, some patients will be unable to use it in this way. One patient might have seen the interpretation as an accusation: as if all misperceptions were culpable. The patient might then have begun defending himself against the suggestion: 'How was I to know that?' or 'Well, you *looked* as if you were going to collapse under the strain.' Or the defence may take the form of an attack: 'I don't believe you: you are just saying that you don't want me to go'; or 'You don't understand *anything* do you?' Confusion may set in if a correct interpretation simply arouses the patient's envy so much that they cannot bear to admit that the analyst is right, and would rather not know. The more subtle patients find the therapist's weak spots and attack there.

In all of these attacks, the patient is not looking closely at what has been offered in terms of understanding. No links are going to be made by the patient while everything the analyst says is being treated like this. Little is going to be changed – except, perhaps, that eventually the patient may come to see the kind of attacks he is making, and to discover with gratitude that the analyst or therapist can survive them in spite of his phantasies that he was turning her into a weak and damaged person, or a wounded and raging lion. It makes sense, perhaps, to wonder if a mother's offered help might at times be greeted in much the same attacking and devaluing way. Some babies and children do seem to reward their mothers more, for just as much or as little as another child would greet with derision, or demands for more.

The patient can behave as couples sometimes behave in conversations or arguments. Some inaccuracy may be picked on and 'corrected' or used to make out that the whole is useless: 'No, it didn't happen last Friday, it was Wednesday, you can never get your facts straight, just like a woman ...' The quarrel can 'take off' from there and leave anything valid in the original point entirely lost and unused. This is the difference between destructive criticism and constructive criticism: some people draw back from any kind of criticism because they have not sorted out the difference between the two. The destructive kind concentrates on the parts that are wrong and uses these to destroy the whole. The constructive kind picks up what is useful and valuable and perhaps does no more than to register the inaccuracies: 'Well, I think it was Wednesday, but yes, you are right about this bit ...' The exploration of just what it means for the statement to have been right can continue.

Another weapon used against analysts and therapists (as well as members of the family) is to lapse into silence. The patient may feel that everything he says is misinterpreted by the analyst who refuses to see him as purely good, innocent in his motives and able to understand himself and everyone else perfectly. The patient may be 'saying' with the silence 'If I can't do it right, I shan't let you do it either!' as if understanding oneself perfectly were a sign of virtue or superiority which could be given up only at the cost of a great struggle. This kind of 'withholding' behaviour may effectively prevent the analyst from doing her job, and may be directed at stopping her from having any satisfaction. It may be used for this purpose in marriages too, or against parents. Sex, physical or eye contact, or words may be withheld from other members of the family – or from colleagues at work – preventing them from showing their capabilities for fear that the self might feel put down by seeing them doing something well. It may be felt to be protecting them too: by preventing them from enjoying life, it may be felt to be protecting them from the workings of envy which would really attack any signs of full enjoyment. But this is one of those mechanisms which is both an attack and a defence: the defence against envy is almost indistinguishable from the expression of it.

Silence can also be used to deny reality: 'If I don't say it, it isn't true.' 'If I don't tell my wife I am having an affair, it won't be a threat to our marriage.' 'If we don't talk about grandma's death, perhaps nobody will notice that she has died.' It sounds silly, but the phantasy is not so far from this.

There are many other subtle ways of using and misusing the analytical situation. One I will mention in case you are reading this book because you know someone who is in analysis. Often the work of recognizing reality, reducing idealizations of the self and others, is so painful or difficult that the patient makes an attempt to distance himself from it. He may claim that the analyst is doing it all, that if it is going on in the analyst's head that is enough. And part of this may sometimes involve getting someone else to attack the analyst for him. Often the wife or husband of a patient will be encouraged to express or feel doubts which the patient dare not feel himself or herself. Even a mother may be used to express a part of the self which does not want help, either through fear or through anger at having to give up some crippling phantasy, perhaps. The patient may be saying to everyone how WONDERFUL the analyst or the analysis is, and provoking a perfectly healthy scepticism, both in those around outside and in the analyst too, that this idealization is perhaps based on a feeling that the whole thing is actually nonsense. Sometimes people do actually arrange or get caught so that someone else makes it impossible for them to continue the analysis. Outsiders of course have their own reasons for fearing the analysis: mothers are afraid they will be blamed by it, and spouses often fear they will lose their partners for one reason or another as a result of the analysis.

Responses to the analyst's failings

When the analyst has in some way misunderstood, as may happen, the patient still has a choice of whether to accept or reject what she has said. A wrong interpretation may be rejected in a triumphant way or sadly; as evidence that the analyst and the analysis is no good at all, like the rest of the world (and the self too, deep down). Or it may be seen as a sad fact of life, that we are all fallible but we can use the good experiences and the good parts of life and people, and enjoy them for what they are. Feelings that the analyst is really 'not good enough' for the (highly superior) patient may be short-lived; very soon the patient may begin to feel that the analyst is trying to get her own back for this devaluation of everything she is and stands for; certainly no help can be expected or received. A more realistic recognition of the analyst's failings may not be achieved until the end of the analysis; looking at them more closely, these failings may then appear to be both greater and far smaller than they appeared in the devaluations and the idealizations of the beginning of the analysis. The fact that some help has been given will be more easy to hold on to without it being lost in feelings of hopelessness or triumphant 'I've done it all myself' feelings. There will then be a real ability to forgive the analyst, the world and the self for faults and imperfections, and a corresponding hope that there is something to be salvaged.

Alternatively, a wrong interpretation can be taken in uncritically, perhaps in a misunderstanding way which *makes* it wrong. Where the patient dares not judge for himself – perhaps out of fear of either the sadness and regret of seeing the analyst as wrong, or out of fear of the triumph which is felt to be so dangerous that it cannot be allowed out – confusion may set in. There may be a feeling that right and wrong are utterly confused and can never be sorted out; that reality and unreality, truth and falsehood, are all indistinguishable from each other. There may be feelings of dizziness and sickness too, as if the patient had eaten something which disagreed with him, while all the time he maintains that the analyst is right. Anne-Marie Sandler, an analyst, describes one of her patients who seemed to take in what she said uncritically at the beginning and then to 'throw it back in her face' later. Patients can do this with 'undigested' interpretations, right or wrong. In my own analysis, how I took my analyst's words and made them into something quite different from what he had actually said was sometimes very frightening. When I eventually plucked up the bitter courage to throw them back at him – 'You said ...' – he was able to show me convincingly that he had said something completely different. Sometimes it is important to be able to reject what someone says, if only to find out that they did not say *that* after all.

This too is a kind of interaction which can happen at home. It may feel almost impossible to challenge anything your husband or older brother or sister says: they are always right, even if you think they are wrong. Mostly you may not dare to think they are wrong, perhaps for fear of what you would do to them if they were. A man told me once how he thought of women, after their husbands had died, jumping on the grave: for him women overtly obeyed men, but secretly hated them and disagreed with everything they said. When death intervened, the disagreement came out as triumph. (In fact, I think this was a reversal of the way he felt about women as well; he kept his own hatred and envy of them hidden behind a pliant exterior too.) I think the thought about challenging people's opinions may sometimes be quite close to: 'If he is wrong I shall kill him and jump on his grave!' And not wanting to kill him, you may not dare to see that he is wrong.

Testing the truth

Each analysis is a process of testing hypotheses. The analyst makes a hypothesis about what is going on in the patient's mind, and then tests this with an interpretation. The patient too has to test these hypotheses and this is by no means easy. Someone who can never hold on to any 'good' perceptions of themselves may find it very difficult to tell if there is any truth in a suggestion about what they are doing to their goodness: anything the analyst says which can be interpreted by the patient in this way may be greeted in a misunderstanding way.

But the testing of the interpretations is going on both consciously and unconsciously. A patient may say 'No, no, no, it's not like that at all', and the next moment produce some memory or statement which seems to imply that it was precisely 'like that' – with a few more details added. The patient may be able to see this when it is pointed out, or may then deny what he has said. Gradually the patient may lose some of his more unrealistic fears: his fear that his triumphant attacks are deadly; his fear that his guilt is so huge that he can never repay his debt to the world; his anxiety that any expression of sorrow would mean he was thrown out into the cold again. Gradually the patient and the analyst may begin to sort out what is being rejected because it is false, and what is being rejected because it is true but painful, in the analysis and outside too.

We can perhaps begin to see that this third level of analysis shows us some of the ways we take in and 'spit out' what the world offers us. We can see that this level of analysis tells us how people feel about asking for help, about being dependent upon somebody else and about having to be constructively, but not destructively, critical about what they take in. It shows some of the ways we try to get rid of painful perceptions which, at one level, we know are true, and painful feelings which arise from what we do to the world, and from our own bodies. It shows how the task of seeing certain aspects of the truth is painful but possible; that it is possible to hold on to these painful perceptions and to allow them to become more bearable of their own accord.

Patients' assumptions about the analyst – and their parents

Studying the assumptions patients make about the analyst has led to a lot of startling discoveries.

One of these discoveries involves the way we transfer expectations from the past on to the present. One of Freud's patients was suddenly aware of a fantasy of Freud kissing her: when he finally got her to admit that this was what was in her mind, Freud was able to trace it to a previous disturbing experience of being kissed by another man, which was extremely relevant for the analysis of her symptoms. Frequently analysis uncovered the fact that such fantasies in particular had been first experienced with parents in the role of seducer or seduced. The way was then open for discovering the way children have sexual fantasies – conscious and unconscious – about their parents, and so the whole issue of infantile sexuality in all its complex ramifications was opened up, as was the importance of phantasies as distinct from actual experiences. The picture of Freud kissing his patient was disturbing her ability to talk to him: there was no question of him actually kissing her. Similarly, with parents, sexual feelings felt by the child towards parents can upset the child considerably – or be enjoyed – while the actual experience never happens, or, if it does, arouses far more upsetting feelings.

The mechanism of projection also emerged as extremely important partly through studying the assumptions patients made about their analyst. This mechanism was observed by Freud: Melanie Klein added considerably to our understanding of it, and its effects on the relationship between parents and children.

Melanie Klein analysed children from the age of two and three quarters who had behaviour and emotional problems. She found that they had quite explicit fantasies about the analyst and their parents biting them to pieces, eating them up, swallowing them whole or taking all their insides out for their own purposes, and so on. Such fears made sense of many adult fears towards the analyst too. Not only did patients see the analyst as wanting to throw them out, take them over, take away their sanity completely, grind them into little pieces and then cast them out exhausted, but they would do this where there was no such intention on the part of the analyst. The fact that the analyst's job satisfaction might reasonably be expected to depend upon the patient's becoming more sane and more secure was frequently wholly forgotten. What is more, these attacks on and fears of the analyst, Melanie Klein noticed, would arise even more after a particularly good and helpful session, and less after a session in which the patient seemed to have obtained no relief at all. The fact that even good and helpful 'mothering' intentions, and understanding which made the patient feel better, could be experienced the next day as persecuting and painful led to her discussion of envy and gratitude and how they seem to permeate our world, attacking our enjoyment of it as soon as it arises.

Much of the child's and the adult's view of the world seemed to make little sense in terms of how real people, real parents, could ever have been. Parents do not swallow their children in fact, however much popular fantasies or Greek myths about devouring parents may suggest they can. Parents seldom cut their children into little bits and scatter them to the winds, eat them or throw them out of the house for being miserable, even if our literature has plenty of examples of such behaviour. Such phantasies began to make more sense when they were seen at least partly as reflections of the child's own infantile desires and fears.

What Freud called the super-ego, the 'internal parents' of the child which told the child what was right and what was wrong, became understood gradually as the child's own creation, out of real parents but seriously distorted by its own phantasies and desires. The child was seen to be seeing the parents through its own phantasies, taking these distorted parents in, and then behaving and feeling as if these parents were inside *and* outside. Children and adults were seen to have extravagant phantasies of attacking, punishing and devouring greedily as well as passionately loving and carefully looking after the parents inside and outside, and also every part of them and what they gave the child.

The child's own jealous desire to take the mother away from the father would be attributed to the father and felt as his desire to take her away from the child; this aspect of it would often be much more important in terms of future feelings than any real desire the father might possibly have to do it. The child's desires to take over its mother's power and ability to feed, to make real live babies and to love could be experienced as the mother's desire to take over the child's power and ability and creativity, for various reasons and in various ways. The resulting fear of being sucked out and depleted, found in many adults, could often be traced back to the adult's infantile desire to suck its mother out – and, interpreting this, the fear of being empty as an adult could sometimes be quite amazingly reduced.

Analysis at this level also showed up the omnipotence of the child's phantasies. For the child, and the child part of the adult, thought can be deed. Many people as adults would hesitate to verbalize the wish that someone were dead – as if such a verbalization could actually cause it. Such a hesitation does not really make sense in terms of adult understanding of the power of words; but it does make sense if it is seen as resulting from a judgement made at a time when we did not have the means to know that words were not so powerful.

Loss of the analyst's approval, for example, is probably not really a life-or-death matter as it can appear to some patients. But loss of the mother's approval may be seriously life-threatening for the small child. This is complicated by the child's projections, so that the child attributes to her its own fury when its mother fails to come up to expectations. As a result the child may expect to be viciously punished for failing, just as it would like viciously to punish the mother's breast when it does not turn up exactly on time. But there is an element of reality in the child's need to keep the mother sufficiently 'on the child's side'. Unless a baby can really please the people around sufficiently, given their own desire to be pleased, the baby's life may really be at risk. At times this may seem for the baby an impossible task, especially if the baby feels for any reason – realistic or unrealistic – that it must do this task of 'mother supporting' entirely on its own. Her own ability to support herself may be ignored, or really shaky; the presence of others to help may at times really be lacking. It is not surprising that some babies do become so terrified of not being able to keep the world going single-handed that they dare not look to see how miserable their mother really is, or how much she is still managing to feed her baby. Their desperation to please her, to keep her going, may not be able to find reassurance in the fact that she does survive, and so does the baby. Quite early on, such frightening phantasies can seem to close down perceptions, and so take away from the child the ability to take in much in the way of help. This process can be observed as it repeats itself in analysis. Analysis offers understanding and help; food for thought and outside suppport; this can be enough to evoke in the adult the experiences of being a baby when such help was also offered. What the patient does with the situation can be enormously revealing.

Fortunately, in spite of feelings to the contrary, analyst and patient are not working alone, any more than mother and child are. Each may be doing their best – at least at times – to help the other. The mother who at times loses her patience and feels she could willingly murder the child may be calmed not only by other parts of herself, but also by something the child does to make her feel better. The baby who feels it wants to punish and destroy its mother may calm down under the influence of her presence and gentle rocking. The analyst who feels he or she is working entirely without the patient's cooperation may be rewarded with a sudden leap of understanding on the patient's part. The patient who feels quite hopeless about the analysis may be positively helped by the analyst's careful behaviour and interpretations.

An adult's attempt to hide angry or nasty feelings towards the analyst does not make sense in terms of the agreement between them about how to work. But a tiny baby cannot know, for example, that its greedy attempts to use her up, or its fury towards her, are not strong enough to destroy her. Baby and adult do somewhere know that devaluation of the mother's contribution, or screams of anger when she has offered something good and worth having, are in fact destructive of pleasure both for her and for the baby. Until the baby has experienced losing and regaining the mother, her love and her food, and gradually come to realize that it is the same, loved mother coming back time and again – not a wicked one at times, or a newly created one each time – phantasies of having wiped her out, of destroying not only pleasure but the source of all pleasure for the eternal Now, and of the child being wiped out by her, may make some sense. The adult who is trying to hide things from the analyst may be re-experiencing such fears which have never before been 'named' and so contained and made more realistic.

In order to make sense of the adult patient's unrealistic assumptions and fears about the analyst, analysts found themselves forced into tracing them back to a time when these assumptions could have made sense, given the experience of reality which was available at the time. As a result, a whole new set of ideas about the ways small babies perhaps saw the world began to emerge. In particular, it seemed, links could be made between ways we experience speech and the ways we experience – or used to experience – eating, defecating, getting rid of pains of all kinds, the mess inside and outside us, love and hope; between holding on to what is true and real in the face of attacks on that reality by ourselves and other people, and the process of understanding and caring. These new ideas about the very primitive processes of the mind arose in the context of making sense of adult behaviour and feelings: sometimes people forget this, and wonder what the reliability, relevance or importance of such ideas are. These things are not a matter of dead history or of purely academic interest. They continue to influence daily life in extremely far-reaching ways, affecting our digestion and our speech; the way we eat and the way we listen to others. The reality of how our mothers and fathers behaved to us when we were small may be only part of the influences upon us now; what matters is what we chose – and still choose – to do with that reality, in our phantasy. And that we can change. Life sets us problems; we do have some control over the kinds of solutions we use.

Having said that, there is another side to the interest aroused by what has been discovered about infancy. I shall be looking in the next chapter at baby observation, which arose out of the desire to see how much of these ideas could be tested or observed in the behaviour of small babies. Many people are of course interested in improving ways in which children are brought up; finding ways of helping them to avoid some of the miseries we or others have been through, and which might be avoidable if we knew more about them. For these purposes, analytical observations have some-times been taken as hypotheses which can be tested out in other ways –

as in the experimental schools of A. S. Neale and Susan Isaacs – and have also been used as a basis for other kinds of observation which I shall describe in the next chapter. There are serious methodological problems in using non-analytical methods for testing analytical ideas; and the methodological problems in using analytical methods for developing these ideas in the first place must at least make us very careful of the claims made about these ideas. On the whole I take the view that we can say little more than 'Somebody saw this, there; does it make sense in your situation?' But I suspect that my beliefs in fact do not entirely follow my cautious academic training: I do think these ideas have an enormous validity; that they make sense of the world in many ways even if we cannot hope to 'prove' them. I sometimes have to restrain the enthusiasm of my students who want to treat the ideas as if they were gospel truth, to be told to all and sundry in the hope of magically making every conflict disappear. It is terribly important to hold on to the fact, when speaking to others of these ideas, that they are hypotheses; plausible guesses which may or may not hold true.

Controls

Analysts, however, cannot avoid the fact that they must be very careful to make their interpretations as accurate as possible. The difficulties introduced into the analysis by interpretations which are not good enough cause trouble not only for the analyst, but also of course for the patient, who has a right to expect the best possible service. The analyst, unlike the psychotherapist or counsellor working in a different way at longer intervals, has plenty of opportunity to observe daily changes and immediate responses to the interpretations made. Analyst and patient are doing a lot of work together which less frequent therapies require the patient to do away from the therapist. As a result, the analyst has both more evidence to support her assertions and more opportunity to restrict herself to making only those interpretations which seem to be supported by the evidence in the particular patient. A counsellor may be able to help a client by saying 'Sometimes people feel like this ... Does it make sense of what you are feeling?' I often find myself telling people in counselling that I am offering them ideas to play with; ideas which the clients themselves must test and explore and modify and probably eventually discard. I cannot offer them anything more certain than this. But an analyst will be able to help the patient to decide whether it does or does not make sense and will only offer something she feels pretty certain about. The controls on the feeling of certainty in the analyst then become very important.

The main control over the analyst's interpretations is of course the patient. The patient has a mind of his own, whatever he or others may fear to the contrary, and the patient's behaviour and feelings are a close check on the analyst's hypotheses.

If the patient, for example, is talking animatedly about somebody else being jealous, and it seems from details in the situation that the patient themselves might be having problems with jealousy and showing the analyst something about it in this way, the analyst can make an interpretation to this effect, thereby testing the hypothesis. How the patient reacts to this interpretation – perhaps with relief and a deepening rapport with the analyst; perhaps apparently ignoring it; perhaps getting angry, tells the analyst something about the accuracy of the interpretation. It does not prove the hypothesis to be true; but it may confirm the feeling that such hypotheses are worth testing out for the additional material they bring up.

Over the years since psychoanalysis began, numerous repeated observations of this kind with many patients by many analysts have lent weight to the hypotheses as well as modifying and refining many of them.

Deductions about the relationship between paranoia and repressed homosexuality were tested in analysis. Freud thought that paranoia arose from hidden homosexual desires: 'I love him' being perceived/changed by the male patient into 'I hate him' and 'I hate everyone/they all hate me.' Rosenfeld found that however much he analysed hidden homosexuality, the paranoia did not go away as it should have done if the hypothesis were correct, but seemed to increase. He eventually concluded that the fear of being attacked – the paranoia – was more fundamental than the repressed homosexuality. Working on this new hypothesis he was able to be of more help to his patients in reducing their unrealistic fears. Freud himself corrected many of his own hypotheses throughout his lifetime as his own observations widened.

All this of course depends on the theory which is used to facilitate observations. Analysts are dependent upon their theoretical understanding being good enough to enable them to make useful observations. Where the body of theory does not encompass enough, observations made are likely to be partial and, for the patient, the result may be that the benefits in the long term of the analysis are not as long-lasting or as far-reaching as they might be. Melanie Klein's discoveries about envy and gratitude and their importance in psychic processes, especially those of learning and enjoyment, enabled her to analyse these processes in her patients far sooner than she had previously; the patients, she felt, benefited considerably from this improvement in her technical awareness. Equally, improved understanding of primitive processes of thought made it possible for Bion and other analysts to begin analysing schizophrenics: the theoretical understanding of the mind which these analyses brought has contributed enormously to the analysis of people who do not suffer from anything like schizophrenia. The restrictions and the advances which arise from inadequate or improved theory are of course common to all sciences, just as they must apply to the phantasies which function as such theories in our day-to-day life. Inadequate phantasies hinder our perceptions; improvements in them can open up whole areas of life to our enjoyment which previously were denied to us.

Another control over the analysis, imperfect though it too may be, is the analyst's own analysis and supervision. Analysts have to undergo years of analysis themselves, in order to be reasonably sure that they are emotionally fitted for analysis of others. There has to be reasonable certainty, for example, that they are not desperately trying to prove something about themselves, or unconsciously wanting to punish their patients or make them suffer for the analyst's own purposes. The analyst must be reasonably sure that when an emotion such as sexual desire, boredom, frustration or a strong desire to *do* something wells up she can tell sufficiently accurately where it is coming from. She has to be able to sort out the elements which arise from her own situation, and those which arise from the patient. She also has to have sufficient internal freedom for a wide range of emotions to be 'evocable' if she is to be able to detect an equally wide range of emotions in the patient. She has to be prepared to fall into the abyss of confusion and misery with the patient for long enough and securely enough to be able to help the patient to climb slowly out. This depends on being able to receive help herself, and on knowing how difficult and painful it is to discover deeply unpleasant facts about herself.

When Mike was convinced that the therapist was going to throw him out for being too miserable, the fact of the clear, well defined therapeutic situation made it very much easier to show him that his expectations arose from him and not from the therapist. In ordinary everyday life the people around might really have thrown him out for it. Sorting out what was 'him' and what was 'them' became much easier for him once he realized that he did make unrealistic assumptions about being miserable. He was able to discover that his parents perhaps really would have been very upset and panicky, but his wife had in fact always responded very positively when he did show her how upset he was. The clear, well defined therapeutic situation; the precisely kept time boundaries; the anonymity of the analyst – all contribute to the controls which enable analyst and patient to sort out truth from fabrication, as well as functioning to arouse particular phantasies in the patient which are causing trouble. (Someone who has little sense of boundaries between himself and others, who 'doesn't know who he is', who feels unsure of his identity, may try very hard to break the time boundaries or the anonymity which are felt to come between him and the analyst. Refusing to give in to these attempts can not only arouse anger, but also tremendous relief, as the anxieties about facing or destroying the boundaries around the self are evoked and can be dealt with in the analysis. Because the agreement about times and the task in hand is firm, a sense of firm reality may be regained by the patient, and patient and analyst have a basis against which to measure the patient's attempts to mess it up. Coming five minutes or fifty minutes late has exact meaning when sessions are at a precise time and finish at a precise time, come what may.)

In ordinary conversation we can sometimes try to sort out what is 'us' and what is 'them', as far as uncomfortable situations and feelings are concerned, and we can to some extent learn how far we can trust our own judgements. Analysis can speed this process up, or help with observations it would be very difficult to make on our own or with friends, but we frequently use conversations with other people in our attempts to make our understanding of ourselves and others more realistic. Some people seem to make us feel warm and comfortable; others seem to be 'prickly'; others arouse anger or frustration in us; others seem able to calm us down; some people make us feel invaded or taken over; some seem to leave us feeling satisfied and well fed. As we grow older and have more experience of such people we may learn to distinguish between their effect on us, and our response to them; discussing these feelings with other people we may discover that such effects are not limited to us. 'It's all right, she does that to everyone!' may be very helpful when you come back from visiting someone feeling strung up with some powerful emotion. One of the important functions of lovers may be to help you sort out your feelings for your parents; how much your troubles are because of them and how much they are your fault. A lover may help give weight to a definition of reality which you believe in and which is quite contrary to one your parents maintain. The sense of relief this can give can be enormous. The lessons learnt from friends or lovers who confirm or alter your perceptions of reality include useful information about yourself and about other people; that you can react in this particular way and that they can evoke such reactions. We thus get to know ourselves better emotionally, just as we learn how much alcohol our bodies can tolerate, or which particular foods invariably give us stomach pains or headaches. We thus learn more about the boundaries between ourselves and others too.

The analyst's own analysis should have given her something of this kind of knowledge. She learns to recognize the good foundations in herself, as well as her own destructiveness; this makes her less likely to be taken in by a patient casting doubts on her goodness in a very absolute way, or by a patient idealizing her. She learns to distinguish between her own feelings better, so she is less likely to confuse one with another or to make herself believe she is feeling something when underlying it is something quite different, as anger may underlie guilt, or guilt anger, for example. As a result, she is less likely to confuse her own belief in her own worth, her own attractiveness, her own power or impotence, with that temporarily aroused by the patient. She has a sense of guidelines in herself which she can check her present feelings against, and so discover what is temporary and what is permanent. The analytical training also of course stresses the need to look for evidence for any idea or hypothesis about what is going on in the patient or herself, both for the accuracy of her judgement and for the source of her feelings, as well as in order to convince the patient that her observations are indeed observations, and not merely unfounded speculations.

Of course analysts are by no means perfect. Part of the problem the patient must learn to cope with is how to get help from people who are not infallible; a perfectly 'real-life' problem. It is not always easy to judge whether it is the analyst or the patient who is distorting things. (Melanie Klein warned analysts not to be too complacent about their imperfections, and not to use this view of them as an excuse to avoid working hard and continually on improving their perceptions.)

A woman told me once that she had been to an analyst in America who had, she said, kept wanting to know why she was neglecting her husband to pursue her own interest in painting. When she came to England, she said, she was amazed to find that her analyst here wanted to know why she felt so guilty about painting, and why she seemed to believe she had no right to be anywhere other than at the kitchen sink. The problem is how to interpret this. Perhaps there were straightforward cultural differences between the American analyst and the British one. Perhaps, on the other hand, mere personal differences were involved. But equally, the difference between the two could have been exaggerated by the patient who might well have preferred to see what was an internal conflict of hers expressed in the two analysts: *they* were conflicting, not her own feelings. I am sure that all of these possibilities exist and that it is extremely difficult to tell which is more important, and which less important, in any one case. The patient might have known on some level; I am not sure that an outsider could ever know for sure, whatever the patient said.

Clearly, part of the control on the analysis, and on the truth of interpretations made, must include the social and cultural environment of the analyst and patient. Where the analytical culture is severely opposed to sexual relations between analyst and patient, even for several years after the analysis, the analysis will be affected by this whenever it emerges as a desire. Part of the patient's security, and freedom to express sexual phantasies about the analyst, will depend on knowledge of such standards amongst the analytical community. The analyst's freedom to interpret such feelings may also depend on such a prohibition.

Differences of opinion amongst analysts

Obviously analysis is a very personal matter which depends to an enormous extent upon the personality, and the strengths and the weaknesses, of the analyst and the patient concerned. It is very difficult for an outsider to have much idea of what is actually going on in an analysis: any form of recording of sessions is generally considered to be an interference, but would also be unsatisfactory since it cannot be complete. We are therefore dependent upon what people say about what they do or think they are doing; the analyst may be no more reliable than the patient when it comes to describing accurately what has gone on, particularly as our concepts seem to me to be woefully inadequate still. The processes involved are as much non-verbal as verbal; all we can do is to try to evoke in each other some awareness of what we are talking about; this is why analysts sometimes despair of getting over to people who have never been analysed the kind of events they are describing. We find it hard to describe music or tastes in words which make sense; some of the most effective pieces of analysis, I suspect, are equally inappropriate subjects for verbal discussion.

In analysis, the relation between culture and the individual has emerged as complex and two-way; individuals influence their immediate social and cultural environment and are also influenced by it. The parents' real behaviour affects the child, but so does the child's interpretation of it, and the child's interpretations and behaviour in turn influence the parents. Similarly, the analyst's real behaviour is important, but so is the patient's interpretation of it.

Both of these points – about the inadequacies of words and the two-way influence of patient's and analyst's interpretations – affect the importance of differences of opinion amongst analysts. It has often been maintained by analysts of different schools that the different theoretical orientations matter less if the analyst is a good one – and exactly what makes a 'good' analyst is very hard to define. As far as I understand it, the deepest phantasies can be evoked, modified and understood in many analogies, and which particular one is used may be less important than, for example, *how* it is used. Since we are talking of phantasies which are themselves not limited to concepts, words, even pictures in a simple sense, but more to sensations running through the body, convictions with a definite and precise content but which have never before been put into words, a large part of the analyst's work consists in getting in touch with these sensations and convictions in a way which cannot be more than a kind of evocation. The particular 'sense' which the analyst helps the patient to make of their world is bound to be partial and to rely to a large extent on the patient's own ability to translate the analyst's words into something meaningful for themselves. The analyst must struggle to check up on this translation system, trying to make sure that the language each is speaking is sufficiently close to what is happening, but it must remain in some sense a translation. The analyst's sensations, phantasies, are translated into words and actions which are then translated by the patient in his own phantasies in the process of 'digestion'.

Precisely how the sense is formulated may at times be less important than whether the words are being used to make loving and creative sense which liberates the patient's ability to love and be grateful in a deeply enjoyable way, or whether they are being used to make someone feel small or inadequate in an unrealistic way.

In some cases, though by no means all, it may make little difference if the phantasies of having a good object (that is, someone/something who is 'not me') inside the self, giving strength to the good self and helping to fight off bad impulses, are described in terms of breasts or in terms of, say, a perception of God, a belief in the Eternal Mother, or a conviction that the world is good; or that the analyst is felt to exist inside the patient, giving support instead of condemnation, or that the real parents are felt to do this as invisible spirits. Clearly all these formulations are subtly different from each other and may be used for different purposes, but they can all be used to reduce anxiety levels, and to make sense of fears and anxieties about being able to destroy such sources of strength and goodness. The similarities may at times be more important than the differences. Many belief systems, including many theories of how the mind works, help to reduce people's sense of responsibility for unrealistic guilt; for many people the relief obtained by a partial understanding of what is going on will be sufficient for all practical purposes, if only for a limited period of time. Most people do function with quite unrealistic and partial understanding of themselves and their world; it can be harmless or it can be very harmful. Problems with solutions or beliefs which are too partial arise when, as a result of the new understanding, a set of phantasies which were previously kept under control for good reason are encouraged to emerge without being themselves understood well enough. There are stories, for example, probably apocryphal, of people in (American, as told by the British) therapy groups 'learning' that their fear of their mother was quite unrealistic – and so verbally abusing her in a quite sadistic way, because they have not learnt at the same time that the fear of their mother was more related to fears of the sadism in themselves than to her actual behaviour. I have no evidence that such stories are true; they make up the general set of myths about analysis and related forms of psychotherapy which help add to the suspicion of them. Some of this suspicion is well founded; some much less so.

Just as in gossip, so in our everyday life and in analysis people are continually testing their own perceptions against other people's. And the shared phantasies may not be more true. Such shared phantasies which we consider unrealistic we may call 'collusive' phantasies. These phantasies can have great power, as social psychologists have demonstrated. I have seen people in one so-called 'therapy' group indulging in certain defensive manoeuvres in a way which seemed to me far from therapeutic. The group culture apparently allowed and even encouraged people to fend off any potentially painful insight by suggesting that it was merely the result of projection on the part of the person who made it. 'Why did you suddenly start rejecting the idea of having an observer, Caroline?' was immediately denied by Caroline saying 'Don't you think you are putting that on me when it is your own feeling?' There was plenty of evidence to counteract this, but no apparent ability of the group to use it. In families there are often extremely powerful collusive phantasies which forbid the saying of certain things: the 'family secret', which, as family therapists have pointed out, everybody knows and everybody pretends not to know, may never be spoken aloud.

Other groups and other families, in other situations, can reinforce far more helpful mechanisms and phantasies about ways to behave, and to feel, which allow far more useful learning to go on. Groups and cultures can enable people to feel safe and creative or under threat and sterile in a quite powerful way. Political groups too, of course, work on the basis of developing collusive phantasies about the world and how to change it: some much more realistic than others; some destructive and some more healing. Such phantasies, shared by so many people, can be at times very hard to resist. But in spite of this they are resisted by some, even at great personal cost.

The question I am often asked in my teaching is whether psycho-analytical ideas about people are no more than a set of unrealistic collusive phantasies. Are analysts simply taught to see what is not there? Do they simply put ideas into people's heads? Is the whole theory of the Oedipus complex simply an invention of Freud's which has been slavishly followed by dirty-minded or gullible analysts ever since?

If we are to consider this question before leaving the chapter, it is worth remembering that Freud himself had to stand out against the prevailing Viennese collusive phantasy which forbade doctors to talk with their female patients about sex. One reason he did this was simply that that is what the patients themselves talked about, and when he began to help them discuss it, he found their symptoms became explicable and were sometimes actually removed. In the *Studies on Hysteria* which Freud wrote at the beginning of his discovery of psychoanalysis, Freud's struggles to deal with the material his patients brought before him come to life. A present-day reader would see signs of sexual conflicts in the material he presents, where Freud apparently failed to notice it at all, or only after weeks of painstaking work. Clearly, Freud has shown what we can look for, and as a result of his work we see far more than we would probably have seen otherwise.

But perhaps there is no point in stating the obvious, that I think that the ideas of psychoanalysts are based on careful observation, on the pressure exerted by patients (for it is patients, I think, who teach analysts as much as anyone does), on theories honed down over the years and over enormous numbers of repeated observations. The basic ideas of the Oedipus complex have been seen to fit patient after patient, all showing signs of loving their parents passionately and wanting to kill one or other, seen as a rival, and at the same time feeling extremely guilty and fright-ened by such feelings. Clearly, my opinion is no help for some people who think I have simply been brainwashed myself. Some people may interpret my suggestion that you try out the ideas for yourself, and that you may not be able to understand fully all that lies behind them without having been in something like psychoanalysis yourself, as a way of saying that people cannot see these things until they have been brainwashed too. I have, unfortunately, to leave these questions for you to judge, on evidence you find in your daily life, and on your assessment of what is fact and what is undecidable, what is useful and what seems totally useless.

It sometimes seems that the idea of suggestion has been carried to extreme lengths, and I detect a similar process happening with the idea of projection. People at times seem to be carried away with the idea that the observer can influence what is observed, and to take it to quite ridiculous lengths. Of course we have to teach each other to see things the way we do; our whole language and culture is formed in the process of trying to make our experience as shared as possible. But people sometimes speak as if there is nothing more to be said or seen beyond what is brought by the observer, as if what is 'out there' can *always* be safely ignored when discussing what people see, and not simply under the special conditions and aims of psychoanalytical sessions, and even there not entirely. What we see is dependent upon both what is out there and what is in our minds ready to make sense of it; we cannot safely ignore either the one or the other.

Just as a baby is not actually putty in its mother's hands, so readers and analysts and patients are not just waiting for revelations with open mouths ready to swallow them indiscriminately. Everyone is continually judging and assessing what they take in and what they refuse; even a baby, whose dependence and lack of experience make the judging process much harder, will when presented with something it does not want turn its face away or screw up its eyes or spit it out. An adult has far more realistic alternatives for deciding what view of the world seems worth bothering with. It seems to me much more likely that psychoanalytical ideas will continue to be found unpalatable and rejected, or only half-digested and distorted, for reasons which are to do with their painfulness, than that they should be unjustifiably swallowed. A useful question to ask may be how much, and precisely what, you stand to lose or gain by either rejecting or trying out some of these ideas. How you try them out is of course important. As I have said before, it is better to confine your observations mainly to the beam in your own eye and leave the mote in other people's as their responsibility. Even objective truth can often be used unreasonably to make life worse rather than better. A little knowledge of psychoanalytical ideas should be used with extreme care. No analyst would dream of interpreting to a friend or relative, and amateurs should certainly avoid doing this if they want to keep friends. In particular the psychoanalytical community has learnt the hard way that it is not a good idea to interpret to one's children. But these questions I take up in the next chapter.

TEN

EVIDENCE: (2)
IN THE OUTSIDE WORLD

Let us now look, if only briefly, at another source of information about the development of basic phantasies: the observation of babies and small children outside the consulting room. I am aware that I am neglecting two other important sources of information: one is that of literature, which can offer detailed and fascinating information about the ways we see and feel and treat the world around us; and the other is the vast collection of academic studies which in recent years have begun to look at the ways babies reach out to and interact with their world. To take the second first: my excuse is simply that I have not read enough of the academic literature. I have tried to encourage the reader to fill this gap in my book for themselves by adding a list of some of the relevant research in the bibliography. My neglect of literature as a source owes more to pressure of space. Not only literature itself, but also the studies of literature undertaken by analysts and others using similar ideas have sometimes produced fascinating illumination or confirmation of psychoanalytical work. They tend to be relatively easy to read: again, I list some of the more notable of them in the bibliography. My own paper 'Mother, Sex and Envy in a Children's Story', is in this tradition. Using a work of literature I was able to examine somebody's (the author's) public fantasy in a way which seemed to me ethical, whereas using private interviews or confidential material would have been far more difficult. Applying psychoanalytical ideas to books, films or plays seemed a relatively harmless and simple procedure, whereby I could test the ideas and explore the implications without having access to patients. Like-minded readers might try it themselves. Because it does not raise such complex issues of influencing the observed, and because in a sense it does not matter very much what we read into the literature around us, it seemed less pressing to discuss it here. But with baby observation, as with the process of psychoanalysis itself, the intermingling of observation and influence, of collecting evidence for hypotheses and changing people's lives, is important.

There are two main ways in which babies are observed. First is the normal observation made by parents and others as part of the process of understanding a particular child and trying to bring it up as best they can. Here the effect of the observation is likely to be immediate and long-term on the behaviour and feelings of the child and the observer.

Second is observation undertaken, usually by outsiders, to see what can be discovered about babies in order to make or test hypotheses which may be important for theoretical purposes, for analytical or therapeutic purposes, or for evidence about what kind of care is best for babies. The effects of such observation are probably less direct for the child observed, unless some gross kind of experimentation is being carried out. We cannot assume that the effects are negligible; when I interviewed adult women, simply listening to them talking about anything that came into their heads, once a week over a period of time, it was clear to me that the attention I was giving them had an effect on their state of mind: making them more relaxed or more tense, for example. I think it likely that a baby too can be affected both directly and through its mother by being given attention of a concentrated kind.

Here I wish to discuss the kind of baby observation undertaken by many people, including myself, with the Tavistock Institute's Baby Observation Seminar. Such observations, taken in conjunction with other sources of information, have deepened many people's understanding of babies and adults.

Once a week I visited a baby, beginning as soon after birth as possible, for an hour. I was simply to watch what the baby did and how it and its mother interacted: not judging in any way but trying to describe as accurately as I could what I saw, with as few interpretations as possible. For example, I might write up afterwards: 'The baby turned its head and looked towards the door: I could hear the mother through the door calling from the kitchen.' Not even the obvious interpretation that the baby was also listening, or possibly watching for her return, went down in the notes. In the seminar we discussed various possible interpretations of this kind, and the evidence for them or its absence. In spite of this careful attention to description without interpretation, it was very difficult not to perceive all kinds of intentionality in the baby's movements. It was amazing to see how the most minute changes of expression and movements of hands, feet, eyes, head and body seemed to fall into patterns and make sense. Even when the baby was asleep, its hands and face twitched and moved, and long-term observation, coupled with sharing those observations in the seminar, made it very difficult to maintain that all these movements were random, unmotivated and accidental, as many people were maintaining (for example, in the universities) at the time.

Obviously I do not mean that the baby was always moving its hands or feet in a consciously intended way, as we might pick up a pen in order to write a letter. I looked in more detail at some of the ways we can talk about motivation which is less conscious in the chapter on 'Blame, Intention and Responsibility'. But listening in the seminar, observing 'our' babies, we discovered that each baby had its own characteristic hand movements; the way it played with the breast or bottle could be seen to be closely akin to the way it played with its hands and fingers, its tongue or its bedclothes. The apparently motiveless waving about of hands and feet could often be seen to be related to what was going on at the time, to what the baby had just experienced, and to what it might plausibly be experiencing internally. Sometimes it seemed as if the baby wanted to be with someone else, to reach out to them even when it was not hungry and when its motor control was severely limited. Sometimes the baby seemed to want to be picked up, to join the conversation, to see what was going on or to find something like the feeding experience, especially just before going to sleep. Sometimes the observer's interpretation of the baby's movements would receive direct testing in the mother's speech or behaviour. How the baby responded to what she offered or what she seemed to ignore gave further evidence which sometimes seemed to confirm or modify the observer's interpretation.

It was fascinating in the seminar discovering how the babies were so different from each other, how the mothers treated the babies (and the observers) in quite different ways, and how the 'fit' between baby and mother – and observer – developed, with adjustments on all sides, over the year of observation. Other members of the family were sometimes also observed with the baby and could be seen to have a great influence on the baby by their presence, their absence or their demands.

A lot of the work in the seminar consisted of looking at the evidence we thought supported our interpretations. This dramatically increased our ability to observe closely and to begin to see where we were making assumptions without much evidence and where we could seek evidence. We also learnt to tolerate a lot of ignorance and undecidability; to keep hold of the fact that our hypotheses were more or less plausible rather than true or false. One of the important lessons was in the attempt to distinguish between hypotheses, interpretations and observations, though our use of language of course is seldom really neutral, and may embody interpretations without our being able to avoid it. Trying to describe how a baby takes the nipple into its mouth may involve us in using words like 'pouncing' or 'grabbing' or 'lethargically', all of which seem to have vast meaning tied up in them. But this attempt to distinguish what cannot really be separated out totally is essential for what is called the 'scientific method'. When it comes to babies, it is important to look at the relation between observation and interpretation.

Observations and interpretations

Clearly the interpretation we put on our observations can be influenced very strongly by our own expectations; our own phantasies do determine what we see. If we see a baby lying quietly staring at the ceiling we may 'understand' what is going on by reference to ourselves. We may, to take extreme cases, be afraid the baby is about to fade away and die because it is not kicking energetically, or we may feel the baby must be all right because it is not causing any trouble to anyone.

But our phantasies not only lead us to categorize what we see: they also affect what we do. Some of our interpretations will lead us to look further, and some will lead us to ignore the baby. Being afraid that the baby is on the verge of death, we may be satisfied with looking to see if it is a good colour, if it is breathing, if it looks back at us when we lean over the cot, or we may feel impelled to provoke some more 'lively' response, by touching its feet, or even picking it up, in order to see if it is all right. A different response would be to turn away from the baby and to find something else to do to take your mind off the fear of the baby's imminent death.

Some people talk and behave as if the expectation or the fear – that the baby will die, in this case – were enough to make it happen; as if such fears can never be calmed by observation; and as if the baby's actual behaviour played no part in the adult's state of mind. In some cases, where the adult's response to the interpretation is such that further observation is too feared or simply not felt to be necessary, what the baby is or does may not influence the interpretation. Perhaps at times the adult's perception of the baby's behaviour is so strongly influenced by such a frightening phantasy that everything the baby does is interpreted in a terrifying way. But this is not the case all the time. Not everyone deludes themselves all the time; many people do have phantasy worlds which are open to change. This is why life is so hard for new parents; they are having to change their phantasies about babies all the time if they are only reasonably sensitive, and this process is exhausting. It is not only the physical effort of producing milk which tires mothers out; it can also be the emotional effort of having to look at the world through new eyes, and to make new phantasies to predict what is going to happen next, at a rate which is far greater with a new baby than at most other times in adult life. Fortunately or unfortunately for the new parents, not all expectations are self-fulfilling prophecies.

Let me give an obvious example. My neighbour's first child, she says, slept through the night from the day he was born, and she quite naturally assumed that her second would do the same if treated the same. Sadly for her, this prophecy remained unfulfilled.

The problem for the observer is one of how to make the process of observation as accurate as possible, or as accurate as necessary for the purpose in hand; and how to ensure that the interpretations are borne out by the evidence. In a simple way, knowledge of possibilities will affect both of these processes.

If we know that a child who is being quiet and withdrawn may be 'all right' or may be far from 'all right', we can choose more realistically what further observations to make to satisfy ourselves as to which is the case. The Robertson's films of children in hospital make it very clear that there was a kind of withdrawal and failure to respond to the environment which at the time was interpreted as 'being good' and which in fact seemed to signify utter despair and hopelessness that augured very badly for the child's future development. Because of those observations, stimulated in their turn by psychoanalytical discoveries, nurses and parents are now encouraged to treat their children's crying and distress on parting in hospital with far greater tolerance, and so to be able to keep in touch with the child and prevent the child suffering such feelings of desertion, and ultimately from cutting off large parts of its ability to feel anything. Knowing that there are such situations can enable us to look to see what kind of quietness the child is experiencing at any particular time. Once we have posed the question, the answer may or may not be clear, but we may be less likely to jump to conclusions as to which applies here.

Clearly our own phantasy worlds must also influence our interpretations. Normally in daily life this does not seem to matter very much: if I interpret my children's behaviour through my own knowledge of my own behaviour and feelings, some of the time I will come close enough to enable them to feel understood, and sometimes I will be distorting or giving a particular emphasis to their situation which is felt by them to be unfair, or idealizing perhaps. Either way they will find other ways of trying to make me recognize the parts of them which they want to be noticed, and which I perhaps tend to ignore. My perceptions of them may be changed by behaviour of theirs which I am eventually forced to notice: this will produce perhaps a somewhat distorted view of them, but it is part of the normal problems of being a parent, and may not matter much in terms of upbringing. In terms of the objective status of my observations it may of course matter quite a bit. It may not be a simple matter to confirm or disprove my observations about my own children if those observations include interpretations.

More seriously, if I have no awareness of certain feelings, for example, my observations which depend on such feelings may be very distorted. If I have been pushed by circumstances, either in my present situation or in my past, to shut off certain feelings as soon as I become aware of them, I may find it very difficult to make some observations which another person could easily make. This kind of situation may occur, for example, in the old-fashioned kind of hospital where nurses are discouraged from 'having feelings' about or for patients. Long exposure to such a culture may result in nurses who are apparently quite unable to see certain kinds of distress in either themselves or their patients. Similarly, some parents, under the influence of theories about children which see them simply as grasping and demanding and manipulating in a greedy and uncaring way, may be unable to perceive a child's expression of love, mistaking it for wanting food, for example. But such an interpretation of the child's gesture may be difficult to demonstrate if the parent has no acknowledgement of their own love or that of others in general.

With her first child Sue suffered from a kind of blindness, as many mothers do; every time her son bit somebody she interpreted his behaviour as a sign of love – Dr Spock mentions that it might be and Sue had read his book and found it helpful. It was not for years, that she was able to accept what people often tried to show her, that his biting was *also* aggressive and destructive and *intended* to inflict pain. A mother differs from a more neutral observer because of her own more intense emotional involvement: Sue cared far more about the biting than an observer would have done, or she herself would have done observing someone else's child. At the same time a mother has to *act* where an observer can reflect upon feelings and ideas aroused by the observation.

Making observations of people's behaviour outside the consulting room we have to take into consideration these influences on their and our phantasy worlds. This is not quite the same as being afraid that our knowledge will so affect what we observe that we can trust nothing. Many people have the fear that an analyst or someone else can put ideas into people's heads which were not there before, and then use these ideas as evidence for their hypotheses, in a circular manner. At times this may go on; but at other times it does not. Often enough, we can actually examine our hypotheses against the agreed evidence and can judge them realistically; or we can simply remain open enough to what is going on around us to allow ourselves to see what is incontrovertibly there.

Recently I received unexpected and direct confirmation of some of Freud's ideas about Oedipal fantasies. I was reading to my four-year-old son a New Guinea folk-tale in which a mother takes her son and runs away from her husband who is a pig. (I had not read the story myself before I read it to him, or I might have refused to.) The pig-father followed her and was killed. My son immediately looked at me with sparkling eyes and said 'So she could marry her son!' I am quite certain that we had never put such an idea into his head; it was a quite spontaneous production of his own. My shock is perhaps a measure of my own difficulty in believing Freud; the evidence of my own son I found far more convincing. I expect that you too will find such incidents in my life far less convincing than similar ones in your own. Without Freud's theories I might not have *noticed* what my son said in the same way: but I do not think that my awareness of his theory could have actually *created* such an idea in my son.

Some years ago I was able to observe a small baby whose behaviour also gave me confirmation of some of Melanie Klein's ideas about the earliest processes in the baby's phantasy. This observation, and the interpretation I put on it, depended upon my being prepared to watch closely and see what happened: I think it is again unlikely that I in some way put an idea into the baby's head – or body – which the baby then followed. Though perhaps such a process might be possible, I find my own explanation more plausible.

I was babysitting for a friend's baby when the child was only about three weeks old and had not had the chance to get to know me well. He cried and I took him on my shoulder. He kept his eyes firmly fixed on the back of the chair, as far as I could see; it was the chair his mother normally sat in. Once or twice he moved his head to a more relaxed position, and saw my face. He cried out and moved back so that he could only see the chair. If I sang or spoke or did anything other than rock him gently as his mother did, he again became restless and cried. It seemed to me very convincing that he was using what movement he could control to help him to maintain a phantasy that I was his mother, or some such equivalent phantasy. Whenever anything happened to destroy this illusion, he got upset and immediately moved to restore it, whereupon he calmed down.

When his mother was there, I should point out, he did not cry whenever he saw my face. Later, when he was older, he was more able to see me as I really was, and to relate to me as someone different from his mother, but it seemed at this time of his life that he was not yet prepared to do that.

My observation is of facts: his movements, the stiffening of his body. My hypothesis is about the reason or intention behind these facts. My knowledge and my interest in the subject led me to note carefully what happened, and enabled me to be reasonably sensitive to what he seemed to be 'demanding' with the means at his disposal. I cannot prove that my interpretation is a correct one, nor would I maintain that it is the only explanation for his behaviour, but as a working hypothesis it was good enough; I kept him reasonably calm while his mother was away. I was also able to tell my friend that it seemed quite clear to me that, in spite of his age, he did know the difference between her and me. In one sense I think she already knew this, but she seemed to feel that it was an indulgence to assume it, and she seemed to have little idea that she too could watch and see what evidence the baby seemed to give that he did know the difference.

Neither of these two observations depended in any obvious way on the use of my own feelings; both come more or less in the category of normal scientific observations in this sense. But there is another kind of observation, made both inside and outside the consulting room, where the feelings of the observer may be actually used.

This is a point at which psychoanalytically inspired work differs quite considerably from that arising from other sources. The use of the observer's feelings in other fields is usually confined to decisions whether or not to be involved, or to work in a particular area; as observations, feelings are often considered to be quite useless, and simply to distort what is to be observed. The discoveries made by analysts and others influenced by them have led in some areas to an increasing awareness that the feelings of the observer follow certain patterns, and can be examined for the information they give. Some of the insights into this way of working seem to be extremely useful for people I teach or work with. They can also dramatically increase the observations people are prepared to make.

As I have already pointed out, if somebody seems to make me feel small, or threatened or as if they are about to bite my head off, I can decide to look on this feeling in various ways. I can assume that it is all my fault and the result of some intrinsic fault in me, or the result of my upbringing or culture. Or I can try out the possibility that it is a feeling which has come up in me *now* because of something about the other person. Does it make sense that this is a feeling they have – about me, perhaps, but perhaps about somebody else – which they cannot cope with on their own and in some sense 'want' me to share with them or bear for them?

Such hypotheses can often be tested, with quite startling results. New observations of the behaviour of the other person – and of the self – may follow, and the atmosphere between us may change considerably as a result. The guilt and fear from the feeling aroused, and from the (probably unnamed) assumption that it was all my fault, or all their fault, may be lessened simply by the activity of looking more closely at what was going on. We can make such hypotheses in many situations, and we may or may not be able to make further observations as a result of such hypotheses.

Our 'intuitions' about people are often drastically wrong or partial, just as our intuitions about ourselves may change from day to day. Sometimes they may be more correct than we can justify because our understanding of the evidence is not good enough on an intellectual level, or because we do not realize that the evidence is there if only we look. Those mothers who felt that the harsh upbringing methods advocated by many books in the past fifty years or more were wrong may have felt they had only their intuition to depend upon, and could not bring this against the weight of the 'scientific' opinion that 'spoiling' was wrong. But there was evidence, in the ways the baby interacted with the environment, and in the feelings of the parents when examined more closely, which could give some parents the strength to stand out against the prevailing opinion. Such unfortunate episodes in our 'scientific' heritage lead some people to swing the other way and to reject all attempts to observe objectively; such people may place too much emphasis on the truth of feelings, and may behave as if any attempt to examine them could only reduce and spoil them. It seems to me that we have to be prepared to observe our feelings just as we observe anything else and to use our observations and our scientific endeavours in the service of our values, neither exaggerating nor denying them.

Making observations about people in everyday life can be extremely hard, and sometimes this is because of feelings involved. Let me give some more examples to illustrate this point.

A dentist, a father himself, once told me that children do not experience 'real pain'; 'not like the starving millions in India' he said when I pressed him to explain what he meant. I wondered where he got his evidence from and determined not to send my children to him for dental work. But I can see that his problem in observing the pain children feel is not his alone. Part of the trouble may be that if he were to scream like a new-born baby does, the emotion he expressed would be almost incredible. And yet this perhaps *is* something like an approximation to what the baby is feeling. The perception, the empathic sympathy which arises for the baby, can often produce panic on the part of adults because they find the pain too much and have too little hope of its being bearable. They may respond by feeling attacked themselves, or by denying any feeling at all for fear they would only want to attack the child or themselves if they did perceive the pain. Such a response may lead to all children being accused – as they were by this dentist – of simply manipulating their parents, so that the distinction between a child that is in some way exaggerating or using its pain to gain some other end and one which is suffering 'real pain' cannot be made. In one sense, the suffering of another person can never be more than an 'interpretation' or 'hypothesis' on our part: pain is not directly observable in the way that behaviour is. This can make it an easy target for denial, or for distortion by the misperception of the observer, or for 'lying' behaviour on the part of a malingerer of any age.

I now want to give an account of an incident, where a friend of mine found it extremely difficult to admit to observing her son's distress, which illustrates some of the difficulties which may be involved in seeing precisely what is going on around us.

One day, Sue's son Ben, aged three, was being very bad tempered. He wanted a bottle of shampoo which his father said he could not have, and he kept banging on her door while Sue was trying to work. Normally when this kind of thing happened it was over quite fast, but on this particular day it went on and Ben was clearly getting hysterical. Eventually Sue went to see if she could help, and she and her husband both sat down with Ben for some time. They talked about the bottle and various substitutes he was refusing. Ben's face remained set and quivering into tears every now and then as he wailed that he just wanted the shampoo. After some time, Ben's father commented how he remembered being miserable when he was three, and Sue talked of some miseries from a similar time. Ben was getting interested but was still clearly in a state, until finally they got on to how Sue had missed friends left behind when she moved house when she was two, and how Ben had missed friends he had left behind in Germany eighteen months ago. He chanted the names of the family he best remembered and had seen since, and Sue supplied some more of the names of people they had visited since, and he had liked very much. He asked who they were and she reminded him, and then his whole face and behaviour changed; he began to move again, having been lying almost rigidly still, and he started hunting for her breast saying that he was also sad because

Sue wouldn't give him the breast any more. But he was clearly not quite serious: Sue was able to push him off without much trouble and he simply laughed. He then hugged his father, said he loved both his parents, and asked for the lolly his father had earlier offered him as a substitute for the shampoo. At lunch time later on he played at seeing his German friends in the garden, and then played at shooting Germans. He insisted, to a joking query, that he was shooting Germans 'in the war' and it happened 'a long time ago'.

Later Sue realized that there was a tenuous connection between the shampoo and the German friends, to do with going swimming with them. At the time, too, Sue's husband was arranging to visit these friends without the rest of the family, and they had put off telling Ben of this since they knew he would be both angry and upset.

My point is that it was quite clear to Sue that something about his memories and the loss of the German friends had been upsetting Ben for some time. She had on some level known that she should tell him he could not visit them when his father went, but the trouble of bearing Ben's feelings about it made her put it off. It was not until Ben forced Sue to sit down with him, by actively stopping her working, that she found the hard work of the discussion a lesser evil than avoiding it. It was also interesting, and typical of the difficulties involved, that when the trouble began on this occasion Sue did not think at all about it having anything to do with the German friendships: her immediate assumption was that she had been neglecting him by trying to work too much. This made it very hard for her to allow herself to think of anything else which might be upsetting him. The discovery that it was his feelings about losing and forgetting his German friends was made simply by allowing the conversation to wander, and watching for his reactions. It involved a trust on Ben's parents' part that together the three of them could work out what was going on, and that they could calm Ben by seeking the roots of his awkwardness. It involved being prepared to face the fact of Sue's supposed neglect of him, and the fact of his disappointment about not visiting Germany. All of these seemed to Sue at the time to require self-discipline and courage; not to turn away from what was going on and leave her husband to sort it out on his own as he usually did quite successfully. There was a fear too about implying that her husband was not capable of dealing with it, and all the associated worries about being left with too much responsibility for the children, and devaluing his ability to care for Ben.

All of these feelings made it hard to enter into the discussion with Ben. As with many such problems, it was only solved when the benefits of solving it seemed to outweigh the disadvantages: in other words, when Ben was being so impossible that Sue could not ignore him any longer. When this happened, she was then given immediate reassurance: it was clear, for example, that her simple presence was not all he needed; that Sue had not been unreasonable in leaving him with her husband, but that he was, as they always thought, perfectly happy with his father and without his mother.

This episode not only shows up some of the difficulties facing anyone who tries to work by allowing the conversation to wander on to painful topics, but it also shows how effective this can be. In the process many psychoanalytical insights receive some kind of confirmation.

The first of these insights to be confirmed here is the way in which not only Sue's anxiety – about being a good enough mother – but also Ben's were significantly reduced. Ben changed from a furious, distressed, screaming child to a rigid, rejecting but listening one, to a relaxed and joking child who was able to accept what was offered to him and go off to play on his own in a lively and creative way. Talking about a painful topic had brought about this change in him. Far from 'putting ideas in his head' which made him more distressed, bringing up the topic of his lost friends had enabled him to work with his feelings about them in a more relaxed and enjoyable way.

Another insight which analysts have often noted can be seen here. Ben's immediate association to the loss of his friends was the loss of the breast. It is often clear in everyday life that some trouble of today will trigger memories of similar troubles which arose long ago; it is less often so clear that these can trigger feelings about losing the breast, and losing the close relationship with the mother which this implies. Giving up anything *now*, just as Ben had to give up the bottle of shampoo, can be made very much harder by phantasies connected with giving up the breast. Some people find it very hard, for example, to make any kind of decision to give something up – cigarettes is perhaps the most obvious instance, but it may be which kind of milk or bread not to buy, perhaps – and these decision problems can at times be traced to much older decisions, just as Ben's seemed to be.

(I would like to add an aside about the problem of giving things up, and ways we deal with this. At the time that I was beginning to refuse my son the breast, and he was getting upset and cross about it, there was an occasion one day when he stomped off from such a refusal, went to the piano and banged a few notes on it, singing to himself: 'Mama, d'lidly, mama, d'lidly' – 'd'lidly' being his word for the breast. I was sure that he was showing me the origin of blues singing. It is clear that having the words can reconcile us to the loss of what they stand for: we seem to feel in some way that we keep hold of the thing, or of the ability to conjure the thing up, if we have a name for it. I once calmed another screaming infant – seventeen months and hardly talking – by saying very firmly (against the wishes of his father, who didn't want to mention her name) that 'Mummy has gone to the shops and she will be back at dinner time after we have played in the sand and in the sea.' There were unfortunate repercussions with the father for my having stepped in like this, but the child – having been extremely difficult for the previous half hour – became perfectly contented and played happily until dinner time. I think that naming 'mummy' gave him some reassurance that she still existed and he had not lost her for ever, just as Paul's playing on the piano reassured him about the breast. This interpretation is of course difficult to substantiate.)

The hesitations about what we might see if we look often serve to hinder our ability to make observations. In order to see if our spouse is having an affair or not, we may have to be prepared to face our own jealousy; in order to see if our children mind being left with a particular person, we have to be prepared to face their misery or to make alternative arrangements; in order to see if our children are happy at school, we may have to be prepared to face conflicts over what to do about it if they are not. Often we will have to feel fairly strongly that the advantages to looking will outweigh the trouble which might be caused, and our judgement of this is unlikely to be very balanced in many cases. As a result, we often prevent ourselves from receiving powerful reassurance; we do not find out that our fears were unnecessary, as Sue discovered that she was not being a 'bad mother' when she was afraid she was. On a personality level, many people never allow themselves to be put in a position where others might see 'the mess inside' them because they are terrified of the effects this could have. As a result, they never receive the reassurance of being 'known' or 'understood' – and *still* loved, mess and all. The emotional hindrances to observing and being observed are, I suspect, far greater than the emotional impulses to see something that is not there.

All of this is important when it comes to you, the reader, finding your own evidence for the kinds of assertions made by psychoanalysts and in this book. I cannot expect you to be convinced by the events in my life and my friends' lives which have over the years gradually built up my trust in trying out psychoanalytical ideas, and so led to my deepening understanding of them. It is not easy to take the plunge of exploring your own or someone else's deepest fears, and so discovering for yourself the enormous relief which can be obtained. It may be easier to begin to watch things happening which previously, since they made no sense, would have been ignored. Some such observations can be made without much effort, and some can be made in relative surety that the influence of the observer on the observed was relatively or totally unimportant. Others can be made while allowing for the role of the observer, and the fact that your presence is bound to affect what you are watching. The parallel of the uncertainty principle, and the influence of the measuring on what is measured in physics, is an obvious one. When physics took the plunge of examining such situations, rather than ignoring them, a whole new field of highly significant observations and theories was opened up. We have to make such a plunge in the field of psychology, by beginning to look more closely at the feelings of the observer and so allowing ourselves to use our own empathy and our own incredible abilities to see and feel in ways which dramatically increase our awareness.

Perhaps I should put in a note of caution once again. I am saying, it seems, two contradictory things. I am saying that we can make discoveries about ourselves and others if we dare to look more closely, and I am also saying that we should take more notice of our feelings. Yet these feelings may well, as I have said, be working to prevent our 'jumping in where angels fear to tread', or they may be working to encouraging us to set ourselves up as God-like know-it-alls for our friends and all those who come into contact with us. Perhaps it is clearer if I say that observing our feelings, naming them, is not the same as simply acting on them. Once we have named them, we can then decide what to do about them: whether to follow one set or another – our curiosity or our hesitancy, for example. We can look at the consequences, in our phantasy at least, of following one course of action rather than another and we can ask ourselves, 'What if the worst did come about?' We may be able, in this way, to free ourselves to let our minds wander without always drawing back from the edge.

When it comes to helping other people, as in the case of parents talking with their children, I think we must be very careful. It is no help if we simply become intrusive, invading the privacy of our children, as a teacher at my secondary school was. She used to force her insights on to members of the class without being sufficiently sensitive to the social situation. It did not matter whether those insights were correct or not; in a school classroom they were inappropriate. Social workers sometimes invade the privacy of their clients inappropriately, and parents can do it to their children too. The roles of analyst, teacher, parent and social worker must be kept separate. The first rule of analysis, I feel, should be to respect people's privacy. An analyst I know says very firmly that she only does it when she is paid for it; in this way there is at least some chance that the person who is in the position of receiving the insight actually wants it. The psychoanalytical session is carefully structured to improve the chances of making accurate interpretations; any other situation is very likely to produce inaccurate ones, and these can cause a lot of trouble. Certainly anyone with any power should avoid the temptation to assume that their insights are more valid than those of the people in their power. Insights can be used to test and to observe what is going on around, but they do not make it reasonable to begin to feel superior. I do not like even teaching Kleinian ideas in situations where the members of the class cannot simply leave if they so wish. Rousing in people difficult feelings they have little means of coping with seems to me an unfair thing to do. The abreaction-by-drugs and hypnotic techniques suffer from this problem too; the person whose memories and feelings are thus aroused may well have no more ability to deal with them now than they had when they were originally forgotten. Attempts are being made now to deal with this problem in hypnotic therapy; but where something comes up which feels 'too much', the natural reaction is to close down some area of functioning. Some kinds of attempts to help people can simply lead to more fear and more being 'closed down' in this way. Any reader of psychoanalytical books would be well advised to remember this.

If we are to seek out evidence for some of the psychoanalytical insights in this book and elsewhere, we must proceed with caution. We must assume first that the chances are that we have actually misunderstood what is being asserted. We must also keep hold of our common sense, while allowing some of its assumptions to be questioned and tested, in thought or deed. We may have to be more tolerant of pain in order to relieve it, but we must be careful not to simply inflict it on others in order to relieve our own burden. If we can do this, we may find that the benefits of the new ability to observe what goes on are enormous, not only for ourselves, but also for other people around us. One person who in some way understands something more, is less panicked and less anxious about the situation, can reduce the emotional temperature to such an extent that many people involved can think more clearly and behave more humanely. If this book succeeds in facilitating this process it will have achieved its aim.

BIBLIOGRAPHY AND SUGGESTIONS
FOR FURTHER READING

This list of books is not meant to include everything on the subject, nor even all my own sources. It is a personal choice of books which I have found particularly interesting and useful for myself and for others. Within sections, books are listed in alphabetical order of authors.

LIST OF SECTIONS

I   Basic Freud
II   Books by Kleinian analysts (with comments on their topics and style):
(a)   Basic books on Kleinian theory and practice;
(b)   Other books and papers by Kleinian analysts
III   Selected books and papers on related topics from standpoints similar or opposed to that presented in this book
IV   Fictionalized case histories describing psychotic states of mind
V   A selection of psychoanalytic writings based on works of literature
VI   A selection of non-psychoanalytic books on infant and child psychology

I   **Basic Freud**

Freud, Sigmund, *The Standard Edition of the Complete Psychological works of Sigmund Freud*, ed. J. Strachey, Hogarth Press and Institute of Psychoanalysis (hereafter HP & IPA), 1975. Some republished by Penguin Books.

    It is worth trying to read this edition; some of the earlier editions lose some of their sense in being republished with unacknowledged amendments. *Studies on Hysteria* and *On Dreams* in vols. II and V raise and examine many of the questions newcomers to and opponents of psychoanalysis ask. Freud has a surprisingly readable style.

Jones, Ernest, *The Life and Work of Sigmund Freud*, Pelican abridged version available, 1964; unabridged version, Hogarth Press, 2 vols.

Wollheim, Richard, *Freud*, Fontana Modern Masters series.

11 Books by Kleinian analysts

(a) BASIC BOOKS ON KLEINIAN THEORY AND PRACTICE

Klein, Melanie, *The Writings of Melanie Klein*, 4 vols, HP & IPA, 1975.
    I   *Love, Guilt and Reparation and Other Works, 1921–45*
    II   *The Psychoanalysis of Children*
    III *Envy and Gratitude and Other Works 1946–63*
    IV *Narrative of a Child Analysis*

These volumes include notes describing the papers and their particular importance, which are very useful as a guide to browsing. I particularly recommend the case studies which make up the first half of *Psychoanalysis of Children* and also *Envy and Gratitude* itself. Both these may be found as earlier editions in single volumes.

Klein, Melanie; Heimann, Paula; Isaacs, Susan; Riviere, Joan (eds.), *Developments in Psychoanalysis*, HP & IPA, 1952.

Brought out to contribute to the discussion within the British Psychoanalytical Society between Klein and Anna Freud and their close colleagues, this volume describes some of the new ideas Klein and her associates were working on. As such, it deals with many basic concepts and basic questions which are relevant for a deeper understanding of these ideas. The other authors write more clearly than Melanie Klein herself, not only adding their own contributions but also explaining some of Klein's ideas.

Klein, Melanie; Heimann, Paula; Money-Kyrle, Roger (eds.), *New Directions in Psychoanalysis*, Tavistock, 1955 and 1971.

This book of papers by people including Bion, Riviere, Klein, Rosenfeld and H. Segal collects together papers published in honour of Klein's seventieth birthday. Bion's contributions include 'Language and the Schizophrenic', which is a good introduction to this aspect of his work; elsewhere he can be extremely obscure at times. This paper uses psychoanalyses of schizophrenics to illuminate the disturbances of thought and speech which affect schizophrenics. Jaques's paper on 'Social systems as a defence against persecutory and depressive anxiety' uses Kleinian ideas in a more sociological context.

Rosenfeld, Herbert, *Psychotic States*, HP & IPA, 1965.

This is one of the pioneering works arising from the classical analysis of people who previously had not been considered suitable for the unmodified technique, such as schizophrenics, alcoholics and drug addicts.

Segal, Hanna,

    (1) *Introduction to the Work of Melanie Klein*, 2nd ed., HP & IPA, 1973.

This has for years been the basic introduction to Kleinian ideas for analysts and others. It is clearly written and full of case illustrations.

    (2) *Klein*, Fontana Modern Masters, 1979.

The first Fontana Modern Mistress, this book is a tightly written account of the history and development of Klein's work and the conflicts around it. Biographical details are included.

(3) *The Work of Hanna Segal: A Kleinian Approach to Clinical Practice*, Aronson, 1981.

This book is less condensed and is relatively easy to read. It contains papers describing new developments in clinical practice since Klein died, and several papers making new contributions to various psychoanalytical subjects. These include one of the first papers on the analysis of a schizophrenic using classical analytical technique; the analysis of a seventy-year-old man; and papers on symbol formation, dreams and aesthetics. Many of these papers can be read and enjoyed by people with no previous knowledge of psychoanalysis. Other topics covered include Melanie Klein's technique, countertransference and the curative factors in psychoanalysis.

(b) OTHER BOOKS AND PAPERS BY KLEINIAN ANALYSTS

Bion, Wilfred,

(1) *Experiences in Groups and Other Papers*, Tavistock, 1961.

(2) *Second Thoughts*, Aronson, 1967 (selected papers).

(3) *Seven Servants*, Aronson, 1977.

This is four books in one: *Learning from Experience*; *Elements of Psychoanalysis*; *Transformations*; *Attention and Interpretation*.

(4) *Four Discussions with W. R. Bion*, Clunie Press, 1978.

Bion is not easy to read but repays hard work spent on his writings.

Grotstein, E. S. (ed.), *Do I Dare Disturb the Universe? A Memorial to W. R. Bion*, Caesura Press, Beverly Hills, 1981.

This includes papers by many famous Kleinians written in the seventies.

Gallwey, P. L. G., 'Transference utilization in aim-restricted psychotherapy', *Br.J.Med. Psychol.*, 1978, vol. 51, pp. 225–36.

A technical paper for therapists who are interested in Kleinian insights.

Isaacs, Susan,

(1) *Childhood and After*, Routledge and Kegan Paul, 1948.

A non-technical book that is well worth reading.

(2) *The Social Development of Children*.

(3) *The Intellectual Development of Children*.

These last two collect together observations on nursery-age children. made at Isaacs' Malting House School They have been enormously influential in British nursery and primary school practice.

Jaques, Elliott, *Equitable Payment*, Heinemann Educational Books, Glacier Project series.

Jaques, Elliott, 'Social systems as defence against persecutory and depressive anxiety', in *New Directions in Psychoanalysis*, eds. Klein et al. (see above).

Menzies, Isabel, *The Functioning of a Social System as a Defence against Anxiety*, Tavistock, 1977.

This should be required reading for all those working with the NHS – or any other hierarchy.

Riviere, Joan

   (1) 'Womanliness as a masquerade', *Int. J. Psychoanalysis*, 1929, vol. 10, pp. 303–313.

   (2) 'A contribution to the analysis of the negative therapeutic reaction', ibid., 1936, vol. 17.

   (3) 'Jealousy as a mechanism of defence', ibid., 1932, vol. 13.

III **Selected books and papers on related topics from standpoints similar or opposed to that presented in this book**

Except for those marked * all these books are reasonably easy and pleasurable to read.

Abraham, Karl, *Selected Papers on Psychoanalysis*, HP & IPA, 1927.

Arieti, Silvano, *Understanding and Helping the Schizophrenic. A Guide for Family and Friends*, Penguin Books, 1979.

Axline, Virginia, *Dibs in Search of Self*, Ballantine, 1976.

*Balbernie, Richard, *Residential Work with Children*, Human Context Books, 1966.

Balint, Michael, *The Doctor, His Patient and the Illness*, Pitman Medical Publishing Co. 1957.

Brown, J., *Freud and the Post-Freudians*, Penguin Books, 1961.

*Chodorow, Nancy, *The Reproduction of Mothering. Psychoanalysis and the Sociology of Gender*, Univ. of California Press, 1978.

Freud, Anna, *The Ego and the Mechanisms of Defence*, HP & IPA, 1976.

Fuller, Peter, *Psychoanalysis and Art*, Writers and Readers Coop.

Guthrie, Lorna, and Mattinson, Janet, *Brief Casework with a Marital Problem*, IMS Tavistock, 1971.

Harris, Martha, *Inside Information on Understanding Infants; Birth to Five Years Old*, The Dickens Press, 1969.

Janov, Arthur, *The Primal Revolution*, Sphere Books, 1975.

Kaplan, Helen Singer, *Disorders of Sexual Desire*, Baillière Tyndall, 1979.

Klein, Sydney (ed.), *Sexuality and Aggression in Maturation*, Institute of Psychoanalysis and Baillière Tyndall and Cassell Ltd, 1969.

Kübler-Ross, Elizabeth, *On Death and Dying*, Tavistock, 1976.

Laing, Ronald D., and Esterson, Aaron, *Sanity, Madness and the Family*, Penguin Books, 1974.

Mainprice, June, *Martial Interaction and Some Illnesses in Children*, IMS Tavistock.

Malan, D. H.,
> (1) *Individual Psychotherapy and the Science of Psychodynamics*, Butterworths, 1979.
> (2) *A Study of Brief Psychotherapy*, Plenum/ Rosetta, NY, 1975.

Mattinson, Janet, *The Reflection Process in Casework Supervision*, IMS Tavistock, 1975.

Mattinson, Janet, and Sinclair, Ian, *Mate and Stalemate*, Blackwell, 1979.

Miller, Jean Baker, *Psychoanalysis and Women*, Penguin Books, 1973.

Orbach, Susie, *Fat is a Feminist Issue*, Paddington Press, 1978.

*Orbach, Susie, and Eichenbaum, Louise, *Outside In and Inside Out; Women's Psychology; A Feminist Psychoanalytic Approach*, Penguin Books, 1982.

Perls, Fritz; Hefferline, Ralph; Goodman, Paul, *Gestalt Therapy*, Penguin Books, 1951.

Pincus, Lily, and Bannister, Kathleen, *Shared Phantasy in Marital Problems*, IMS Tavistock, 1965.

Pincus, Lily, *Death and the Family; The Importance of Mourning*, Faber, 1974.

Reich, Wilhelm, *Character Analysis* (trans. V. R. Carfango), Farrar, Strauss and Giroux, NY, 1972.

Renvoize, Jean, *Web of Violence (A Study of Violence in the Family)*, Routledge and Kegan Paul, 1978.

Salzberger-Wittenberg, Isca, *Psychoanalytic Insights and Relationships*, Routledge and Kegan Paul, 1975.

Sandler, Anne-Marie, 'Comments on the significance of Piaget's work for psychoanalysis', *Int. Rev. of Psychoanalysis*, 1975, vol. 2, part 4, p. 365.

Southgate, John, and Randall, Rosemary, *The Barefoot Psychoanalyst; An Introduction to Karen Horney Counselling*, The Assoc. of Karen Horney Psychoanalytic Counsellors, first ed. 1976 (later eds. may be better).

Storr, Anthony, *Sexual Deviation*, Penguin Books, 1964.

Sutherland, John D. (ed.), *The Psychoanalytic Approach*, Institute of Psychoanalysis, 1968.

Tustin, Frances, *Autism and Childhood Psychosis*, Hogarth Press, 1974.

Winnicott, D. W., *The Piggle. An Account of the Psychoanalytic Treatment of a Little Girl*, Penguin Books, 1980.

IV Fictionalized Case Histories describing psychotic states of mind

Berke, Joseph, and Barnes, Mary, *Mary Barnes*, Penguin Books, 1968.

Green, Hanna, *I Never Promised You A Rose Garden*, H, R & W, 1964.

Schreiber, Flora Rheta, *Sybil*, Warner, 1973.

Vonnegut, Mark, *The Eden Express*, Corgi.

v A selection of psychoanalytic writings based on works of literature

(References are to books listed under *Books by Kleinian analysts*.)

Freud, S., *Standard Edition*,

     vol. 9: *Delusions and Dreams in Jensen's Gradiva*, 1907.

     vol. 12: *Psychoanalytical Notes on an Autobiographical Account of a Case of Paranoia*, 1911.

     vol. 21: *Dostoyevsky and Parricide*, 1928.

     vol. 12: *The theme of the three Caskets*, 1913.

Klein, M., 'On identification' (in *New Directions in Psychoanalysis*, and in *Writings of Melanie Klein*, vol. 3).

     'Infantile anxiety situations reflected in a work of art and in the creative impulse', 1929 (in *Writings of Melanie Klein*, vol. 1).

Jones, Ernest, 'A psychoanalytical study of Hamlet'(in *Essays in Applied Psychoanalysis*, IPA Press, 1923).

Riviere, Joan, 'The unconscious phantasy of an inner world reflected in examples from literature' (in *New Directions . . .*).

     'The inner world in Ibsen's *Master-Builder*' (in *New Directions . . .*).

Rosenthal, R. J., 'Raskolnikov's transgression and the confusion between destructiveness and creativity' (in Grotstein (ed.), *Do I Dare Disturb the Universe?*).

Segal, Hanna, 'A psychoanalytic approach to aesthetics' (in *New Directions . . .* and *The Work of Hanna Segal*).

     'Delusion and artistic creativity' (in *The Work of Hanna Segal*).

     'Conrad and the midlife crisis', *Int. Rev. of Psychoanalysis* (to be published).

Segal, Julia, 'Mother, sex and envy in a children's story', *Int. Rev. of Psychoanalysis*, 1979, vol. 6, part 4, p. 483.

vi A selection of non-psychoanalytic books on infant and child psychology

List and notes provided by John Churcher, Department of Psychology, University of Manchester.

Bower, T. G. R.,

     (1) *A Primer of Infant Development*, W. H. Freeman, 1977.

     (2) *Development in Infancy*, W. H. Freeman, 2nd ed. 1982.

    Both books are coherent, well written, theoretically motivated and have selective reviews of recent experimental work on infant perception and cognition (i.e. knowing, thinking). The first is a better introductory book.

Donaldson, Margaret, *Children's Minds*, Fontana, 1978.

A short, readable and thought-provoking account of recent research on pre-school children and its implications for education.

Boden, Margaret, *Piaget*, Fontana, 1979.

A reliable and short introduction to Piaget which does not try to be a substitute for reading Piaget.

Piaget, Jean,

> (1) *The Origins of Intelligence in the Child*, Routledge, 1953; Penguin Books, 1977.
>
> (2) *The Child's Construction of Reality*, Routledge, 1955.
>
> (3) *Play, Dreams and Imitation in Childhood*, Routledge, 1962.

Piaget's trilogy on infancy – difficult to read but rich in observation and theory. The third volume contains a discussion of unconscious symbolism in children's play.

Butterworth, George (ed.), *Infancy and Epistemology*, Harvester, 1982.

A collection of reviews of recent work on infant cognitive development, many of them excellent.

McShane, J., *Learning to Talk*, Cambridge University Press, 1982.

FOR THE BEST IN PAPERBACKS, LOOK FOR THE 🐧

In every corner of the world, on every subject under the sun, Penguin represents quality and variety – the very best in publishing today.

For complete information about books available from Penguin – including Puffins, Penguin Classics and Arkana – and how to order them, write to us at the appropriate address below. Please note that for copyright reasons the selection of books varies from country to country.

In the United Kingdom: Please write to *Dept E.P., Penguin Books Ltd, Harmondsworth, Middlesex, UB7 0DA.*

If you have any difficulty in obtaining a title, please send your order with the correct money, plus ten per cent for postage and packaging, to *PO Box No 11, West Drayton, Middlesex*

In the United States: Please write to *Dept BA, Penguin, 299 Murray Hill Parkway, East Rutherford, New Jersey 07073*

In Canada: Please write to *Penguin Books Canada Ltd, 2801 John Street, Markham, Ontario L3R 1B4*

In Australia: Please write to the *Marketing Department, Penguin Books Australia Ltd, P.O. Box 257, Ringwood, Victoria 3134*

In New Zealand: Please write to the *Marketing Department, Penguin Books (NZ) Ltd, Private Bag, Takapuna, Auckland 9*

In India: Please write to *Penguin Overseas Ltd, 706 Eros Apartments, 56 Nehru Place, New Delhi, 110019*

In the Netherlands: Please write to *Penguin Books Netherlands B.V., Postbus 195, NL–1380AD Weesp*

In West Germany: Please write to *Penguin Books Ltd, Friedrichstrasse 10–12, D–6000 Frankfurt/Main 1*

In Spain: Please write to *Alhambra Longman S.A., Fernandez de la Hoz 9, E–28010 Madrid*

In Italy: Please write to *Penguin Italia s.r.l., Via Como 4, I-20096 Pioltello (Milano)*

In France: Please write to *Penguin Books Ltd, 39 Rue de Montmorency, F-75003 Paris*

In Japan: Please write to *Longman Penguin Japan Co Ltd, Yamaguchi Building, 2–12–9 Kanda Jimbocho, Chiyoda-Ku, Tokyo 101*

PENGUIN POLITICS AND SOCIAL SCIENCES

Political Ideas David Thomson (ed.)

From Machiavelli to Marx – a stimulating and informative introduction to the last 500 years of European political thinkers and political thought.

On Revolution Hannah Arendt

Arendt's classic analysis of a relatively recent political phenomenon examines the underlying principles common to all revolutions, and the evolution of revolutionary theory and practice. 'Never dull, enormously erudite, always imaginative' – *Sunday Times*

Ill Fares the Land Susan George

These twelve essays expand on one of the major themes of Susan George's work: the role of power in perpetuating world hunger. With characteristic commitment and conviction, the author of *A Fate Worse than Debt* and *How the Other Half Dies* demonstrates that just as poverty lies behind hunger, so injustice and inequality lie behind poverty.

The Social Construction of Reality Peter Berger and Thomas Luckmann

Concerned with the sociology of 'everything that passes for knowledge in society' and particularly with that which passes for common sense, this is 'a serious, open-minded book, upon a serious subject' – *Listener*

The Care of the Self Michel Foucault
The History of Sexuality Vol 3

Foucault examines the transformation of sexual discourse from the Hellenistic to the Roman world in an inquiry which 'bristles with provocative insights into the tangled liaison of sex and self' – *The Times Higher Education Supplement*

Silent Spring Rachel Carson

'What we have to face is not an occasional dose of poison which has accidentally got into some article of food, but a persistent and continuous poisoning of the whole human environment.' First published in 1962, *Silent Spring* remains the classic environmental statement which founded an entire movement.

PENGUIN POLITICS AND SOCIAL SCIENCES

Comparative Government   S. E. Finer

'A considerable *tour de force* ... few teachers of politics in Britain would fail to learn a great deal from it ... Above all, it is the work of a great teacher who breathes into every page his own enthusiasm for the discipline' – Anthony King in *New Society*

Karl Marx: Selected Writings in Sociology and Social Philosophy
T. B. Bottomore and Maximilien Rubel (eds.)

'It makes available, in coherent form and lucid English, some of Marx's most important ideas. As an introduction to Marx's thought, it has very few rivals indeed' – *British Journal of Sociology*

Post-War Britain   A Political History   Alan Sked and Chris Cook

Major political figures from Attlee to Thatcher, the aims and achievements of governments and the changing fortunes of Britain in the period since 1945 are thoroughly scrutinized in this readable history.

Inside the Third World   Paul Harrison

From climate and colonialism to land hunger, exploding cities and illiteracy, this comprehensive book brings home a wealth of facts and analysis on the often tragic realities of life for the poor people and communities of Asia, Africa and Latin America.

Housewife   Ann Oakley

'A fresh and challenging account' – *Economist*. 'Informative and rational enough to deserve a serious place in any discussion on the position of women in modern society' – *The Times Educational Supplement*

The Raw and the Cooked   Claude Lévi-Strauss

Deliberately, brilliantly and inimitably challenging, Lévi-Strauss's seminal work of structural anthropology cuts wide and deep into the mind of mankind, as he finds in the myths of the South American Indians a comprehensible psychological pattern.

FOR THE BEST IN PAPERBACKS, LOOK FOR THE

PENGUIN PSYCHOLOGY

Introduction to Jung's Psychology   Frieda Fordham

'She has delivered a fair and simple account of the main aspects of my psychological work. I am indebted to her for this admirable piece of work' – C. G. Jung in the Foreword

Child Care and the Growth of Love   John Bowlby

His classic 'summary of evidence of the effects upon children of lack of personal attention ... it presents to administrators, social workers, teachers and doctors a reminder of the significance of the family' – *The Times*

The Anatomy of Human Destructiveness   Erich Fromm

What makes men kill? How can we explain man's lust for cruelty and destruction? 'If any single book could bring mankind to its senses, this book might qualify for that miracle' – Lewis Mumford

Sanity, Madness and the Family   R. D. Laing and A. Esterson

Schizophrenia: fact or fiction? Certainly not fact, according to the authors of this controversial book. Suggesting that some forms of madness may be largely social creations, *Sanity, Madness and the Family* demands to be taken very seriously indeed.

The Social Psychology of Work   Michael Argyle

Both popular and scholarly, Michael Argyle's classic account of the social factors influencing our experience of work examines every area of working life – and throws constructive light on potential problems.

Check Your Own I.Q.   H. J. Eysenck

The sequel to his controversial bestseller, containing five new standard (omnibus) tests and three specifically designed tests for verbal, numerical and visual–spatial ability.